REVELATION AND DIVINATION IN NDEMBU RITUAL

SYMBOL, MYTH, AND RITUAL
Series Editor: Victor Turner

Bennetta Jules-Rosette, *African Apostles: Ritual and Conversion in the Church of John Maranke*

Frederick Karl Errington, *Karavar: Masks and Power in a Melanesian Ritual*

Shlomo Deshen and Moshe Shokeid, *The Predicament of Homecoming: Cultural and Social Life of North African Immigrants in Israel*

Barbara G. Myerhoff, *Peyote Hunt: The Sacred Journey of the Huichol Indians*

Victor Turner, *Dramas, Fields, and Metaphors: Symbolic Action in Human Society*

Frank E. Manning, *Black Clubs in Bermuda: Ethnography of a Play World*

Raymond Firth, *Symbols: Public and Private*

Nancy D. Munn, *Walbiri Iconography: Graphic Representation and Cultural Symbolism in a Central Australian Society*

Mircea Eliade, *Australian Religions: An Introduction*

OTHER BOOKS BY VICTOR TURNER

Dramas, Fields, and Metaphors: Symbolic Action in Human Society

The Ritual Process: Structure and Anti-structure

The Drums of Affliction

The Forest of Symbols: Aspects of Ndembu Ritual

Lunda Medicine and the Treatment of Disease, Occasional Papers of the Rhodes-Livingstone Museum, No. 15

Essays in the Ritual of Social Relations (with D. Forde, M. Fortes, and M. Gluckman)

Schism and Continuity in an African Society: A Study of Ndembu Village Life

Lunda Rites and Ceremonies, Occasional Papers of the Rhodes-Livingstone Museum, No. 10

The Lozi Peoples of North-Western Rhodesia

Editor of:
Profiles of Change: African Society and Colonial Rule

Political Anthropology (with M. Swartz and A. Tuden)

REVELATION AND DIVINATION IN NDEMBU RITUAL

VICTOR TURNER

Cornell University Press

ITHACA AND LONDON

First published 1975 by Cornell University Press.
Published in the United Kingdom by Cornell University Press Ltd., 2-4 Brook Street, London W1Y 1AA.
First printing, Cornell Paperbacks, 1975

International Standard Book Number (cloth) 0-8014-0863-6
International Standard Book Number (paperback) 0-8014-9151-7
Library of Congress Catalog Card Number 75-1623
Printed in the United States of America by Vail-Ballou Press, Inc.

TO MUCHONA,
friend and educator

Foreword

Recently both the research and theoretical concerns of many anthropologists have once again been directed toward the role of symbols—religious, mythic, aesthetic, political, and even economic—in social and cultural processes. Whether this revival is a belated response to developments in other disciplines (psychology, ethology, philosophy, linguistics, to name only a few), or whether it reflects a return to a central concern after a period of neglect, is difficult to say. In recent field studies, anthropologists have been collecting myths and rituals in the context of social action, and improvements in anthropological field technique have produced data that are richer and more refined than heretofore; these new data have probably challenged theoreticians to provide more adequate explanatory frames. Whatever may have been the causes, there is no denying a renewed curiosity about the nature of the connections between culture, cognition, and perception, as these connections are revealed in symbolic forms.

Although excellent individual monographs and articles in symbolic anthropology or comparative symbology have recently appeared, a common focus or forum that can be provided by a topically organized series of books has not been available. The present series is intended to fill this lacuna. It is designed to include not only field monographs and theoret-

7

ical and comparative studies by anthropologists, but also work by scholars in other disciplines, both scientific and humanistic. The appearance of studies in such a forum encourages emulation, and emulation can produce fruitful new theories. It is therefore our hope that the series will serve as a house of many mansions, providing hospitality for the practitioners of any discipline that has a serious and creative concern with comparative symbology. Too often, disciplines are sealed off, in sterile pedantry, from significant intellectual influences. Nevertheless, our primary aim is to bring to public attention works on ritual and myth written by anthropologists, and our readers will find a variety of strictly anthropological approaches ranging from formal analyses of systems of symbols to empathetic accounts of divinatory and initiatory rituals.

"Chihamba the White Spirit: A Ritual Drama of the Ndembu" originally appeared as Rhodes-Livingstone Paper No. 33, 1962; and "Ndembu Divination: Its Symbolism and Techniques" originally appeared as Rhodes-Livingstone Paper No. 31, 1961, Rhodes-Livingstone Institute, Lusaka. Each was reprinted in 1969 by Manchester University Press for the Institute for Social Research, University of Zambia.

I am retaining the vernacular in the texts, not only for the sake of those familiar with Bantu languages, but also for American, English, French, and Italian symbolic anthropologists who are currently engaged in an extensive and lively debate on the explanation, interpretation, and translation of symbolic forms among different cultures. Readers not interested in these controversies can skip the vernacular texts; but responsibility to professional colleagues demands their retention. The texts are my considered selection from field material and best demonstrate my theoretical position concerning ethnographic description and interpretation.

VICTOR TURNER

University of Chicago

Contents

Introduction   15

PART ONE │ CHIHAMBA THE WHITE SPIRIT: A
          RITUAL DRAMA OF THE NDEMBU

  1. *Chihamba* the White Spirit   37
  2. Some Notes on the Symbolism of *Chihamba*   159
  3. Some White Symbols in Literature and Religion   179

PART TWO │ NDEMBU DIVINATION: ITS
          SYMBOLISM AND TECHNIQUES

  4. A Preliminary Analysis of Ndembu Divinatory
     Symbolism   207
  5. Some Kinds and Methods of Ndembu Divination   243

  Appendix   339
  Bibliographical References   343
  Index   345

Illustrations

PLATES

1. *Yileng'a* rattles   48
2. An adept draws a cross on her arm   49
3. Adepts chase candidates   94
4. Ritual joking   95
5. Candidates sit with their backs to *Kavula*   96
6. *Kavula*—candidate's view   110
7. *Kavula*—adept's view   111
8. Doctor applies castor oil to tree   124
9. Doctor anoints the wounds of the white spirit   125
10. Doctor "sings at the root"   126
11. Preparation of *yibi* shrine   127
12. Preparation of candidate for symbolic execution at *yibi*   128
13. The *yibi* shrine left as a memorial   129
14. A candidate's personal *kantong'a* shrine   130
15. An Angolan diviner and the tools of his trade   287
16. Disfigurement of the Angolan diviner's hand   288

FIGURES

1. The divining objects   294
2. The divining objects   300
3. The divining objects   304
4. The divining objects   307

REVELATION AND DIVINATION
IN NDEMBU RITUAL

Introduction

The two essays reprinted here, neither readily accessible in its original form, together present an important theme of the religious ritual of the Ndembu tribe of North-West Zambia (Northern Rhodesia during the time of research). This theme is *kusolola*, making visible, whether as the disclosure of what has previously been concealed (divination), or as the· manifestation of what resists conceptualization in the linguistic terms available to the Ndembu (revelation). Divination is specially concerned with uncovering the hidden causes of ills brought about by the immoral or self-serving thoughts, words, and deeds of incumbents of positions in an institutionally structured social system. Revelation is the exposure to view in a ritual setting, and by means of symbolic actions and vehicles, of all that cannot be verbally stated and classified. Thus divination is a mode of analysis and a taxonomic system, while revelation is a prehension of experience taken as a whole. The action sequences of these two processes of exposure are likewise antithetical. Divination proceeds by a sequence of binary oppositions, moving stepwise from classes to elements. Revelation, on the contrary, begins with authoritative images or root metaphors, manifested as sets of connected symbols, and is culturally contrived to give those exposed to it a sense of what Walt Whitman might have called "the rondure, the cohesion of all." Divination is dualistic, revelation nondualistic. Divination seeks to uncover the private malignity that is infecting the public body, while revelation asserts the fundamental power and health of society and nature grasped integrally. Because of their sense of wholeness—a sense continually restored by performances of the *Chihamba* ritual—the Ndembu are distrustful of all that is withdrawn from public view or company. In Ndembu thought religion is emphatically *not* what an individual does with his solitude. Inveterately solitary persons among the Ndembu are prime targets of witchcraft accusations.

All structures, whether of language or society, arise from a division of the unitary flow of experience into elements that become "parts" when they are reconnected by native rules of logic to form a system set aside from that flow, that is, an abstract system. When the parts are components of social statuses and roles whose ensemble make up a social system, and when the incumbents of such status roles happen to be conscious, feeling, and willing human beings, a tension is set up between the living whole and the abstract system. The individual human being attributes reality to the system and identifies himself with that part of it which he happens to occupy. He identifies his aspirations with upward movement in the hierarchy of the system and thus disconnects himself from the open flow of life, hides his thoughts and wishes from others, and subordinates the concrete whole to the abstract part (which is itself a component of a system of such abstract parts). The seeds of dualism are sown: subject/object; one/many; body/soul; incumbent/office; ego/alter, and so on. From this point of view social structure is masking, while a ritual like *Chihamba* points to a direct apprehension of reality. Divination is the process of unmasking the privative drives of those who seek personal gain at the expense of the corporate welfare. Revelation and divination both unmask, but divination unmasks the culturally defined sins and vices of those who voluntarily separate themselves from the living flow of society, while revelation uncovers that flow itself. I have recently been rereading Dante's *Inferno*, *Purgatorio*, and *Paradiso*. If the reader will recall them and then turn to the inventory of divinatory symbols discussed in Chapter 5, below, he will see that the hypocritical, the fraudulent, the simulator, the dissimulator, the greedy, the cannibalistic, and the adulterous are types of secret malefactors as well known to the Zambian forest dwellers as to the immortal Florentine. I direct the reader's attention to the Ndembu exegesis of such evil symbols as *katuwambimbi* (p. 295), *chamutang'a* (p. 293), *chimbu* (p. 303), *matang'isha* (p. 312), and *ilomu* (p. 310). On the other hand, the white imagery of revelation in the *Paradiso*, Canto xxxi, recalls the pervasive white symbolism of *Chihamba*. To quote at random from Dante (1950, Canto xxxi, pp. 590–591):

In form, then, of a white (*candida*) rose displayed itself to me that sacred soldiery which in his blood Christ made his spouse. [v.1]

They had their faces all of living flame, and wings of gold, and the rest so white that never snow reached such limit. [v.5]

The first verse echoes the way in which candidates for *Chihamba* initiation are transformed into adepts through the symbolic death and blood of *Kavula* and partake of the whiteness of that deity. Both the *Paradiso* and *Chihamba* reveal the deepest values of their respective cultures in images of sacred communitas. Both combine white and red symbolism as images of purity and sacrifice.

I mention Dante advisedly because I have been taken to task in a review by Robin Horton (1964) [1] for propping up this kind of analysis (further exemplified in Chapter 3 below) with Thomist concepts. Although Dante has been said to have based the conceptual structure of *The Divine Comedy* on the *Summa Theologica* of Thomas Aquinas, it is now widely held that Dante's work is far less Thomist than was formerly thought, and is precisely non-Thomist in the way my argument is non-Thomist. Etienne Gilson writes (1956:368; also cited below): "It is quite impossible to come to the act-of-being by an intellectual intuition which grasps it directly, and grasps nothing more. To think is to conceive. But the proper object of a concept is always an *essence*, or something presenting itself to thought as an essence; in brief, an object. An act-of-being is an *act*. It can only be grasped by or in the essence whose act it is. A pure *est* is unthinkable; but an *id quod est* can be thought. But every *id quod est* is first a being." In this passage the French philosopher was trying to find in scattered statements by Aquinas expressions of a position that would render him congenial to the young philosophers who would later burgeon into the existentialist and phenomenological schools. But in truth the vast architectonic of the Summa is one of "essences," even though it rests on the acceptance of "revealed truths." I am not a Thomistic essentialist in this sense. In Chapter 3 I attempt to find in a wide range of cultural expressions, whether by individual writers

[1] This review article, "Ritual Man in Africa," has been republished in M. H. Fried, *Readings in Anthropology*, vol. II (New York: Crowell, 1968), pp. 651–673, and in W. A. Lessa and E. Z. Voget, eds., *Reader in Comparative Religion* (New York: Harper & Row, 1972), pp. 347–358. It has been cited frequently, an index of its influence on anthropological thought. Horton's summary of the description and theoretical argument of *Chihamba the White Spirit* has been the only access many readers have had to my text.

or in folk myth and ritual, some recognition of the universal fact of human experience that reality is continuous, while language, and the systems of thought that depend upon it, are discontinuous. Often the experience of pure act or *durée* (time perceived as indivisible) hits the individual with "blinding force," "is revealed in a flash," or may be expressed in other metaphors drawn (like many in *Chihamba*) from meteorology, especially sun and thunderstorms. *Satori* and *samadhi*, in the vocabularies of Zen and Hinduism—as well as the revelation experienced not long before his death by Aquinas himself, which made him declare that the *Summa* was "so much straw"—seemed to refer to such global intuitions of the seamlessness of process. There is, I think, an affinity between the thump on the head delivered by a Zen master to his pupil and the aggressive verbal thumping administered by the thunderous *Kavula* to the *Chihamba* candidates. The strong element of practical joking in the Zen training recalls Mary Douglas' characterization of the central episode of *Chihamba*, the killing of *Kavula*, as a "joke rite" or a "ritual mock killing" (1968:375).

As Horton points out, African ritual systems contain, *inter alia*, explanatory models of the cosmos and the place of society within it (utilizing metaphors drawn from relations between persons, rather than, as with Western man, between things), and this view is correct as far as it goes. I have pointed out many connections between symbolic actions and vehicles in *Chihamba* and aspects of Ndembu social structure and social dynamics. Also I devoted an entire chapter of my book *Schism and Continuity in an African Society* (1957:Chapter 10) to a detailed study of the major social effects of a specific performance of *Chihamba* on Mukanza Village and its field of intervillage relationships. Many people, indeed, see the gist of my work as consisting in the study of the relationship between social process and symbolic action. But *Chihamba*, of all Ndembu rituals, proved intractable to this approach in its central symbolic emphasis. That is why I had to go further and have recourse to Western philosophical notions, even invoking Kierkegaard with his insight that paradoxes are the inevitable result of man's reflections. As Mary Douglas wrote in the article cited above, "Forget his [Turner's] presentation in scholastic [Thomist] terms; it could as well have been presented through Kant, or Kierkegaard, or modern phenomenologists" (p. 375). When I wrote *Chihamba the White Spirit* there was as yet no wide public for the various "emic" studies, ethnoscience, ethnomethodology, ethnobotany, ethnozoology, ethnomusicology, and so on. I now see that I was looking to Ndembu culture for some evidence of ethnophilosophy or ethnotheology, or for some "metalanguage," which, because the Ndembu have no specialized class of professional theologians or philosophers, would probably be in the main a nonverbal language, a language of symbolic forms and actions, like the Zen master's thump on the head or the token decapitation of the *Chihamba* candidate. These assaults on the head were not assaults on cerebration or reason; rather, they were attempts to say the unsayable. Mystical experience and cosmic joke: both exceed the just or even possible limits of thought. They are to cognitive approaches what such approaches are to pragmatic immersion in the stream of events. Indeed, in some ways they replicate the pragmatic; the silhouettes of the pragmatic man's activities and those of certain mystics and cosmic jokers may be almost indistinguishable to common sense perception. For the postcritical person recovers spontaneity not out of weariness from thinking too much, but from overcoming the dualism inherent most prominently but not exclusively in the Western philosophical tradition. *Chihamba* and other African ritual manifestations have taught me that it is not enough to counterpose West and East as the archmodalities of human articulate experience. If "heart-shaped Africa" (as Blake always called it) may be considered mankind's civilizational South, we have there an autonomous set of linked world views which validly enrich our ways of understanding ourselves. For African thought (the South of the world) embeds itself from the outset in materiality, but demonstrates that materiality is not inert but vital. *Kavula* in the *Chihamba* ritual humanizes this vital materiality. African religion, as Horton rightly divines, begins with man thinking about the universe. *Kavula*, whose very name is the fertilizing but brutal rain and thunder and lightning, which impregnate, illuminate, and overawe, is yet almost incarnate in a fierce old hunter, the lightning of whose guns bring meat to the people and health to the children. He is not so much, he is not at all, a system of categories, binarily or any other way ordered. He is that which sustains all orderings and, when they become limiting and tedious, destroys them "with a flash of the fire that can," and an answering rumble of his inchoate yet fertilizing voice.

I have frequently written about communitas, meaning by this relationships which are undifferentiated, equalitarian, direct, extant, nonrational, existential, "I-Thou" (in Ludwig Feuerbach's and Martin Buber's sense), between definite and determinate human identities. The empirical base of this concept was to some extent my experience of friendship during the war as a noncombatant private soldier in a British bomb-disposal unit. But it was mainly village life in Africa which convinced me that spontaneous, immediate, concrete relationships between individuals not only were personally rewarding but also had theoretical relevance. *Chihamba*'s dramatic, if not chronological, climax in the social antistructure of universal friendship, following the ritual slaying of *Kavula*, seems to me the epitome or concentrated essence of African village communitas raised to metaphysical power by symbolic action. The hypothesis that African ritual models having the explanatory capacity of scientific models for the industrial West are founded in the experience of social relations does not take into account the experience of communitas. Communitas is a nonstructured relationship, or, better, a spontaneously structured relationship which often develops among liminaries, individuals in passage between social statuses and cultural states that have been cognitively defined, logically articulated, and endowed with jural rights and obligations. Communitas, too, may provide the foundation for African explanatory models. Such models would not represent the cosmos as hierarchically arrayed, but as possessing a common substratum beyond all categories of manifestation, transcending divisible time and space, beyond words, where persons, objects, and relationships are endlessly transformed into one another (as in the multiple transformations of *Kavula*). The social experience underlying this model—which is the *Chihamba* model—is an experience of communitas, the corporate identity between unique identities, the loss of the sense of number. If I appear to be using the language of Hindu nondualism, this may be because the classical Sanskrit texts of ancient Hinduism seem to contain social intuitions of the same order as may be found in African metarituals, such as *Chihamba*. There is nothing, I must insist, mystical about all this. We must not dismiss what cannot be framed within our own cognitive traditions as "non-sense." Our own philosophical traditions have sensitized us to structures of many types and to the structuring of the manifold in general. But the very success of structural discoveries, and the energies we have deployed in working under this paradigm, may well have diverted us from attempting to understand what all things deeply share, the continuum underlying relative space and time, the creative process underlying all explicitly formulated systems of thought. In the language of the German mystic, Eckhart, communitas may be regarded as the "Godhead" underlying Emile Durkheim's "God," in the sense that Durkheim's "God" was a shorthand for all social-structural actualities and possibilities, while "Godhead" (though not too distant from Durkheim's "effervescence") is the performative communitas reality from which all social structures may be endlessly generated. Communitas is the primal ground, the *urgrund* of social structure. *Chihamba* is an attempt to transmit to Ndembu the inherited wisdom of their culture about this primal ground of experience, thought, and social action and about its fitful intrusions into the ordered cosmos which native models portray and explain.

But if *Chihamba* may be said to represent a ritualization of Ndembu protophilosophical speculation about determinacy and indeterminacy, order and disorder, and dualism and nondualism, there is little that is philosophical about the divinatory process. If divination is a "mentifact" of diviners, and if a fortiori witchcraft/sorcery are part of divination, then real diviners create suspected witches. Since the symbolic trappings of divination and witchcraft manifest paranoid attitudes we must conclude that an influential majority of diviners must have had paranoid tendencies. Many diviners are marginal men, through physiological abnormality, psychological aberrancy, or social-structural inferiority or out-siderhood. It may be held that these disqualifications qualify the diviner to respond sensitively to stresses and strains in social relationships. Marginals and outsiders, since they possess little pragmatic power or influence, may be thought to be more objective than those involved in struggles for goods and prizes. There are certain dangers in allocating judgmental roles to near-paranoiacs, for their early experience, which may have involved the swallowing down of anger in the face of taunts and insults, gives them clairvoyance into the ill-natured motivations of others, but also imparts a "paranoid style" into their mode of sifting truth from falsehood, or as Ndembu would put it, of "making secret things visible." W. H. Auden's line "The desires of the heart are as crooked as corkscrews" epitomizes the prevalent attitude of diviners toward human nature, that is, the view that the most common qualities of human beings are inhumane. The paranoid style does not impair the diviner's ability to sift evidence in a rational way, but it does mean that he explains misfortune by positing a complex, often logical scheme of delusory persecution, aimed at undermining delusory aspirations to grandeur (such as claims to high office which may not actually be staked), as the evaluative frame in which he judges relationships, assigns guilt, and recommends ritual remedies. Diviners as a class may be said to exact a subtle revenge on a society which has rejected or belittled them as individuals. They know that even the most powerful or fortunate are vulnerable to death, disease, or misfortune, that they fear rivals and envy the more successful. In such crises diviners provide for the solid citizens a coherent if illusory system which translates into cultural terms the mental structures of paranoia. Divinatory séances into the secret causes of outstanding misfortune provide a kind of resolution of the social relationships disturbed or broken by the crisis, but resolution is achieved only at the cost of a running total of hate, and sometimes of the actual ostracism or physical punishment of the secret plotter, "the witch." The diviner has now reduced the successful and orthodox villager to his own original marginal position. The "reality" he professes to reveal is not communitas, but a secret war of all on all.

The conditions of life in African rural society determine that there are a sufficient number of connections between the components of experience and those of a paranoid system, such as divination, to render the latter plausible as an explanatory model. High morbidity and mortality rates (and an exceptionally high infant mortality), low nutritional levels, plagues, droughts, blights, and famines, and, in the past, slave raids and blood feuds, combined to make life short, arduous, and dangerous. Most of all they often left the villager with little control over his life. Diviners counteracted the fears and anxieties produced by such indeterminacy through the frequent interposition of their overdetermined schemata, which restored coherence, even at considerable cost, to lives fractured by misfortune. It might even be said that the paranoid style was functional in such a milieu. But this would be to overstate the case. Excessive disorder at the objective level cannot be successfully neutralized by delusory order. It is into this irresoluble problem that Kavula leaps, giving his lightning flash of an ultimate reconciliation between contrarieties. For this reason the Ndembu regard *Chihamba* as the strongest medicine, the panacea for all ills. In a sense the very redundancy of white symbols reveals to the Ndembu what life, including social life, could be if there were no witches or malignant spirits (we would say, if they had a

higher standard of living and much less disease). But
Ndembu, like all peasants, do not expect to live in perennial
communitas, cared for by *Kavula*. Rather do they pit their
misfits (the diviners) against their misfortunes. And although
we might say, from the standpoint of Western wealth, that
this combat constitutes a delusory system, for the Ndembu it
mirrors their own experience fairly faithfully. It also gives
them motives for action, discriminates just from unjust con-
duct, and purges society of its real as well as imaginary malefactors. For, as I said, a good deal of reality has become
mixed up with fantasy in the divinatory complex. If its deep
structure has paranoid features, its surface structures contain
many of the facts of daily experience. I shall not take up this
point here since I have covered it in Part Two, below, in my
description and analysis of the divinatory process in its social
and cultural settings. But the divinatory process has much in
common with the judicial process in its techniques of interrogation and its scrutinizing of evidence. Where it differs
most markedly is in its attribution of magical power to motivation; in judicial action it is assumed that physical power,
controlled by some rational adaptation of means to ends, is
the source of injury. But diviners say that the grudges of
men and women are themselves powers (*jing'ovu*) which can
stir up malignant entities, such as familiars (*andumba, tuyebela*), or render medicines efficacious, to kill their fellows.
Such powers are often beyond rational control, killing even
when their owners have repented of the lethal impulse, and
they kill in ways beyond rational comprehension.

I am, of course, well aware that divination has many positive qualities. In the past few pages I have focused attention
on the Ndembu basket diviners, whose main pragmatic function is to detect witches. But as the section on divination

shows, there are many other kinds of diviners and modes of divination which relate more frequently to the complex of rituals of affliction and to the veneration of ancestors. On the whole, the rituals of affliction are less imbued with paranoid attitudes, but, instead, constitute a set of practical paradigms for moral action. They are more deeply embedded in the corporate life of villagers and express various degrees of its "moral density." But the paranoid clairvoyance of the great flawed basket diviners uncovers the individual motivations that lurk incipiently beneath the surface of a society which even in the throes of change could be classified under Durkheim's rubric of "mechanical solidarity." The spiky, indefeasible contours of the individual—awareness of which as a social category is one of the marks of societies with a high degree of differentiation—appear in the context of this book as marks of asociality, stigmata of the "enemies of society" (with whom the paranoid diviners feel a strange complicity).

To conclude this comparison, then, *Chihamba* expresses the implicit Ndembu theory of goodness (even although *kuwaha* and its derivatives stress components of experience which the more puritan West might regard as hedonistic or materialistic), while divination incorporates their theory of evil. Both genres of social action must be studied as phases in social processes before we analyze them as cultural structures. Divination is itself a public response to a mounting crisis in the life of the community whose representatives decide to have recourse to it. *Chihamba* is the most important of that class of Ndembu rituals I have called "rituals of affliction"; one of the manifest functions of such rituals is to overcome precisely such hidden intentions as divination had previously revealed to be fracturing the social body. *Chihamba* may be regarded as the quintessence of its class of rituals, for more than any of them it stresses the white symbolism which is at once the mark of goodness, revelation, the overcoming of secret malignity, and the reconciliation of covert and overt foes. When all is revealed, by the very fact of revelation, for Ndembu thinking, all is fertile, healthy, strong, and pleasurable. But it is clear from the account of *Chihamba* that to obtain these delectable ends sacrifices are required. The demigod *Kavula* is sacrificed by the neophytes of his cultus, who are, in turn, sacrificed to him by his adepts. It is as though all social structural statuses, roles, and rules cancel one another, leaving a liminal space that is at once pure act and pure potentiality, a zero that is all. This limen is also the Ndembu *locus classicus* of communitas.

When the moment of communitas is over—and it must be remembered that the moment follows the episode in which the candidates have been shown that the effigy *Kavula* is literally a social construction, an artifact of culture—its efficacy is symbolically transferred to the personal shrine set up for each candidate. These shrines consist mainly of seeds and cuttings, as though *Kavula* were being "planted" in the personal symbolic space of each of his worshipers, whom he has slain and who have slain him, the fecund emptiness of their mutual death. When the cultural icons, the *signifiants*, the symbol vehicles of *Kavula*, have been exposed and dismantled, his invisible and potent meaning (*signifié*) is planted in the literal and the natural shape of seeds, there to regrow the cosmos and society, with which the new adept is now one, and therefore good, healthy, and fertile.

The religious ideas and processes I have just mentioned belong to the domain of performance, their power derived from the participation of the living people who use them. My counsel, therefore, to investigators of ritual processes would be to learn them in the first place "on their pulses," in coactivity with their enactors, having beforehand shared for a considerable time much of the people's daily life and gotten to know them not only as players of social roles, but as unique individuals, each with a style and a soul of his or her own. Only by these means will the investigator become aware of the communitas in the social structure and of the infiltration of social structure into communitas, as the scenes of the local drama of living succeed one another. He may then come to know how it is that all societies develop a need both for revelation and divination and construct appropriate cultural instruments for satisfying these needs. Divination, for example, may involve manual mantic techniques, astrology, or psychoanalysis; revelation may be sought by liturgical action or contemplation, by group therapy, or through psychedelic drugs. Man cannot tolerate darkness; he must have light, whether it be the sunlight of revelation or the flaring torch of divination.

The reader who knows my later work will see at once that my theory and methodology for the study of ritual and other cultural symbols have undergone certain changes, under the influence of contemporary linguistic theory (particularly the neo-Saussureans such as Roland Barthes) and the philosophy of language (through my encounter with the work of Max Black). Although my recent work is almost entirely uninfluenced by the views of Jung and Freud, I have thought it useful to retain the original text, which does reflect this influence. Anthropologists collect data often by a blind instinct that they may be later pressed for a rich theoretical yield. When they reflect upon these stubborn and puzzling facts they devise a number of makeshift frames, sometimes borrowed from other disciplines (and hence having the status of metaphors in the anthropological domain), and sometimes constructed ad hoc with an eye to the nature of the materials they confront. Only after a good deal of experimentation the investigator learns how to make a workable fit between data and frame. The papers on *Chihamba* and divination may perhaps be said to reveal an anthropological diviner in action, at the beginning of a long séance that has by no means been concluded. It should be remembered that when I was in the field in the early 1950s my only theoretical guidelines were derived from the school of Durkheim and the British functionalists. Then the majesty of the Freudian symbology of the unconscious appeared to me in the role of a master paradigm. I have elsewhere (*The Forest of Symbols* 1967:Chapter 1) stressed the crucial difference between psychological and cultural symbols and have warned against the danger of crude interpretation of cultural symbols by psychoanalytic concepts. But Freud's sense of the complexity of symbolic forms and actions, his discrimination between levels of meaning, and his insistence on the polysemous nature of dominant symbols and key metaphors, all these stimulated me to pursue inquiries into ritual processes with eyes opened to the richness and subtlety of the phenomena under observation.

But the Freudian model could not to my mind adequately account for the dramatic and performative aspects, not only of rituals themselves, but of the social and cultural processes in which these were embedded. Here I had to have recourse to the insights of dramatic and literary critics, for rituals are moments in the unending stream of developing and declining relationships between individuals and groups. These relationships are informed with reason, volition, and passion, and they are subject to fatigue, misunderstanding, and malevolent and benevolent manipulation. The problem of meaning in symbolic action derives as much from intent in the execution of actions and processes as from any underlying cognitive structures. The latter may set some as yet undetermined limits on human capacities for thinking and doing, but the free variables available for communication and manipulation in symbolic action are so diverse and numerous, and the rules for their combination so simple yet fruitful for the production of messages (including inspired and prophetic messages), that free will virtually reigns during important phases of the social process. Limits impose themselves mainly in the course of juridical, divinatory, and ritual action, for it is primarily in these settings that the moral order of a society is firmly reasserted as a set of constraints on malign (or merely random) personal or factional actions performed under the influence of self-serving passions. The account of the divinatory process given here and the exegeses of dominant symbols in *Chihamba* illustrate this moral circumscription of anticommunitarian action on the level of religious ritual. I have not been immune to the symbolic powers I have invoked in field investigation. After many years as an agnostic and monistic materialist I learned from the Ndembu that ritual and its symbolism are not merely epiphenomena or disguises of deeper social and psychological processes, but have ontological value, in some way related to man's condition as an evolving species, whose evolution takes place principally through its cultural innovations. I became convinced that religion is not merely a toy of the race's childhood, to be discarded at a nodal point of scientific and technological development, but is really at the heart of the human matter. Deciphering ritual forms and discovering what generates symbolic actions may be more germane to our cultural growth than we have supposed. But we have to put ourselves in some way inside religious processes to obtain knowledge of them. There must be a conversion experience. M. N. Srinivas, professor of anthropology at Delhi, recently spoke (in a series of lectures delivered in May 1974 at the University of Chicago on Indian culture and society) of anthropologists as thrice-born. They leave their natal culture to study an exotic culture, and return, having familiarized (as well as they may) the exotic, to an exoticized familiar culture wherein their social identity is reborn. So it should be with our religious traditions. We are born into the faith of our fathers, we distance ourselves from it, and then, in a movement of return, we re-enter it in sophisticated naiveté, civilized earnestness. Religion, like Watergate, is a scandal that will not go away. We have to live it through; it cannot be dispelled by a magical incantation or reduced to a non-sense by positivist or linguistic philosophy, for it is concerned with negative or midliminal experiences of the sort which perhaps provoked Ludwig Wittgenstein's ultimate aphorism "whereof one cannot speak, thereof one must be silent" (*Tractatus Logico Philosophicus*, Aphorism 7). That is why scientists of culture who ignore the implications of *Chihamba*, *Moby Dick*, the Transfiguration, the aphorisms of the Zen masters, the Sufis, and Wittgenstein's final surmounting of his own propositions (recalling Aquinas' final comment on the *Summa*, mentioned above) are in peril of crippling their understanding of the human condition. The obvious and the commonsensical must be seen in the light of the revealed, the manifest in that of the unmanifest (for which there may be no code, but which can be understood as the plenitude of an experience that indicates the emptiness of all codes). I am not, of course, arguing for silence (sterile *or* pregnant!), nor for a cessation of the scientific quest for a greater understanding of cognitive order, both in its simplicities and complexities. I am merely putting in a plea for greater attention to the properties of processes. Hegel has not said the last word on this matter, and process for man, still evolving, is the central problem—even if progress, creative ideas, new practices, often appear to sidle in from the margins and to emit from the weak, the marginals, the liminaries, and the outcasts. Let us go to Arnold van Gennep for his liminality, to Durkheim for his "effervescence," and to Max Weber for his "prophetic breaks" rather than to the more conventional wisdom of these seminal thinkers. And to Georg Simmel for his "conflict" and "problematics," rather than for his typologies. Today's liminality is tomorrow's centrality. Consideration of the negative instance provokes science to a grasp on general laws. Evolving species push back boundaries, so that it is on boundaries that creative thought must dwell. Inner space, like outer space, has boundaries, and these often prove to be the boundaries of symbolic systems. Man has to be continually extending the limits of the sayable by active contemplation of the un-sayable. Silence is not the answer, as many of our counter-cultural friends would suggest. Silence is our problem, not our answer. We are provoked by silence, negativity, liminality, ambiguity, into efforts of extended comprehension. I hope that this analysis of *Chihamba* may serve to open up a difficult area in the developing science of culture.

PART ONE

CHIHAMBA THE WHITE SPIRIT: A RITUAL DRAMA OF THE NDEMBU

CHAPTER 1

Chihamba the
White Spirit [1]

In my book *Schism and Continuity* (1957:Chapter 10) I out-
lined some of the main features of the *Chihamba* ritual, de-
scribing it as one of the "cults of affliction." Cults of affliction are performed for individuals, who are said by Ndembu
to have been "caught" by the spirits of deceased relatives
whom they have forgotten to honor with small gifts of crops
and beer, or whom they have offended by omitting to mention when prayers are made at the village shrine-trees
(*nyiyombu*). People may also be "caught" for quarreling with
close kin or as representatives of kin groups torn by quarrels.
Being "caught" means to be afflicted with bad luck at hunting in the case of men, with reproductive disorders in the
case of women, and with illness in both cases. A distinction
is made by Ndembu between the spirit (*mukishi*), which af-

[1] I wish to express my appreciation to the Rhodes-Livingstone Institute
for financing my field research, to the Center for Advanced Study in the
Behavioral Sciences for providing the opportunity, in the form of a fellow-
ship, to write Part One, and to the University of Manchester for leave of
absence to avail myself of that opportunity. I am most grateful for the sec-
retarial help of Mrs. Jean Pearce at the Center. My field work among the
Ndembu of Mwinilunga District in Zambia was carried out during
1950–1952 and 1953–1954 as a Research Officer of the Rhodes-Livingstone
Institute.

flicts, and its mode of affliction. The afflicting spirit is a known and named deceased relative of the afflicted person or patient (*muyeji*). The patient is at the same time a candidate for initiation into the curative cult; the doctor (*chimbuki*) is an adept in that cult. The mode of affliction refers to certain characteristics of this spirit which are correlated with outstanding features of the sufferer's misfortune or illness. The name of the mode of affliction is the name of the ritual performed to treat the afflicted person. The treatment is carried out by a number of doctors or adepts (*ayimbuki* or *ayimbanda*), both male and female, who have themselves been closely associated with previous performances of this kind of ritual. They form a sort of ad hoc cult association. The doctor-adepts are arranged in a loose hierarchy of ritual prestige, and each performs a different task. Between doctors and patients there may be no ties of kinship or affinity.

Each cult of affliction has exoteric and esoteric phases, the former attended by anyone who can come and the latter by initiated and initiands only. Esoteric phases take place either in the secrecy of the patient's hut or in the bush behind a sacred fence or screen. In the past doctors drove the uninitiated (*antondu*) away from such sacralized areas with bows and arrows.

Several cults have the classical *rite de passage* form, involving the performance of two successive rituals, separated by a period during which the patient undergoes partial seclusion from secular life. The first of these rituals, in cults where women constitute the senior patients, is called *ku-lembeka* or *ilembi*, and the second, the more elaborate and important, *ku-tumbuka*. A candidate who had undergone *ku-lembeka* may play a minor role in the cult, but cannot become an officiant until she has "passed at" (*ku-hitaku*) *ku-tumbuka*.

Chihamba is a typical cult of affliction, with *ilembi* and *ku-tumbuka* phases. After *ku-tumbuka* a number of taboos are observed for about a month, during which time the candidate undergoes partial seclusion from secular affairs. Two types of supernatural beings are believed to afflict the living in *Chihamba*. The first is an ancestress of the senior patient (who is a woman), and the second is a nature spirit or demigod, called *Kavula*. *Kavula*, spoken of as male, is an archaic term for 'lightning,' perhaps connected etymologically with *nvula*, rain. *Kavula* is described as the husband and the ancestress as the wife. The ancestress is said to catch the patient, while *Kavula*, impersonated in various ways and during different ritual episodes by male doctors, gives each patient a special adept name from a limited stock of such names. The *Chihamba* manifestation of spirits [2] afflicts its victims in several ways. Most commonly it is said to cause pains in the whole body, especially in the neck, and a feeling of extreme cold. Sometimes it is said to induce decay in crops planted by the objects of its wrath. It may also afflict women with various reproductive troubles. Men who have experienced bad luck at hunting allow themselves to be caught by female *Chihamba* doctors so that *Kavula* may remove their misfortune. The *Chihamba* manifestation is, in fact, a sort of compendium of misfortunes recognized by Ndembu. *Chihamba* is the most important of the cults of affliction and is attended by many

[2] A spirit is a named known person; a manifestation is a set of traditional traits. We distinguish them but the Ndembu do not. I shall italicize such manifestations to indicate that these are Ndembu concepts. To distinguish, for example, *Kavula* or *Kayong'u* (see below) as personalities from their denomination as instrumentalities for ancestor spirits, by using roman type, would be to introduce a Western distinction not made by the Ndembu.

more people than come to any other ritual except boys' circumcision.

Sources of Data

I observed only one performance of *ilembi daChihamba*, the first or lesser phase of this ritual, and that was early in my first period of field work. Many of the implications were lost on me, although I recorded many observations. Later in my first trip I attended part of a *ku-tumbuka* phase. Again my information was not really satisfactory, for I was tactfully kept away from the esoteric episodes. But toward the end of my second field trip, in circumstances described in *Schism and Continuity* (1957:303–317) I was fortunate enough to be able to observe and describe the whole of a performance of *ku-tumbuka* as well as the antecedent social events in the sponsoring village, Mukanza. Indeed, my wife and I were classed as candidates, although we did not personally undergo the questionings and trials that were the customary lot of *Chihamba* candidates. Nevertheless, we were permitted to see, and even to photograph, most of the episodes, including some of a highly secret character. Many of the adepts discussed the symbolism and procedure with us during and after the performance. All the adepts gave us permission to publish a full account, for they were aware that it would not be long before most of the Ndembu rituals would be forgotten by the young people, as labor migration became more extensive.

As well as observing these performances, I collected several accounts of *Chihamba* from informants. The fullest of these was given me by a *Chihamba* adept named Muchona. This man was by far my best informant on ritual matters.

He was himself a doctor-adept in most Ndembu cults of affliction. Better than this for my purposes, he was highly articulate and had a passionate enthusiasm for everything to do with religion. I spent many hours with him, discussing not only Ndembu ritual, but also Christianity and Judaism. We were usually accompanied in these sessions by an intelligent young village schoolmaster, Windson Kashinakaji, who helped me to sort out knotty points of Ndembu religious terminology—for the ritual vocabularly was highly technical. Muchona's Lunda (the language spoken by Ndembu) was extremely idiomatic, condensed, and allusive, and Windson helped me to record texts from him. I took down, with Windson's aid, a full account of *Chihamba* procedure from Muchona some months before I observed *ku-tumbuka* in detail at Mukanza Village. There are many discrepancies between his narrative and my observations. Muchona himself played a leading role in the performance I witnessed, but several other doctors contributed their knowledge of *Chihamba* procedure. The result of their deliberations and wrangles was a series of compromises, departing in many respects from Muchona's picture of the correct form. From my experience at many performances of other kinds of ritual, where senior practitioners of approximately equal status were present, I am prepared to assert that no performance of a given cult ritual ever precisely resembles another. Where there is no political or ecclesiastical centralization, no liturgical literature, and practitioners in a mobile society came from widely separated birthplaces, it is only to be expected that there is no authorized version of a given ritual. The wonder to me was that so much agreement did exist in the details of different performances.

In order to present my data so as to give the reader as accurate a picture as possible of the various categories of information I use in the subsequent analysis, I first divide the *ku-tumbuka* ritual, on the basis of my own observations, into consecutive episodes, each of which constitutes a culturally defined task. Next I take each episode in turn, first recording my own observations, then giving Muchona's account if it does not tally with mine. After this, I present indigenous explanations of the procedural items and indigenous exegesis of the symbolism. Where it is practicable, I give the names and describe the relevant social characteristics of my informants and attempt to estimate the relative merits of their interpretations. Finally, I append comparative observational and exegetic material from other kinds of Ndembu ritual. Wherever I consider that Ndembu explanations raise points of key theoretical importance, I insert vernacular texts to support them. From time to time, at important stages in the procedure, I interleave the narrative with photographs. Since my data on the *ku-lembeka* phase of *Chibamba* are thin, I use them only to throw light on some point in the *ku-tumbuka* phase.

The order of episodes at the *Chibamba* ritual performed at Mukanza Village is as follows:

First Day (March 6, 1954)
  1. The sending of the arrow
  2. Ceremonial beer drink
Second Day (March 7, 1954)
  1. Prayer before the village ancestor shrines
  2. "Taking an ember from the chief's fire" (*kwokola kesi*)
  3. Blowing powdered white clay on *Chibamba* rattles
  4. Anointing arms with white clay

5. Collecting *isaku* medicine
6. Preparation of *isaku* medicine
7. *Ku-tumbuka* night dance
   a. Preparation of *nsompu* washing medicine
   b. Entry of patients into principal patient's hut and interrogation by *Kavula*
   c. Public dance

Third Day (March 8, 1954)

1. Rousing the candidates with cock's feathers
2. Inserting the arrow in principal patient's hut thatch
3. *Isoli*
   a. Marking out the sacred *mukoleku* barrier
   b. Sacralizing the *musoli* tree (*ku-bola* or *ku-busa musoli*)
   c. Dragging the meal mortar to *isoli* site
   d. Preparation of *isoli*
   e. Fitting the arrowhead to the shaft
4. The chasing (*ku-hang'a*)
   a. Beginning of chasing (*ku-tachika ku-hang'a*)
   b. The *mpanda* slave yokes
   c. Interrogation of candidates
5. Greeting *Kavula*
6. The killing of *Kavula*
7. Concluding oration at the village

Fourth Day (March 9, 1954)

1. The cutting of the *ikamba daChihamba* root and collection of components of *kantong'a* and medicines
2. The *yibi* epidode
3. The making of *kantong'a* shrines
4. Beheading of a white hen
5. Cutting medicines for the pots (*ku-teta mazawu*)
6. Planting beans and maize round *kantong'a*

7. "Stopping up *Chihamba*" (*ku-jika Chihamba*)
8. Ceremonial payment of adepts
9. Taboos

Four weeks after beginning of *ku-tumbuka* (April 3, 1954), lifting of taboos (*ku-jilola*)

The First Day

1. The sending of the arrow

In the late afternoon on March 6, 1954, the main organizer of *ku-tumbuka*, Sandombu, brought a calabash of beer brewed by his wife Zuliyana, one of the two principal patients,[3] to the kitchen of the female organizer, Nyaluwema. There a number of *Chihamba* senior and junior adepts were gathered. The headman of Mukanza Village then sent an arrow to Nyaluwema, confirming her appointment as senior organizer and ceremonially inaugurating the performance. Each of the male adepts in order of precedence, beginning with Sandombu, then dipped the point of the arrow in the beer and licked it. Order of precedence depended partly on the number of occasions an adept "had been to *Chihamba*" and partly on the role assigned to him jointly by Sandombu and Nyaluwema. Not all the male adepts had arrived by that time, and some *antondu* or uninitiated men "gate-crashed" the proceedings in the hope of getting some beer. After all the adepts had licked the arrow, it was draped with a necklace of white beads, provided by the older principal patient, Headman Mukanza's wife, and taken away by Nyaluwema.

2. Ceremonial beer drink

At the beer drink which followed, adepts were served first by Sandombu's order. One of the uninitiated men grumbled

[3] The other was Nyamukola: see Turner 1957: passim.

that he had not been selected as a candidate (*muyeji*—also "patient") for initiation. Theoretically this is done by capture, as we shall see, but in practice, persons chosen by a meeting of adepts are told in advance that they will be captured on a certain path. He pointed out his close kinship connections with several adepts and candidates. But the others laughed at him, saying that kinship did not establish claims to be caught at *Chihamba*. Only those suffering from some obvious misfortune might be chosen; the grumbler had a paid job at a European store; why should he complain?

The conversation turned to degrees of ritual status. It was agreed that a woman with the *Chihamba*-name Katendi was allowed to approach closely the sacred site called *isoli* (see pages 78–86 below), a sort of tabernacle, while a woman named Kalukeki had to remain at a little distance from it. While this was going on, a very senior adept, Sakutoha, was carving a wooden arrowhead, one of two used by adepts to drive uninitiated persons ceremonially away from the area of bush sacralized on the third day of *Chihamba*. Nyaluwema later entrusted her bead-hung arrow to this adept, Sakutoha, for she feared that she had forgotten many of the customs of *Chihamba*.

After the beer drink Sandombu discussed the procedural form of the ritual with the other adepts. The whole village was in a ferment of pleasurable expectation.

Indigenous exegesis

White beads. Nyaluwema explained that the white beads stood for "the *mufu* of *Chihamba*." *Mufu* means a dead person and is a term often applied to dangerous ghosts, rather than moral ancestor spirits (*akishi*). Such ghosts are believed to have power to kill living persons who clap eyes on them. In other contexts I have heard the term *mufu* used interchangeably with *mukishi*. *Chihamba* manifestations of spirits are nevertheless regarded as exceptionally dangerous for, while most other manifestations cause misfortunes only, *Chihamba* can kill the person it afflicts.

White beads are used, said Muchona, because *Chihamba* is a "white" spirit. Many things representing *Chihamba* have a white color, as we shall see. In some forms of divination powdered white clay (*mpemba*) represents the *Chihamba* spirit.

My observations and informants' accounts show that beads often represent in ritual various manifestations of ancestor spirits. For example, white beads symbolize the *Mukala* manifestation of a hunter spirit. This is also a dangerous manifestation, for *Mukala* is believed sometimes to lure lost hunters into swamps at night in the guise of a white light, like the will-o'-the-wisp of English peasant superstition. The *Kayong'u* spirit-manifestation, which "catches" a man with various asthmatic and bronchial troubles and which, when propitiated, becomes the tutelary of a diviner, is symbolized in ritual by red beads. *Kayong'u* is also a violent spirit capable of causing death.

On the other hand, during various episodes of *Nkang'a*, the girls' puberty ritual, white beads often represent female fertility or many children. For example, they are draped around a miniature bow (*kawuta*), placed at the apex of the novice's seclusion hut. The bow, too, stands for procreative ability (*lusemu*).

When my wife mentioned this meaning of white beads in *Nkang'a* to Nyaluwema, she was told that the *Chihamba* beads also represented fertility. But she added that for a patient over childbearing age, like Nyamukola, the beads did not mean fertility but strengthening (*ku-kolisha*). The term "whiteness" (*wutooka*, *chitooka*, or *kutooka*) and its concrete ritual expression, powdered white clay (*mpemba*), are said by many informants to mean, among other things, *wukolu*, "strength" or "good health."

The arrow was said by all informants also to represent the spirit (*mukishi*).

The Second Day (The Day of "Medicine" Collection)

1. Prayer before the village ancestor shrines

In the morning I was told that "the adepts will pray at the *nyiyombu* shrine-trees of Mukanza Village." Heavy rain prevented this while I was with the adepts, and I did not observe such a prayer at any time, although it may have taken place. Petitions are normally addressed to the ancestor spirits at the village shrines before the great life-crisis rites of boys' circumcision (*Mukanda*) and girls' puberty (*Nkang'a*), but not before rites of affliction.

2. "Taking an ember from the chief's fire" (kwokola kesi)

A member of the village returned from Chief Kanongesha's capital with the news that the chief's permission had been obtained to hold *Chihamba* that day. The villagers had sent him to the chief with a calabash of beer and presents of food as a notification of the ritual. In the past, it is said that a glowing piece of charcoal from the chief's fire was sent to kindle the sacred fire of *ku-tumbuka*. Today his verbal permission is enough.

3. Blowing powdered white clay on Chihamba *rattles* (1 P.M.)

First, Sakutoha inserted the arrow decorated with white beads in the earth about six yards in front of the hut of the principal patient, Nyamukola. A *lwalu* winnowing basket,

1. *Yileng'a* rattles, no two alike.

used in all rituals for the collection of medicines, was put beside it. All the *yileng'a* rattles, peculiar to *Chihamba*, and carried by adepts, were placed in the winnowing basket. A male adept, Sandombu, picked them up, tested them for sound, and replaced them. He picked them up again and licked them. Then he blew powdered white clay over them to bless them. All the female adepts picked up their rattles and shook them in time to the song, *kamukombela*, in which the male adepts joined.

Exegesis

Inserting the arrow. According to Sakutoha, to insert an arrow into anything is to become its owner (prefix *mweni-* or *mwini-*). The *Chihamba* spirit has become the owner of the patient (*mwenimuyeji*). It is the same idea as that expressed in

2. An adept draws a cross on her arm in white clay.

the notion catching the patient (*ku-kwata muyeji*). Later the patient's personal shrine will be erected where the arrow was fixed.

Rattles. The handles of *yileng'a* rattles, according to Muchona, are made from laths, split off from trees by adzes. On the one hand this is to provide woodcarvers with a smooth surface on which to work patterns, and on the other the strokes of the adze resemble those of lightning (*nzaji*). This is because *Kavula* himself "is the lightning." Chips (*yibalu*) from lightning-splintered trees are actually inserted in the smaller rattles (*nzenzi*), used at the *isoli* (see below). The sound of rattles is said to resemble that of thunder (*ku-dolomwina*) when it rattles in the distance (*kwakulehi*). This sound "has power" (*ng'ovu*). In the large *yileng'a* rattles, grains of maize make the noise. Maize, as we shall see, plays an important

role in *Chihamba*. Each adept's rattle has its own carved de-
sign, and *yileng'a* are made from different species of trees,
including *mukula* (*Pterocarpus angolensis*), *katawubwang'u*, and
muteteli—on account of "the smoothness of their bodies,"
says Muchona. The sound of rattles, like those of drums and
singing, at the beginning of any ritual is to "rouse the spirit"
(*ku-tonisha mukishi*).

When a *Chihamba* adept gives his *chileng'a* rattle to someone, he does not let go until the other tugs at it. This again is
a sign of strength.

Winnowing basket. Muchona explains the use of the *lwalu*
winnowing basket for collecting medicines as follows: "All
medicines are put in *lwalu* because a person's food is always
placed in *lwalu* which means the cassava meal (*wung'a*) he
usually eats; in the winnowing basket they separate fine meal
from coarse and lumpy—medicines are like fine and good
food."

Blowing. Nyaluwema said that the *mpemba* was blown onto
the rattles "to please the spirit" (*nakutiyisha kuwaha mukishi*).
Blowing *mpemba* on a person or object, an act known as *ku-
pumina*, means to bless (*ku-kiswila nkisu*). The act of blowing
is common to a variety of ritual contexts. Ndembu blow on
their food before eating as a sign of gratitude to the ancestor
spirits who have given them good crops. Here the act is
known as *ku-seng'ula*. In *Chihamba* the whiteness is specified
by informants as standing for the *Chihamba* spirit-manifestation, for "*Chihamba* is a white spirit."

4. Anointing arms with white clay

Nyaluwema, the principal woman organizer, put white
clay on the inner side of her lower arm, although some
adepts said that she did this prematurely. Soon the others

followed suit. One female adept, Manyosa, normally very knowledgeable in ritual matters, drew a cross shape in *mpemba* on her upper left arm.

Exegesis

According to Manyosa, the cross shape represents *Samuseng'a*, one of the esoteric names of *Kavula*, derived from *ku-seng'uka*, "to multiply" (of fruits, crops, and offspring). We shall find further examples of the white cross as a symbol later.

5. *Collecting* isaku *medicine* (c. 2 P.M.)

The adepts encircled Nyamukola's hut, singing. Then they stopped near the arrow. From this point they set off through the village in complete silence to the bush to collect *isaku* medicine. After they crossed the Boma motor road into the bush a fierce dispute arose when Sandombu declared that he would collect as *ishikenu* or principal medicine the roots and leaves of the *mudyi* tree (*Diplorrhyncus mossambicensis*). Everyone opposed him saying that the *mucheki* tree was the true *ishikenu* "for *isoli*." Some whispered that he was drunk. Eventually Sandombu agreed that *mucheki* should be collected. Down they went on the precipitous slope to the source of a small stream, for *mucheki* tends to grow in such a habitat. After taking some leaves from a small *mucheki* bush, they found a large *mucheki* which they declared was *ishikenu*. First the adepts encircled it, then Sakutoha made invocation before it (using white clay) to the afflicting ancestress Nyamakang'a, while the female adepts crouched in a circle to listen. Then they set about digging up the whole tree in order to get at the root, a woman doing the hoeing. When the tree had been lifted out bodily by the adepts, Sakutoha cut off the root with his ax, divided it into four pieces, and then re-placed the tree in an upright position "so that the patient might be cured," he said. About a dozen leaves were re-moved from the *mucheki*. Then the adepts returned to the dry bush, taking leaves from *munkalampoli*, *musoli*, *mucha*, *museng'u*, and *mutuhu* trees. Arguments went on all the time about what medicines to collect. All the vegetable medicines were placed in the flat, round winnowing basket carried by Sakutoha.

Exegesis

Isaku. An *isaku* is a skin pouch containing medicines. San-dombu told me that the *isaku* used at *Chihamba* was made from the skin of the giant rat (*Cricetomys*), called *chituba* in ev-eryday speech but known as *kambidyima* during *Chihamba*. I asked Muchona why its skin was used in *Chihamba*. He re-plied as follows: "When *chituba* walks in darkness it gives many sounds by walking on dead leaves and sticks; it causes fear. That is why it is used. Women with babies are not given this animal to eat, otherwise their children will not be able to control their defecating.[4] When *chituba* makes its bur-row it fills up the entrance (*wina*), literally 'hole' afterward." I could not make much sense out of this at the time, but it occurred to me recently that Ndembu might associate the noise of rattles and the nocturnal rustling of the *chituba*. The noise of the rattles is often described by informants as "terri-ble" or "causing fear," and, as we shall see, *isaku* medicine is placed on the butt of the *yileng'a* rattles and given to adepts and candidates to eat.

[4] Cf. the joking derivation of *Chihamba* from *ku-hambuka*, "to defecate as infants do."

Encircling. To encircle (*ku-jing'amuka*) has the general meaning in Ndembu ritual contexts of "to sacralize" (*ku-jilisha*). We shall come across other instances and forms of ritual encirclement (see pages 80–81 and 124) where this process may be more appropriately discussed. When Nyamukola's hut was encircled this meant that it was now regarded as a sacred site. *Ku-jilisha* means "to taboo" or "cause to be forbidden."

Mucheki. The *mucheki* tree, as the first tree from which medicines (*yitumbu*) were taken, was also encircled. In this respect it might be said to represent all the other trees and plants visited, for these are not encircled. Another term for a place, object, or person thus sacralized is *chakumbadyi*, "something aside or set apart." It is as though the object were placed outside ordinary routinized life.

Ishikenu—First tree. The term *ishikenu* is connected with the customary greeting "*shikenu mwani*," "please arrive," made to a respected visitor. The first medicine tree usually receives an address of greeting; in some rituals or episodes of a ritual directly, in others as the symbol or dwelling (there is much ambiguity here) of the afflicting ancestor spirit. Another term for the first tree visited is *mukulumpi*, "the elder," for the first tree is the elder or senior of the set of trees whose parts comprise a specific type of medicine. The *ishikenu* may be regarded as substantival in function and the others as adjectival, qualifying and extending its meaning.

Invocation. Sakutoha's invocation was typical of its kind and I give the vernacular text:

Mpemba oyu Nyamakang'a. Lelu neyi eyi wakwata iwu muntu Nyamukola muChihamba lelu mumbuku. Ng'oma yindi ching'a ayihang'ani chachiwahi. Kumadiki nawa cheng'i ching'a kumusefwila nyitondu chachiwahi

swayi swayi yindi. Wumwinki wukolu. Mpemba oyu, walwa nawa owu.
Enu mwading'i nakuuka chachiwahi Chihamba, twayenu tukenu.

(That [is your] white clay, Nyamakang'a. Today if you catch
this person Nyamukola in *Chihamba*, today release her. [At] her
drum they must dance for you well. And also tomorrow there must
be an increase in numbers of [her] vegetable medicines well and
quickly. You must give her strength. That is [your] white clay,
that is also [your] beer. You who were curing well, [o] *Chihamba*,
come, fly [hither].)

Medicines. At this episode the prayer is made to Nyamakang'a, the afflicting ancestress, on behalf of her matrilineal kinswoman Nyamukola. In *Chihamba* special stress is laid
on the candidates acquiring correct knowledge of the medicines vested in the cult. The term *yitumbu,* "medicines," is
applied widely to mean not only vegetable substances, possessing nonempirical power to heal, but also portions of animals and birds, minerals, and even physical structures—
everything that is thought to confer mystical benefit on the
patient. The term *nyitondu,* however, literally "trees," is reserved for vegetable medicines, whether used as potions,
poultices, or external applications, or as components of
shrines or sacred fences.

White beer. The reference to beer is to a libation poured by
the invoking adept at the base of the tree. When invocations
are made to ancestor spirits only beer with a white color,
such as maize beer (*walwa wakabaka*) or kaffir corn beer
(*walwa wamasa*), may be used. Its use exactly parallels the use
of white clay which is sprinkled on the ground in three
(sometimes one or four) lines from the shrine (whether a
village *muyombu* tree or a bush "medicine-tree") to the person
praying. Whiteness (*wutooka*) is a polysemous term signify-
ing, among other qualities, goodness, harmony, good will,

health, purity, and candor.[5] The appropriate attitude to adopt when invoking is a "white" attitude. Not only purity of thought and feeling are implied, but an earnest wish for the harmony and well-being of the whole social group.

It is possible to infer from a series of such invocations, although this was not explicitly stated to me by Ndembu, that the afflicting spirit is exhorted to come and fly into the tree itself and invest the medicine with its propitious, as contrasted with its punitive and harmful, qualities.

According to Muchona and Sakutoha, the *mucheki* tree is the *ishikenu* or dominant medicine not only of the *isaku* episode, but of the whole *ku-tumbuka* ritual. Both of them told me that it was used "because of its white root, which is just like white clay—it is completely white." Because of its whiteness it is also a "symbol" (*chinjikijilu*, from *ku-jikijila*, to blaze a trail by cutting marks in tree trunks or by breaking and bending branches) of *Chihamba* itself. As I have mentioned, *Chihamba* is conspicuous for its many white symbols. We shall come across many more, and I shall discuss the particular characteristics of each in addition to its color as they appear in serial order. But I cite here a text given me by Muchona on the pervasive white symbolism of *Chihamba*, since it formed a parenthesis in his discussion of the meaning of *mucheki*:

Yawaha kutookesha nachu mujimba wamuntu kudi akishi hela Chihamba muntu ashakami chachiwahi; neyi wunakoli dehi kulonda akatong'ojoki kumulembeka nayena nyitondu oyu.

(It is good to whiten a person's body with it [i.e. with *mpemba*] toward [or on behalf of] the ancestor spirits or *Chihamba* so that the person may stay well; [it is good too] if he is strong already, so that

[5] It is worth mentioning that the English words candor and candidate are both derived from Latin *candidus*, "white."

he should think about the *ku-lembeka* ritual and also those vegetable medicines.)

He went on to say that "when white things are grouped together, the spirits can see them and make a patient free from diseases."

White clay, *mpemba*. Several attributes of *mpemba*, as a white symbol, are mentioned here by Muchona. It is thought of (1) as having intrinsic efficacy (so that a person should stay well); (2) as a reminder to an adept of *Chihamba* and its medicines; and (3) as the embodiment of a wish directed toward the spirits that the patient should recover. It thus represents a present, past, and future condition. It implies cohesion and also continuity.

Uprightness. With regard to the replacement of the tree in an upright position, Muchona told me: "If the tree was left lying on the ground, this meant that the patient's sickness would go on. But if the tree was planted again the patient would stand up." In Ndembu ritual there are further instances of this theme of uprightness; in *Chihamba*, in *Mukanda* (boys' circumcision)—where it is connected with the notion of the erectile penis, in *Nkang'a*, and in hunters' funerary rites where the corpse is buried sitting upright. At *Chihamba* the *mucheki* tree itself was doomed, for the root taken was its taproot, source of its strength. Its upright position was only a symbol for the patient's wished-for recovery.

The fact that a woman adept cut down the tree, and not, as was usual in Ndembu rituals of affliction, a male adept, was discussed by Nyaluwema in the following terms: "Women made the first *Chihamba*, and then the men caught it. Women used to be the big doctors, now the men are; a long time ago the men followed behind."

There was general agreement among the senior adepts about the meanings of the other trees used for medicines.

Munkalampoli. *Munkalampoli*, according to Muchona, with the agreement of Sakutoha, Sandombu, and others, "has little thorns which catch someone passing, just as a disease catches a person. If *Chihamba* catches a person in this way, it must release him today."

Musoli. *Musoli* is a tree used in various ways in nearly all Ndembu rituals. Its meaning is partly a function of its natural properties and partly of its name. Young shoots of *musoli* and its fruits are much appreciated by duiker and other woodland antelope at the beginning of the rainy season. They emerge from concealment in the deep bush to eat these and may be readily shot or trapped by hunters. Ndembu derive the term *musoli* from *ku-solola*, "to make seen" or "to produce to view." In their thinking, the *musoli* tree reveals the coveted game to hunters. Forked branches of *musoli* wood, peeled of bark to make them dry and resistant, are used as shrines to hunters' spirits in the *Wubinda* and *Wuyang'a* hunting cults. Its wood is described as hard and termite-proof. String cannot be made from its bark, and so Ndembu say that it "does not tie up huntsmanship." In the hunting cults and in *Mukanda* the senses of *musoli* paramountly stressed are the masculine values of toughness and strength and the production of many animals to view. In women's reproductive cults it signifies fertility, since it bears many fruits. But in whatever ritual context it appears, it has the pervasive meaning of to reveal, to disclose openly what has been hidden. As a medicine it is believed to have special efficacy in what one of my informants described as "making things appear quickly." As I have said, the main processual theme of Ndembu ritual is to make known what has been hidden, partly by naming the afflicting spirit, so that "it is remembered by many people," and partly by expressing by means of symbols the order of the universe (including the social order) as Ndembu conceive it. It also has the meaning, so Muchona told me when explaining the *Nkula* ritual, of "speaking private matters in public," for often in Ndembu ritual hidden grudges (*yitela*) are brought to light by adepts and candidates in an endeavor to locate the cause of a spirit's anger. We shall return to this symbol later in the indigenous exegesis of *Chihamba*, for it has great importance in the *isoli* episode—*isoli* is also derived from *ku-solola*.

Mucha. *Mucha,* too, is frequently employed as a symbol, and its products as medicine, in Ndembu ritual. The *mucha* tree (*Parinari mobola*) bears a delicious fruit (*incha*) like a peach in color, with a hard stone. Like *musoli* it produces fruit at the beginning of the rains, and is regarded as an indicator of their onset. In the *Musolu* [6] ritual, performed by a chief or senior headman to bring on the rains if they are unduly belated, the *mucha* tree plays a leading role. Because of the hardness and long-lasting properties of its stone, the *mucha* tree is known in the esoteric language of divination as *mwaka,* which means either a season or long ago. Its senses therefore include: (1) fertility (from its fruits and as harbinger of the rains that promote growth); (2) toughness (from its stone); (3) longevity (from its stone). [7] It is sometimes known as the tree of God (*mutondu waNzambi*), presumably from its imputed relationship with the seasonal and productive cycle. In *Chi-*

[6] The term *musolu* is yet another derivative of *ku-solola*. The avowed aim of the *Musolu* ritual is "to make the rains appear."

[7] See page 306 below for an interpretation of the *incha* stone as a divinatory object. There it has the general sense of taking a long time.

hamba it seems to be connected with *Kavula*, whose manifestations include lightning, rain, and fertility.

Museng'u. The *museng'u* tree has a similar range of senses to *musoli* and *mucha.* Sakutoha told me that in addition to bearing numerous snall fruits (*museng'u* is derived from *ku-seng'uka*, "to increase and multiply") and having a tough wood from which hunting shrines (*ayishing'a* or *nyichanka*) are made, *museng'u* has many flowers, full of honey. *Museng'u* is used in ritual to attract many people to the public performance, just as bees are attracted to the flowers. "The spirit will be pleased that many people will hear its name mentioned and remember it." Sakutoha thought that the name *museng'u* might be connected with *ku-seng'ula*, "to bless food by blowing on it." Muchona, however, did not agree with this derivation.

Mutuhu. Muchona derived *mutuhu*, the last medicine collected, from *ku-tuhuka*, meaning to leap out and usually applied to the way a mole leaps out of the ground. In the same way a disease must *tuhuka* from the patient's body.

6. Preparation of isaku medicine

The adepts returned to the village. All circled the principal candidate's hut again. A mat was placed on the side of the arrow away from the hut. All circled the arrow, singing; their circlings became wilder and more exuberant all the time. A young female adept carried the winnowing basket. A cloth was spread over the top to hide the medicines it contained. When the dance was over, the winnowing basket was laid on the mat. A female adept took the cloth off, then replaced it to expose the *mucheki* roots only. Sakutoha took these roots and began to scrape off the white outer covering on top of the cloth (which had been contributed by a female adept). All the adepts crowded round shaking their *yileng'a* rattles and singing "*Kamukombela, mayonde,*" while Sakutoha scraped the root, its whiteness being dramatically obvious. Whenever children approached they were driven off violently.

Some logs were placed side by side, a mat was laid on them, and the cloth, covered with scrapings of *mucheki* root, was spread out on the mat. The scrapings (*nyemba*) were then left to dry. The senior female adepts took the winnowing basket containing the rattles and leaves to one side. Sakutoha took the bead-hung arrow and put it to lean against principal patient Nyamukoila's hut. Nyamukoila was sitting in her hut by that time.

Other *mucheki* scrapings were pounded by a senior female adept, together with fine *ibanda* salt, to sweeten the medicine (*ku-towesha yitumbu*—meaning both to sweeten and to salt medicine). She did this just outside Nyamukoila's doorway. Women stood the the left, men to the right, of the hut.

Sandombu put salt on the butt of his rattle and gave it to both adepts and patients to lick. The scrapings were finally collected and put into an *isaku* pouch.

Exegesis

Mucheki waluseng'a. According to Nyaluwema, the bark scrapings of *mucheki* are called *mucheki waluseng'a*. This medicine is to be eaten a little at a time, mixed with salt (*mung'wa webanda*—from salt deposits), taken on the tip of the tongue off the end of the rattle. It is to strengthen the body and is for all the patients and for those doctors only who have passed through *ku-lembeka*, the first ritual of *Chihamba*.

Ibanda salt. The medicine, said Muchona, is pounded with

ibanda salt, because *ibanda* "has renown" (*mpuhu*), and "is liked by *Kavula*." Indeed, many wars took place in central Africa for control over salt deposits [8] before European overlordship was consolidated. Bundles of salt seem to have constituted a form of currency among the west-central Bantu. For example, we find Chinguli (Turner 1955:17), the Lunda founder of the Bangala state, according to Carvalho, the Portuguese explorer, exhorting his people to work their salt deposits (Portuguese *salinas*) at Quilunda and Lutona, for these were "their good fortune; in them they had the wherewithal to buy many slaves in his sister [Luweji Ankondi]'s state, and they would lack neither sustenance nor the means of clothing themselves like the sons of Muene Puto [the Portuguese]."

Eating without hands. Eating food directly from an object without the use of hands is a recurrent feature of Ndembu ritual behavior. For example, in the hunting cult of *Wuyang'a,* lumps of cassava mush are eaten off a gun by adepts and candidates, and in *Mukanda* newly circumcised boys eat mush from a circumcision knife. I could get no satisfactory explanation of the meaning of this from Ndembu.

7. Ku-tumbuka *night dance* (7 P.M.). *a. Preparation of* nsompu *washing medicine*

After dark a ritual fire was lit in front of the principal patient Nyamukola's hut. A large heap of *mukula* firewood was piled near the initial site of the *Chihamba* arrow. Some said *mukula* was the sacred firewood of *Chihamba*, others that any kind of wood could be used. The main thing was to have a huge fire, "so that everything could be clearly seen." Two *manung'u* clay pots were placed near the fire, one quite close to it, for holding medicines respectively. A *chizanda* potsherd

[8] See, for some examples, Turner 1955: 17–18.

was also used. All contained warm water and pounded-leaf medicine (*nsompu*) for drinking and washing with. The medicines were those collected in the afternoon.

A tremendous dispute about the procedure broke out. Koshita, who had recently officiated at an *Ihamba* [9] ritual for Nyamukola, and who was also a senior *Chihamba* adept, angrily claimed that Sandombu had omitted to collect certain medicines, such as *muntung'ulu* and *mwang'ala*, in the afternoon. More than that, it was his job that evening to bring in a winnowing basket, maize, grains, beans, kaffir corn grains, sweet potatoes, and cassava. He had not shown up yet. Some spoke up in his defense, saying that he had been drunk in the afternoon. But others said that the job of organizer was too much for Sandombu—that he "spoke much but knew little." When Sandombu did arrive, an extremely wise and able old adept called Lambakasa very gently but firmly told Sandombu to fetch all the foods mentioned by Koshita and also to fetch a calabash of maize or kaffir corn beer. As we have noted these are "white" beers and are used for invoking the "white" ancestor spirits.

Sandombu brought the things mentioned on a winnowing basket, and Lambakasa then invoked the ancestress "who had come out in *Chihamba*," and afterward poured beer to the left and right of the winnowing basket. Then he took some beer in a mug and went well beyond the ritual fire to pour a little beer to the spirits of the malevolent dead, known as *ayikodjikodji* (singular: *chikodjikodji*). All the adepts broke off portions

---

[9] Not to be confused with *Chihamba*. An *Ihamba* doctor applies cupping horns to his patient's body with the aim of extracting from it the upper front incisor tooth of a dead hunter, which is believed to be "biting" the patient.

of cassava root and threw them round the gathering. Adepts, candidates, and uninitiated alike then cast some bits in the medicine containers and others on the mat where the two principal patients, Nyamukola and Sandombu's wife Zuliyana, were sitting. Other pieces were thrown over the fire. The adepts then formed a dancing circle and sang, shaking their *yileng'a* rattles. This was to make the patients *kuzakuka*—tremble violently. The songs were the theme song of the *Nkula* ritual, *"mwana moye,"* "only one child," [10] and *"chawahi munkondu,"* "it is good, the position of clasping a baby in one's arms."

Exegesis

Invocation. I give here the text of Lambakasa's invocation:

To-o mpemb' oyu enu awenu nkaka, ejima wenu, enu aNyamakang'a, ejima wenu twayenu, afu etu. Ifuku dalelu neyi yenu mwamukatishang'a iwu muntu, ifuku dalelu hitukwimba ng'oma yenu, ching'a iwu muntu akoli. To-o mpemba oyu.

(Completely white [is] that white clay, you yourself grandfather, all of you, you Nyamakang'a, all of you come, our dead. Today if you are making this person sick, today we will sing your drum, this person must become strong. Completely white [is] that white clay.)

Kwimba ng'oma, "to sing [to] a drum," is a common expression for performing a ritual. The *nkaka,* "grandfather" or "grandmother," may refer either to *Kavula,* who is called grandfather in later episodes, or to the afflicting ancestress Nyamukang'a. The emphasis on the whiteness of the *mpemba*

---

[10] "Only one child" is compared with "a reed or split cane that stands alone"—it is unsupported and useless—it should be woven into a mat.

in the common formula of invocation stresses the moral purity and good intention of those making invocation.

Ayikodjikodji. These are the spirits of sterile persons, witches, sorcerers, mean and inhospitable men and women, lovers of brawls and quarrels, murderers, and idle persons. They are believed to weaken the efficacy of the medicines. Unlike the respected ancestor spirits who are addressed by their names when alive, the *ayikodjikodji* are regarded as a crowd "without names." Many Ndembu have told me, however, that even though they are not loved, they must still be given beer and food—the pieces of cassava thrown beyond the ritual fire were for them—because, after all, they were once human beings.

Mukula firewood. I asked Muchona about the ritual fire, and he asserted strongly that *mukula* was appropriate firewood. At *kulembeka,* he said, the *ishikenu* medicine-tree was *mukula.* *Mukula* plays a prominent part in the symbolic systems of *Nkula* and *Chihamba,* two rituals of affliction. When cut this tree exudes a dusky red gum, which Ndembu compare to blood. It is used in all rituals that relate to situations where "blood is clearly seen," as Ndembu put it. Thus it is used in the boys' circumcision ritual, in hunting ritual, and in ritual concerned with menstrual disorders and with parturition. Muchona told me that in *Chihamba* it stands for the blood of killing (*mashi akutapana*) because *Kavula* is symbolically slain by the candidates, as we shall see.

Sacred food. The food crops represented at *Chihamba* stand for the fertility of gardens, as well as providing a communion feast for the adepts in the cult, who eat, they believe, with the ancestor spirits and with *Kavula.*

*7b. Entry of patients into principal patient's hut and
interrogation by* Kavula

At about 10 P.M. a great surge of adepts bore the two principal patients into Nyamukola's hut. The patients entered first, guided by female adepts, followed by male adepts who entered the hut backward. A few of them then guarded the door against intruders. It was whispered that "*Kavula* had come." The beer was then taken inside. Only the two patients "caught" by the spirit of Nyamukang'a were allowed inside. Although I could undoubtedly have entered I thought it tactless to do so at the time, for I did not want to claim special privileges before the main ritual on the following day. When I had lived in Chief Ikeleng'e's area during my first period of field work, I had entered a *Chihamba* patient's hut at the *ku-lembeka* ritual—at the request of the patient's husband. The hut had two rooms and was made of sun-dried kimberley brick. In one room the candidates and patient gathered round a fire, on which beans were cooking in an open clay pot. In the other room, hidden by a matting screen, the "big doctor" Chimbila (who was also headman of that village) had concealed himself and was enacting *Kavula*. He spoke in a gruff, throaty voice, asking each of the candidates why they had come and punctuating his questions with sexual swearing. Everyone laughed at his remarks, but rather uneasily as though they were frightened at the same time. I did not then know enough Lunda to follow the proceedings, and my interpreter was debarred from entering the hut.

Nyaluwema told me that on the night of *ku-tumbuka* at Mukanza Village, *Kavula* was not present. The adepts just spoke to the candidates, she said. The adepts drank beer and ate food in the hut, but the patients were allowed beer only.

According to other informants, *Kavula* "appeared" at that time. What form *Kavula* takes when "he" enters a single-roomed wattle-and-daub hut, I cannot say. Informants denied that his impersonator was masked, covered in a blanket, or hidden by a mat-partition from the patients. Nor would they tell me whether patients were forbidden to look in his direction. Lambakasa merely said that "he comes in his form as *Kavula*." According to Muchona's account, *Kavula*'s interrogation of the patient does not take place on the day *isaku* medicine is collected but on the following day, the day of *isoli*—in fact, after *Kavula* has been ritually slain by the candidates.

I give Muchona's account in full here, since it vividly illustrates at least how a believing adept regards the situation.

Muchona's account of *Kavula*'s interrogation

"When people came from *isoli* they found cooked beans were ready outside the patient's hut on the fire of *Chihamba*. *Kavula* is the one who first enters the hut. Everyone followed *Kavula* one by one until the hut was filled with adepts. Then they kept silent. [Muchona now changed to the present tense.] Now beans are brought in. Patients believe *Kavula* comes through the apex or topknot of the hut [*ntung'u yetala*]. He comes with *yileng'a* rattles. [Muchona seemed hesitant and afraid to explain further, at this point, saying that he had 'just heard some sounds of *Kavula*!']

"*Kavula* reviles all the adepts and gives them a name. New names are given to those who want to become doctors. When *Kavula* has eaten his beans, he reviles people just as he likes. The doctors in the hut begin to cry [*ku-dila*], saying:

Nkako, nkako, bayi wutujahaku, ching'a tushakami naneyi, nkaka wut-wanakenuku etu tukoli, etu antu eyi yeyi watukeshang'a mbutu jejima,

yeyi wakotolong'a antu nshing'u nayikatu, yeyi wakatishang'a antu ma-
kasa; lelu dinu tushakami ejima wetu chachiwahi.

(Grandfather, o grandfather, do not kill us, we must sit with
you, grandfather, feel pity for us here that we may be strong, we
your people, you who cause all seeds to be watered, you who break
people [in] the neck by sickness, you who make people ill [in] the
arms; today however may we stay, all of us, well.)

"*Kavula* is lightning, which comes with *yileng'a* rattles.
Lightning always strikes the apex or topknot of a hut, for this
is in direct line from the sky. Thus it is a strong spirit which
goes directly. It has come to give names to its people.

"*Kavula* is a great doctor who has been to many *Chihamba*
drums. He instructs the other doctors [or adepts]. He speaks
as follows:

Munantambiki dehi munantambikili nsang'winyi?
(You have called me already, why have you sent for me?)

"They reply:

Tunakutambikili muntu wakata, tunakutambikili muntu wakata ku-
londa eyi wumukoleshi.
(We have summoned you [on account of] a sick person, we have
called you [because of] a sick person, so that you may make him
strong.)

"He says:

Chachiwahi nayiwani dehi. Chakatayi muntu ninami natiyi kutama,
ami nenzi dehi nukumukwasha lelu muntu chachiwahi.
(Good, I have found you already. When the person was sick I
have felt bad, I have come already, I will help him today, the person well.)"

Muchona continued: "If it is a woman, *Kavula* says:

Mwitaku dindi hanyinkang'ahu makunduku ninshima nehi ni walwa nehi, lelu dinu namuvuluki dehi namuwani. Lelu ami nukudya makundi ninenu.

(In her vulva! [imprecation] she does not give me beans, nor cassava mush, nor beer, but today I have mentioned her by name, I have found her. Today I will eat beans with you.)

"They reply:

Tukudya nenu hamu.
(We will eat together with you.)

"He says:

Mpang'a jenu, nayiwani.
(Your swollen scrotums, I have found you.)

"They answer:

Enga, nkaka, wunatuwani dehi.
(Yes, grandfather, you have found us.)

"He comes with rattles, he falls on the ground crash! with his rattles.

Eng'a tunakutambiki dehi ching'a wutukwashi, etu tukweti wubinda, waya dehi, wutukwashi eyi Chihamba.

(Yes, we have already called you, you must help us, we had huntsmanship, it went already, you must help us, you *Chihamba*.)

"He says:

Eng'a ami nenzi dehi.
(Yes, I have come already.)"

Naming. Muchona described how *Kavula* mentions people by their *Chihamba* names:

Mukanzu wakola-a? Wudi naWubinda?
(Mukanzu, are you fit [or strong]? Are you a hunter?)

"He says:

Eng'a mwani, ami nidi naWubinda.
(Yes, sir, I have huntsmanship.)

"Kavula replies:

Chachiwahi. Musamba Njita Kapepa wakola-a?
(Good. Musamba Njita Kapepa, are you well?)

Eng'a mwani nakola.
(Yes, sir, I am well.)

Eyi wunakujaha nihanu-u?
(Are you one who kills over there?)

Wubinda watwala dehi eyi.
(You took away huntsmanship already.)

Chibanda ami nenzi dehi eyi nakwinki dehi wubinda weyi, katataka wukujaha. Eyi Shindamba Munshinshi wakola tahindi?
(Chibanda, I have come already, I have already given you your huntsmanship, soon you will kill. You Shindamba Munshinshi are you well, eh?)

Ami nayekela dehi nakukata, eyi Chihamba yeyi wankotolang'a.
(I was already ill, you, *Chihamba*, break me.)

Eng'a, lelu nakwiteji wukami tulu. Eyi Nzaji Wanwamwikonki wakola?
(Yes, today, I agree that you should sleep. You, Nzaji Wanwamwikondi, are you well?)

Ami mwani nyendu yakotoka yafwa yaching'umuka dehi, yeyi Chihamba, wankotola dehi.
(I, sir, [my] legs are broken, dead, already sprained, you, *Chihamba*, broke me already.)

Eyi wanvulamenang'a, mpang'a yeyi. Ching'a wunyinkang'ahu makindi nawalwa.

(You always forget me, your swollen scrotum! You must just give me beans and beer.)"

Muchona then proceeded to comment on some of the details of the two episodes, the preparation of *nsompu* washing medicine and the interrogation by *Kavula*. First he spoke of the importance of cassava in *Chihamba* as a whole and its role in episode 7a, above.

"Cassava [*makamba*] is used instead of powdered white clay [*mpemba*] to purify, that is cassava meal [*wung'a*]. Indeed, if people have no white clay to invoke with, they should use cassava meal.

"Now *Chihamba* causes cassava roots to decay in the gardens when he catches a person. Cassava is important both at birth and death. When a child is born it is given thin porridge [*kapudyi*], made from cassava meal. If a sick person is nearly dead, before he dies he asks for thin cassava porridge. He drinks it and dies. These things act together both at birth and death. Again, when women pass a grave they throw down cassava roots for the dead. They are food for the dead. Think of the pieces of cassava the adepts throw at *Chihamba*. Cassava is the most important food of the Lunda. Truly meat is just an addition to it."

Beans. "But the big food of *Chihamba* is *ikundi* [singular form, meaning bean]. It is to cause love [*ku-kundisha*] [11] between *Chihamba* and the people. *Chihamba* goes attached to the group of doctors just for a little time. Those who want children would not ask *Chihamba* for children. [But many other Ndembu have told me that *Chihamba* is performed for

[11] *Ku-kundisha* is the causative form of *ku-kunda*, "to love." Ndembu derive *ikundi* from *ku-kunda*.

women with reproductive disorders.] [12] *Chihamba* is for huntsmanship, for cultivation [*ku-dima*], and for sickness [*yikatu*]."

Naming, continued. Muchona then carried on with his description of the episode in the principal patient's hut:

"Then *Kavula* begins to give names to the patients, as follows:

Muyeji wami yeyi Kaluswika Nyanzenzimeka.
(My patient [novice] you [are] Kaluswika Nyanzenzimeka.)

"They say:

Bulenu nying'ula.
(Make a joyful noise by beating your hands on your lips.)

"All the people who are outside trill thus with joy:

Yeyi Katayi Kamahamba Yikosa Yileng'a, bulenu.
(You [are] Katayi Kamahamba Yikosa Yileng'a, make a joyful noise.)

"Nyanzenzimeka comes from *nzenzi*, 'a rattle'; it means 'she who shakes rattles.' The other name means 'Katayi of the *mahamba* spirits with cleansed rattles.'

"If there had been a third patient, her name might have been Nyakantemba Mumbanda Waditemba Muyileng'a. But there are many *Chihamba* names. People keep the same names through many performances."

Taboos. "After naming the patients, *Kavula* tells them: 'You must not eat the meat of the hippopotamus, nor of the *mu-*

---

[12] And note the singing of *Nkula* songs, from a rite to restore female fertility, on page 63, above.

sonji [a kind of catfish], nor of the yellow-backed duiker [*kasenda*], nor must you eat with other people.' "

Muchona explains these taboos: "If someone ate hippo, it would mean that he ate the spirit of *Chihamba*. He would become very sick. The *musonji* catfish has a very slippery body; if a patient were sick the medicine would become too slippery and would not stick to kill the disease. The yellow-backed duiker sleeps in the *itu* [streamside evergreen forest] where the spirit of *ng'uvu* [hippopotamus] lives. The patients must avoid eating white beans, that is, beans with the outer skins removed, because *Chihamba* is white. A patient must not eat with 'impure people' [*anabulakutooka*], not even with *Chihamba* adepts who are impure. [Impure people, literally 'who lack whiteness' in the context of *Chihamba*, are menstruating women, breakers of *Chihamba* taboos, or people who have just had sexual intercourse.]"

Climbing the apex. "When *Kavula* has instructed the patients he climbs up to the apex of the hut, then drops the *yileng'a* rattles down in a terrible fashion. The people shout:

Tunafwi yayo, wuyang'a hohu.
(We have died, alas, this is mere huntsmanship [with guns].)

"*Kavula* replies with a song:

Ami nayi kwatung'a mulondu kunu.
(I have gone to the place where the cormorant dwells, to this place.)

"The people answer:

Wuyang'a hohu, kwatung'a mulondu kunu.
(Huntsmanship only, where the cormorant dwells.)

Kavula is really talking about the place he is going to, near the water where the cormorant lives.

"After that the doctors [adepts] collect the *yileng'a* rattles and put them in the rafters. Then they say to the patients: 'Stay well, we shall see you tomorrow.' "

Forms of Chihamba. I asked Muchona why the *Chihamba* spirit was said to be a hippopotamus. He did not give a reason for this but explained that there were two kinds of *Chihamba* ritual, known as *ng'uvu* (hippopotamus) and *katala matung'a* (a cryptic phrase referring to the Livingstone's lourie, *Tauracolivingstoniischalow.*) If *Chihamba* has "come out in *ng'uvu*," the patient has been caught by a spirit from the water or from the river. If it has "come out in *katala matung'a*" a spirit from the bush has caught the patient. It is the diviner, consulted about the patient's illness, who decides whether the hippo or lourie form of *Chihamba* has been manifested. If the former is divined, medicines are first collected in the streamside forest, and afterward from plants in the dry bush; if the latter, the order is reversed. Both *Chihamba* and *Nkula* possess these variant forms of affliction and treatment. Sometimes the "water" form is called *chozu*, "wild duck" and the "bush" form *kalendu*, another term for Livingstone's lourie, (usually called *nduwa*). It is hard to see why the lourie should be held to typify the bush, for it is found far more frequently in streamside gallery forests. Red wing feathers from this bird are used in a number of rituals, including *Mukanda* and *Nkula*, to be described in later chapters, and the two hunting cults. Perhaps it owes its association with the bush to its use in hunting and circumcision ritual, where the bush (*isang'a*, nearly always used with the locative prefix *mu-*, i.e. *mwisung'a*) is the milieu to which many symbols refer.

Kavula. Who or what is *Kavula?* I have never received really satisfactory information on this point from Ndembu. Muchona, after much thought, told me: "*Kavula* is more like

Nzambi, the High God, than an ancestor spirit. He is the grandfather of all people, who makes crops grow, who gives health and good luck to men and women, and who causes animals to multiply [*ku-seng'uka*, the verb from which are derived the name of the tree *museng'u*, and one of the secret names of *Kavula*, *Samaseng'a*]. In the performance at Mukanza Village, Nyamakang'a caused the sickness, but *Kavula*, after the candidates had repented [*chinalembawu ayeji*], made them strong again. Thus women are junior, men are senior in *Chihamba*." It will, of course, be noted that this contradicts Muchona's account of *Kavula's* interrogation of the adepts and candidates, when several candidates blamed *Kavula* himself for their misfortunes.

Nyaluwema, the senior woman doctor, said that *Kavula* was a man (*iyala*), while the ancestress was a woman (*mumbanda*). She agreed that *Kavula* resembles *Nzambi*, the High God. "But God is above, and this spirit [here she used the term *mukishi*, usually applied to ancestor spirits, for *Kavula*] is in the ground." She went on to explain that *Kavula* is not a *mufu*, someone who has died, but yet is a *mukishi*. Other adepts confirmed that *Kavula* was a *mukishi*. However, this is the only instance I have heard of where the term *mukishi* was employed by Ndembu for any being other than an ancestor spirit. The Luba, to the northeast of the Ndembu, often mean by *mukishi*, not an ancestor spirit, but a nature spirit or *genius loci*. Perhaps we have in *Chihamba* a survival of an ancient or perhaps of a more general usage. It is interesting that Nyaluwema, in order to bring out the distinction between ancestress and *Kavula*, felt herself compelled to use *mufu*, "dead person," for the former.

According to Muchona, *Kavula* is "the grandfather [*nkaka*] of all people" because "your grandfather is the one who knows everything. He must always be praised. You can also joke with him [*ku-disenseka*], using sexual swearing. You must give him food when he asks you for it. But you also fear [*ku-tiya woma*] him. Without my mother and father I would not have been seen, and they would not have been seen without my grandfathers and grandmothers. Therefore, I fear my grandparents. My mother's mother's brother [*nkaka*] is the elder of my group. He is an important grandfather.

"Grandfathers teach their grandsons many things, especially to leave off taking mistresses [*andowa*], for many quarrels come of this.

"*Kavula* is the grandfather of all the people."

7c. Public dance

After the episode in Nyamukola's hut, both patients were brought outside again and made to sit on a mat near the ritual fire. During the rest of the night until dawn, doctors washed the patients with *nsompu* medicine at intervals, giving them a little to drink now and then. Practically everybody in the vicinage who was able to come had done so, as well as a number of government employees from the Boma. I counted more than four hundred attenders at one point, and more may have arrived later. Several young men, most of whom had worked on the Copperbelt, asked me for a candle, as they wanted to play guitars in an abandoned hut. They seemed both afraid and scornful of *Chihamba*. Other young people of both sexes formed into two dancing circles and danced the currently popular *Chikinta* dance, brought in from the Belgian Congo, to the rhythm of the *Chihamba* drums. At intervals, *Chihamba* doctors danced in their own circle, singing the special *Chihamba* song "*ng'unda yakuya*" (*ng'unda*, like *mung'ula* mentioned above, stands for the cry made by beating the hand on a shrilling mouth—here in praise of the *Chihamba* spirits).

In between dancing and singing, both initiated and uninitiated had frequent recourse to the beer calabashes which the sponsoring village supplied in generous quantities. Flirtations, leading to illicit sexual intercourse in the bush, are common features of such public dances. At *Chikinta*, indeed, dancers cross the circle and choose a member of the opposite sex to sing with them in the middle. Later the chosen one may slink away to a secret assignation with the chooser. Since "sweethearts" are usually married to others, and since their spouses are also present, much jealousy is aroused, and fights break out between the lawful and illicit mates of men and women.

The public dance went on till the dawn of March 8, 1954, the third day of *Chihamba*.

The Third Day

1. Rousing the candidates with cock's feathers

At dawn the adepts began to sing *chokoloko choko*. Then women doctors took a live red cock and went round every hut in the village, leaving a few of its feathers on each threshold. As they did so they said, "You have seen the chicken."

This circling of the village took place at about 5.30 A.M.

Exegesis

Red cock. Muchona said that "the red cock is to please the *Chihamba* spirit, and it means that the *Chihamba* spirit was visiting everyone. Those whom he visited were cultivators of crops and some were sick. *Chihamba* can help them. Then people knew that *Chihamba* was going to eat his cock. *Chihamba* is a male though the dead person (*mufu*) was a woman."

Nyaluwema told my wife that "the men later eat that cock; for the *mukishi* [*Kavula*] is a man [*diyi iyala*]."

Chokoloko. The *chokoloko* song is reminiscent of the song of the novices in the *Mukanda* circumcision lodge at dawn, "*Eye chekeleke*, drongo bird, we have seen you, we have prayed to you." Sakutoha said that at *Chihamba* they sang *chokoloko*, and not *chekeleke*, because *Mukanda* and *Chihamba* "had different mysteries [*jipang'u*]."

2. Inserting the arrow in principal patient's hut thatch (7:30 A.M.)

The adepts then led the patients, stripped to the waist, round in a dance. Zuliyana, Sandombu's wife, the second patient, wore her cloth tied between the legs. Beans were brought out shelled in a pot. One woman carried a bowl of cassava roots on her head, another carried a basket of cassava meal. Then the senior male adept Lambakasa hopped to Nyamukola's hut with the *Chihamba* arrow (see page 44), draped on the feathered end with a leaf of the castor-oil plant (*imonu*) between the second and great toe of his left foot. He took it to the thatch overhanging the doorway of the hut and thrust it through the thatch with his foot. Other doctors lifted him up so that he could do this, for "the arrow must not touch the ground, that would be bad; and the doctor must not touch it with his hands," said Sakutoha.

Exegesis

Hopping. The act of hopping (*ku-zonkwela*) is a feature of a number of Ndembu rituals (including *Wubwang'u*, *Mukanda*, and *Nkula*). Lambakasa said that in *Chihamba* "if the doctor catches the spirit with his hands, [the spirit] will not cure well." By spirit he meant the arrow which at this stage in the ritual appears to have been identified with the *Chihamba* spirit itself.

Castor-oil leaf. The castor-oil leaf, according to Muchona, represents castor oil, which is used at all life crises, birth, marriage, and death. Oil mixed with red clay (*mukundu*) is placed on the fontanelles of a newborn baby. The same mixture is placed on the head of a girl coming out of seclusion in *Nkang'a*, the girls' puberty ritual. Muchona appeared to argue that it was used in the arrow episode in *Chihamba* as a sign of birth, of starting the ritual chasing.

Sacred foods. All the foods in the bowl are called *yinsang'a*, which may be translated as sacred food. Muchona insisted that beans as well as cassava roots were usually taken into the bush for the chasing episode. At Mukanza Village I saw only cassava roots. Adepts are allowed to eat many kinds of food during the day, but novices must stay hungry, said Nyaluwema.

Lambakasa said that "perhaps the arrow going into the thatch means that *Chihamba* has chosen the patient, and will later help her."

3. Isoli. a. Marking out the sacred mukoleku *barrier*

The adepts went in procession, accompanied by the two principal patients, toward the *isoli* (see below). The *isoli* is always the scene of esoteric ritual. They proceeded along a path between Sandombu's farm and Mbimbi Village and crossed the government motor road which runs between the Mwinilunga Boma and Kalene Mission Hospital. On the opposite side of the road from Mukanza Village the procession halted at the entrance of a footpath. The adepts declared that the head of the path was *mukoleku* and that only adepts and candidates (doctors and patients) were allowed to pass beyond it. Later in the day candidates would rest at *mukoleku* for short periods—not in the village because during that time they are "apart" (*kumbadyi*) from the uninitiated.

A quarrel arose between female adepts and several men who wanted to gain access to the sacralized area beyond *mukoleku*. Prominent among these men was Wankie Soneka, formerly a teacher at the local mission outschool. Now a polygynist and man of influence in village affairs, he wanted to set the seal on his readmission to village life by becoming an adept at *Chihamba*. One of the male adepts, Mboyunga, a man of slave origin, considered malicious and idle, strenuously opposed Wankie's right to pass *mukoleku*, throwing his mission education in his teeth. Others supported Wankie, and his claim to enter was upheld when some old men said that they remembered him as a young boy carried past a *mukoleku* by his father, who "had been a big *Chihamba* doctor." But he had to pay several shillings as *nyishing'u* (payments giving the right to observe a secret ritual object or activity) before he could go on. Other men were turned back. It is a great honor and privilege to become a *Chihamba* adept and one guarded with especial jealousy by those with relatively low secular status such as women and men like Mboyunga. No fence or framework was erected to demarcate *mukoleku*.

Exegesis

Mukoleku is said by all informants to be derived from *ku-kola*, "to be strong or healthy" and from *ku-koleka*, "to make well or strong." In *Mukanda*, *mukoleku* refers to a framework made of three poles of *mukula* wood in the form of a goal erected at the head of a path newly made by lodge officials and leading to the site of circumcision. After circumcision only circumcised males are allowed to pass through it. Some informants said that in the past a similar frame, of *musoli* wood, was set up at *Chihamba*.

3b. Sacralizing the musoli tree

The adepts then went to a *musoli* tree about a hundred yards down the path past *mukoleku*, at an angle of about 45° from the path. One adept was sent further on to locate the *isoli* proper, which had already been marked off by an arrow inserted in the ground. The *isoli* would later be screened off by bent and broken boughs, "made of any trees, for it is just to hide secret things."

The site for *isoli* was about twenty yards from the *musoli* tree, described as the *ishikenu* for the ritual proceedings of that day, the day of chasing. The adepts would later be washed with medicine at the *musoli* before being taken to greet *Kavula*, in what manner we will see.

The adepts then proceeded in single file to *isoli*, with the exception of Muchona, who took a red cock and bound its neck round with grass taken from the base of the *musoli* tree. After that he laid red beads, with red cock's feathers tied to the string, at the foot of the tree. He took the cock and dragged it round the *musoli* tree, leaving a trail of red feathers. Then he dragged it backward from the *musoli* tree to the *isoli* site along the narrow path beaten through the grass by the other adepts. The adepts then went to the *musoli* tree and circled it several times to trample down the grass in a ring around it and mark out the tree clearly as a sacred place.

Exegesis

Circling (*ku-bola musoli*). The trampling down of grass round the *musoli* tree is called *ku-bola musoli*. It is a widespread feature of Ndembu ritual, and we shall meet it again in the other kinds of ritual. It is said to make the tree surrounded sacred and to "take away familiars of witches and sorcerers."

Red Beads. The red beads, like the red cock's feathers, are said to stand for *Kavula's* blood.

Backward approach. The act of dragging the cock backward is guided by the general notion that sacred things should be approached back first. This behavior will also be met with in other kinds of ritual. In *Chihamba*, too, the candidates approach *Kavula* throughout the long day of chasing and questioning with their backs to the *isoli.* Only at the very end do they turn their faces toward the representation of *Kavula.*

According to Sandombu, the cock is dragged "to give the spirit blood."

3c. Dragging the meal mortar to isoli site

This episode took place at the junction of the main path and the new path. Sandombu, who had been carrying the meal mortar in which *nsompu* had been pounded the previous night, stood facing the village, the other doctors behind him in a line, backs to *isoli.* They went through the motions of copulating with the mortar (*iyanda*) as they passed it between their legs (an act known as *ku-hitisha iyanda munyendu*). Then Sandombu dragged the mortar along the path past the *musoli* tree to *isoli.* At this point I was told that an adept, Spider Chanza, had gone on ahead of the other doctors when they stopped at *mukoleku* to mark off the site of *isoli* (*ku-busa isoli*). After he passed the *musoli* tree Sandombu ceased to drag the mortar, but carried it in his arms the rest of the way. Spider Chanza had driven an arrow into the ground to mark the site of *isoli,* and the mortar was placed beside it. The *isoli* itself was then fashioned. Its fence or screen consisted of a rough circle of small shrubs, bent and interlaced to hide the mortar and arrow. Adepts almost immediately began to make within it a representation of *Kavula*.

Exegesis

Dragging the mortar. Sakutoha told me that Sandombu should have dragged the mortar all the way. He said that "big doctors drag the mortar to give it power; it passes beneath *mapanza* [plural form of *ipanza*, the crutch of the legs] where children come from." He described the act as "*ku-sundyikija iyanda*," "causing the mortar to copulate." Muchona strongly denied this and said that it was called *ku-shinjikila iyanda*, "to escort the mortar on its way" (from *ku-shinjika*, "to push") or *ku-kooka iyanda*, "to drag or pull the mortar." The sexual interpretation is supported by an episode in *Mukanda*, the boys' circumcision ritual, where the basket used for carrying circumcisers' medicine (*nfunda*), with the containers (*tudiwu*) of the actual medicine removed—for it may not come into contact with the ground without losing its efficacy—is passed between a tunnel of legs formed by circumcisers and senior lodge officials. Here it is said "to make the genitals of the doctors strong."

In the *Wubwang'u* ritual performed for women who have had or who are expected to have twins (*ampamba*), male doctors dive between one another's legs. This too is explained as "copulation," and the term *ipanza*, for the fork of the body, is used. It may be said that in general, forks in nature or in physical structures, like the forks of trees, the apices of round huts, and forks in paths are ritually regarded as symbols of fertility, human or animal.

Starting (ku-busa) isoli. The term *ku-busa isoli*, "to start a new *isoli*," as Windson Kashinakaji translated it for me in periphrasis, is derived, according to Muchona, from *ku-busa*, "to cut open a belly [of an animal or bird] with a knife, to remove the entrails. Thus it means to start something, an inside thing." When hunters butcher a carcass, they begin by removing the internal organs, some of which are reserved for them and tabooed to those who are not members of hunting cults. It is in these organs and in the head (also reserved for hunters) that the power of a living creature is believed to reside. In Ndembu belief, *Kavula*, at this stage of the ritual, is brought out of the earth, in the same way as the power-filled internal organs of an animal are brought out through the slit in its belly. The theme, mentioned earlier of making visible (*ku-solola*) is also exemplified here.

Muchona's account and interpretation of the preparation of *isoli* differs in several respects from the episode I observed at Mukanza Village. For example, the *ishikenu* or dominant tree was not *musoli* but either *mukula* or *katochi* or *mukeketi*. Here are his remarks in full:

Muchona's account of the preparation of *isoli*

"The day before *kantong'a* [see page 124], at about 8 A.M. all the adepts go to find a place where *isoli* is going to be used. In front go the adepts, the candidates follow them. Every adept is ready to go carrying his *chileng'a* rattle, but the candidates are not given their *yileng'a* then. They sing on the way. When they are ready at *isoli*, the candidates are left behind at one place, but the adepts go in front to *isoli*. Big adepts, the most important first, stand with their legs open at the place where a new path joins the old path, the first one facing the old path, the others with their backs to him toward *isoli*, just as in *Mukanda*. When they are ready a big adept holds the mortar in his hands, with a cock that knows how to crow alive in the mortar, and a bow and arrow [called *itong'i* in *Chihamba*]. He goes under all the legs carrying these things to go to the tree of *isoli*, which is *mukula* for the Bush *Chihamba*, or *katochi* or *mukeketi* for the Streamside Forest *Chihamba*. Small adepts [*ayimbuki anyanya*], i.e., minor adepts, also pass through the legs. The big adept who went first puts all these things near the *ishikenu* tree, then he goes round that tree stamping the grass flat [*ku-bola ishikenu*]. *Ku-bola* is to make a new circle around something by stamping grass. Then all the adepts follow in order of importance. A big adept, who will speak for *Kavula*, instructs the small adepts to make up a fence [*chisolu*] round the *ishikenu* tree, made of leafy branches. A special compartment [*chipang'u*] is made for *Kavula*. This is the *isoli*. Then the big adept, who is *Kavula*, is now ready with a razor [*ntewula*], an ax [*kazemba*], and a hoe [*itemwa*]. He also has a needle [*nguya*], and he has white beads [*wusang'a watooka*] on a string to tie around the ax and hoe, as a sign [*chinjikijilu*] of *Chihamba*. The needle is tied with them. Together they make up a bundle, known as 'Chihamba.' The big adept digs a hole near the foot of the *ishikenu* tree, a few feet deep. In this hole he puts the bundle standing upright. Then the mortar is placed on top of the bundle. Then earth is put around the bundle and mortar to keep them standing upright."

Muchona went on to explain further what the symbols stood for: "When the adepts go through the legs this means *ipanza*, the place where children come from. It means that a child enters a woman's body and comes out alive. It is just the same in *Mukanda*. A cock is used because he is an elder and awakens everybody. To sacrifice [*literally* 'cut,' *ku-ke-*

tula—always by beheading] means life [*wumi*] for everybody. The bow and arrow are *wubinda*, huntsmanship. The mortar is a special place for pounding food for everyone. It is an elder. The razor is a thing for shaving, and cutting the skin for cupping horns [*tusumu*], so it is helpful. Without a hoe, no one can cultivate, so it means cultivation. An ax is for preparing a clearing [*ntema*] for a garden, it is for cutting meat, and cutting down trees to get honey, so it means clearing and preparing. A needle means the pains of disease and is used so that a person should not feel those kinds of pain. The spirit is kept bound in the bundle. The beads stand for the spirit. The hole in which the hoe and other things are buried means the innocence [*ku-ying'a*] of the patient. She is free from the thing that is vexing [or troubling] her [*chuma chaku-mukabisha muyeji*]. An ax is that which begins cultivation, it is an important thing for everybody. A hoe is the second step, it is the cultivation of crops. If a man wishes to live he must have crops. The razor is there because when a person is feeling something painful it must be stopped. The work [*mu-dimu*] of the razor is to shave around the hairline [in many rituals a sign that an important stage has been completed] to let everyone see that the person shaven is all right again. In *Mukanda* the novices are cut [*ku-ketula* again, here meaning circumcise], when they are made to come out of the lodge, they are shaven, their pain has been shaved off. All diseases too that give pain should be shaved off. If a disease is very sharp, it must stop, because of the razor, which means sharpness [*ku-wambuka*]. The needle is the pricking of the disease.

"*Chihamba* thinks that a person is cured when these things are buried. *Chihamba* feels pleased [*natiyi kuwaha*]. A man who is cured can be spoken of as *wunatooki*, 'he is white,' or *wunaying'i*, 'he is innocent,' as well as *wunamuuki*, 'he is cured.'

"The patients are shaved at the end of *Chihamba* with the razor that has been buried."

3d. Preparation of isoli

The preparation of the *isoli*, notably the making of a contraption to represent *Kavula*, coincides in time with the "Beginning of Chasing" (*ku-tachika ku-hang'a*). I will describe these episodes seriatim, for the sake of greater clarity.

First Muchona went to the mortar dumped among the bushes of *isoli*, which he described as "grandfather," took all the *yileng'a* rattles, and banged them down beside the mortar, while another adept planted a flexible stick in the ground on the far side of it and passed it over the mortar and Muchona's legs to the other side, forming an arch approximately one foot six inches high. My wife, who made this observation, was then asked politely to go away, for only very old women were allowed to be near *isoli* when *Kavula* was being made.

At that time I was observing the beginning of the chasing of candidates by adepts. When I returned to *isoli* I found that a frame of sticks had been set up, covered with a blanket whitened with cassava meal. The sticks were planted in the ground at intervals of about a foot and were joined together with bark string, to which were attached small *nzenzi* rattles. The blanket was not quite big enough to cover the whole contraption. A long bark string led off to a strong upright pole hidden in the bush behind *Kavula*. When this was moved the rattles on the frame shook. At the far end was the arch my wife had observed, and it was to this that the "control rod" was attached. The meal mortar had been inverted and placed at the end next to the new path. The *chisolu* fence was roughly three-sided, concealing the *Kavula* contraption from anybody approaching from the *mukoleku* and open at the back. *Kavula* was rather longer than it was broad and was said to represent "something white rising out of a grave." *Kavula* was regarded with awe, even by those who had just made it, and one female adept said to my wife later in the ritual, pointing to *Kavula*, "You have seen the spirit [*mukishi*]."

Exegesis

Nature of Kavula. Discussing this episode with Muchona I mentioned that *Kavula* had been described to me during the performance by someone as a *mufu*, that is, as a dead person. He agreed with this interpretation, in spite of what he had said earlier about the difference between the ancestress and *Kavula* (page 74). I then said that perhaps the ancestress was *Kavula*, who would then have been a woman. "No!" replied Muchona with some heat. "*Kavula* is a man. Do not men perform the most important work in *Chihamba?* They make *isoli* and *Kavula*, they stay by *isoli* which is their place. But only women long past the menopause [*achinyikili mwaka*] can sit at *isoli*, and they cannot sit behind the *chisolu* fence. *Kavula* is for the men!"

Posture of Kavula. Sandombu held that *Kavula* was shown lying on his back, but Muchona insisted that the white covering is "the back of *Kavula.*" *Kavula* shakes and rattles in time to drums placed nearby. Sandombu said that its convulsive jerking represented the movements of the belly during sexual intercourse. When the adept who acted *Kavula* (it was said) in the senior patient's hut the previous night danced with a *lwalu* basket later that day, he faced *Kavula* and jerked his stomach in and out, in time with the jerking of the blanketed frame.

During the day no less than three senior male adepts, including Muchona and Kanyabu, were observed manipulating the framework.

The meal mortar was inverted, said Muchona, so that the candidate (at a later stage of the day's ritual) would not know what was underneath. The concealed razor, ax, and so forth were part of the mystery of *Chihamba*.

3e. Fitting the arrowhead to the shaft

When *isoli* was being prepared, most of the adepts were sitting at the fork between old and new paths, while the two candidates had been taken back to the *mukoleku* (the start of the path leading to the sacred sites). Suddenly Sakutoha, one of the principal male adepts, ordered silence, and everyone, near and far, quieted. Then he took the wooden arrowhead he had been making on the night of the ritual beer drink, now barbed and beautifully carved, and ceremonially fitted it to the shaft of an arrow. Then he took a bow and shot the arrow high into the bush surrounding Mukanza Village, or rather Sandombu farm. Nyaluwema explained that the arrow might not be aimed either in the direction of *isoli* or of the patients' villages. No one was allowed to fetch the arrow at that time, but she herself, the principal woman adept, would have the task of fetching it later. The shooting of the arrow formally opened the process of chasing the candidates.

Exegesis

The wooden arrowhead, said Sakutoha, is called *mbong'ola yaChihamba* and is made from a thick piece of reed (*iteti*). A reed is used "because the hippopotamus is the *Chihamba* spirit" [presumably because hippos live among reeds].

According to Nyaluwema "the people must be silent while they are chasing away a spirit." Nyaluwema, incidentally, mentioned that Nyachipendi, the founding ancestress of Mukanza Village, was "the woman; the man, her husband, is *Kavula;* and the candidates are their children."

The arrow was aimed at the bush between village and *isoli*, according to Muchona, because the ritual of chasing took place between village and *isoli*, and did not stay in either.

4. The Chasing. a. Beginning of chasing
(ku-tachika ku-hang'a)

Shortly after starting to prepare *isoli*, some of the adepts went to the candidates left at *mukoleku* and began to chase them back to principal patient Nyamukola's hut. As they ran they sang *"mpandove-e!"* interspersed with shouts of *"shoku, shoku, sho-o!"* The chasing was highly formalized; an adept held each candidate, stripped to the waist, on either hand or arm, and they ran slowly in rhythm with the singing. The words of one song included, "She has been caught by the Chokwe." The whole rite was reminiscent of the slave trade, for *mpanda*, the word constantly repeated in the main song, means slave yoke. The Chokwe were the terrible slave raiders who ravaged Mwantiyanvwa's empire in the second half of the nineteenth century.

The group of adepts and candidates ran slowly from the *isoli* to the village, but when they reached the village they ran faster. Indeed they entered Nyamukola's hut with a rush and left after a gasp for breath. At first they ran with all their might in the direction of *isoli*. This was appropriate behavior, explained as follows by Nyaluwema: "They want to see the

other *Chihamba* [that is, *Kavula*], at the place of *Samaseng'a*"
(one of the secret names of *Kavula*). Later candidates and
adepts settled down into a slow, steady trot. I was told off
for going too fast when I was chased as a candidate.

When the candidates reached Nyamukola's hut, they were
bundled unceremoniously, if ritually, inside, and forced to
stand facing the wall with their hands spread out on the wall
above their heads. Then they were chased back to the *mukoleku* path entrance, where they were made to sit down with
their backs to the *isoli*. Nyaluwema said that "they sit with
their backs to *Kavula* so that they should not be frightened
by him." Each time they turned from the village they were
chased a little further toward the *isoli*. Whenever they
stopped and sat down, adepts asked them cryptic questions
concerning the names and nature of *Kavula*, whose name was
not to be mentioned at this stage. If a candidate answered
correctly, the adepts made the pleased trilling sound of
ng'unda. If the answer was incorrect, they laughed jeeringly.

The first time the two principal and original candidates
were chased to Nyamukola's hut, a fearful battle seemed to
take place at the door. Sakutoha indeed threw a woman violently out of the hut in the scuffle. A large stick was used to
force the candidates to kneel in the doorway. But this was
not a real fight, Nyaluwema explained, "just matters of the
spirit." Nevertheless, Lambakasa, a senior male adept,
shouted angrily, "Why are you bringing quarrels and
grudges here? You are making this a strange sort of *Chihamba*. Be off with you!" He then grumbled to me, "*Chihamba chakalung'a* [*Chihamba* of the grave] is an important affair, it is to make people stay well and strong. It is not just
playing about [*hachakuhemisha hohuku*]!"

Catching of candidates. Any person not an adept could be

caught by the doctors on the path between *mukoleku* and Nyamukola's hut, made to pay *nyishing'u*, and forced to become a candidate. Some of those captured, as we have noted, expected to be, and even wanted to be. Others regarded it as a great nuisance. One man, Mungongu, for instance, was quietly wheeling his bicycle along the road, taking his wife home from a visit, when he was descended upon by a fierce crowd of female adepts, like bacchantes, and held fast by them. He tried to buy his way out with several shillings, but was led triumphantly before an improvised "court" of male adepts. These men asked him to explain the *mpang'u* (riddles or mystery) of *Chihamba*. When he showed ignorance, he was ordered to strip to the waist and be chased with the two main candidates and other captives, now loudly declared to be the "slaves" (*andung'u*) of *Chihamba*. Mungongu was made to sit third in order, behind the two women. He was then lifted by hand through the press of adepts and then he was run vigorously to the village. Other adepts and the two senior female candidates remained near the *mukoleku*.

About halfway through the morning (just after 10.30 A.M.), the male adepts, now mostly collected at *isoli*, suddenly started like mad for the women at *ishikenu*—the consecrated *musoli* tree. The male adepts, with branches in their hands, did not actually strike the women, but made as if they would do so. Then both groups joined together, all of them adepts of long standing, and went to *mukoleku*, where they beat the junior adepts. Finally, the senior male adepts, with frightful grimaces, beat the ground by the candidates' feet to terrify them and make them run. Only the men were entitled to carry and use the branches as beaters. The adepts abused one another in a ritual joking relationship. Secular joking relationships held good in this context, but had an added intensity. Thus one Ndembu doctor joked with a Humbu doctor, and people from Chief Kanongesha's area joked with those from Chief Sailunga'a area.

By that time, quite a number of people had been captured, mainly by female adepts. They included men, women, and children. Women headed the line of candidates, then men, then children. After the principal candidates (who were also patients in the sense that they had been sick), other women were placed in their order of capture. Men too followed one another in order of capture. Children were not separated by sex, but were added to the procession as they were seized on the path. Most of the children had been told by their parents to let themselves be caught.

At *mukoleku*, shortly afterward, Lambakasa came rushing from *nkaka* (the *isoli* "tabernacle"), tore through the crowd and began beating Mungongu, the recent recruit to the candidates, with both hands. He then put him in front of the row of candidates, though he was later ordered to return behind the women.

Lambakasa then went to the leading candidate Nyamukola and asked her why she had come. She replied, rather shyly, "I am sick." He said, "You have come to *Chihamba*. I will tell grandfather." Then he tried to take Mungongu off to *isoli*. Other adepts shouted, "Not yet!" and chased Mungongu back to the village. But Lambakasa, from his grinning face, was just joking.

People continued to get caught. One victim, an unwilling one this time, was old Headman Mbimbi. He had for years pretended that he was a senior adept in *Chihamba*, and since there had been no performances of *ku-tumbuka* in the neighborhood for more than ten years, many had believed him. Women adepts mocked him and twisted his head when they caught him slinking surreptitiously along the path. Then he was chased vigorously. He covered his head with his hands and made a wry grimace, evidently much ashamed. His son Makanjila and a man from a nearby village were seized and dragged bodily halfway to the *isoli*, arguing and cursing, by two junior adepts. Others caught included Nyamukola's sister's daughter Yana, rather weakly in constitution, and Masondi, Muchona's wife. In the end, there were twenty-seven candidates, including five women, four men (Headman Mbimbi was let off after being chased a couple of times), nine girls, and nine boys. My wife and I were honorary candidates, and we acceded to Sandombu's plea that we should let ourselves be chased from sacred area to village a few times. This gave us the opportunity to see what went on in the principal candidate's hut.

When the candidates were driven into the hut they were ordered to put their hands up high on the wall, standing with their backs to it. All the female adepts cheered and clapped when the hut door was shut. The candidates were sternly warned not to laugh or indeed to speak except in a modest whisper. The candidates, still known as slaves, had to retain their posture (for all the world as though they were manacled to the wall), while the adepts stamped their feet and banged the ends of their *yileng'a* rattles on the closed door. Nyaluwema, in reply to our question as to whether the chasing imitated the Chokwe slave raids and slave gangs, said that she did not think so, for *Chihamba* was older than those raids and "came from Mwantiyanvwa," that is, from the Luunda empire, from which the Ndembu emigrated. Mwantiyanvwa had many slaves, she said.

The female adepts, according to the senior men, "had the work of *tulama*" (police or messengers); they were less impor-

3. Adepts chase candidates into the senior candidate's hut. Note arrow in thatch above doorway and medicine leaves.

tant than the men. Nevertheless, they conducted their tasks with ferocious efficiency and great vigor, though several of the older women complained of leg-weariness, for they had been up most of the previous night at the dance.

Exegesis

Nakedness. Complete or partial removal of clothing is a common feature of Ndembu ritual. A candidate is said to be a poor person (*kazweng'u*), without possessions or status. Both in boys' and girls' initiation rites, the nakedness (*wuzekesi*) of the novices is compared with that of an infant. Nyaluwema also likened the *Chihamba* candidates to infants "*ayeji afwana neyi atwansi.*" This is why, she said, they must keep quiet also. "*Chihamba* must be honored; the *mukishi* would

4. Ritual joking between a Ndembu and a Humbu doctor.

feel bad if there were noise." But the adepts are expected to make a noise; they can revile the patients and one another, or trill, or cheer. Silence is a sign of respect, especially from juniors to seniors.

Joking. I spoke to Muchona about the mutual joking (*wu-sensi*) at *Chihamba.* He replied, "Men can revile women, and women can revile men. Or men may joke with men, and women with women. *Chihamba* is a terrible spirit [*mukishi*],

5. The candidates sit modestly in line with their backs to the sacred enclosure of *Kavula*, while the adepts ask them riddles.

and he is the grandfather of everyone present. We joke with the spirit as with a grandfather. This joking between men and women also rouses sexual desire [*wuvumbi*]. Rough speaking by adepts pleases the spirit and frightens the candidates, just as when *Kavula* speaks to them in the hut. But adepts tell candidates to be calm, they say:

Wundaku muchima weyi; neyi Kavula wudinakuhosha yuma bayi wu-tiya womaku, wundaku kanda wuyisha kumuchimaku.

(Be at peace [in] your liver; when *Kavula* is speaking things do not feel fear, be tranquil, do not put them in [your] liver [i.e., take them to heart].)

"Adepts tell the candidates they must learn from experience, but they must not show either fear or anger under their testing [*kweseka*]. An adept must be a person whose face shows no emotion."

Beating. The beating of candidates by adepts parallels the beating of novices by lodge officials at *Mukanda* and of candidates by officials at the funerary ritual of *Mung'ong'i.* Beating (*kweta*) is a sign of the inferior status of those beaten.

4b. The Mpanda *slave Yokes*

After the chasing (*ku-dihang'a*, literally, "chasing one another") had gone on for several hours, Muchona put a forked branch of *mudyi* wood over his neck and told other adepts to push him by its means to the principal candidate's hut. This forked branch represents the wooden yoke formerly fastened over the necks of slaves. It is called *mpanda*, and it was about *mpanda* that the adepts sang as they chased the candidates—*mpand'oye.* In the past, said Nyaluwema, candidates wore actual wooden yokes linked to one another along the whole line. Now only junior adepts who had shown ignorance of *Chihamba* customs and esoterica wore these symbolic *mpanda* yokes. Muchona only wore *mpanda*, he told me, to show the younger adepts how it was used. Spider Chanza, who was found to have gate-crashed *Chihamba* without knowing its *mpang'u* or *jipang'u* (mysteries), Wankie Soneka, the former teacher, and my cook-henchman Musona, whose admission to the rite I had purchased for a few shillings, were forced into the yoke by Lambakasa, Sakutoha, Muchona, Sachinjungu, Koshita, Sandombu, and other "big doctors," and driven ignominiously all the way to Nyamukola's hut. The village was now crowded with spectators who laughed and jeered uproariously as these "liars" (*akwakutwamba*) were chased by the senior adepts, who shouted *sho, sho,* as if their victims were dogs. Despite my aid Musona was kept well away from most of the esoteric phases of *Chihamba*, and I gained nothing by having had him admitted through *muko-leku*. As the seniors drove they blew piercing blasts on large whistles—also called *mpanda*—made from *mutebitebi* wood.

From time to time female adepts cooked the cassava roots they had brought on a fire not far from *isoli* and shared them with the other adepts.

Exegesis

According to Muchona, "*Mpanda* is part of the *mpang'u* of *Chihamba*. It comes from *Nkang'a*, the girls' puberty ritual, for *mudyi* is the tree of *Nkang'a*. In the old days candidates as well as junior adepts wore *jipanda*. It means they are born again, are pure. A person with *mpanda* tied on the neck is called *wanwa mpanda*, 'he drinks *mpanda*.' This is because *mudyi* stands for breast milk [*mayeli*]. *Mudyi* is the mother of everyone."

It is interesting to note in passing the consistent linkage made in *Chihamba* between the nurturant and disciplinary aspects of authority. Motherhood here comes in the guise of a slave yoke. *Kavula*, the giver of fortune and fertility, bullies and terrifies the candidates.

Mutebitebi. *Mutebitebi*, said Muchona, is a hollow-stalked shrub found on large termite hills. Whistling "pleases the spirit."

4c. Interrogation of candidates

During the day the candidates were chased between hut and sacralized bush beyond *mukoleku*. Each time they returned they were brought a little closer to the *isoli* central shrine or tabernacle. Periodically they were questioned while they rested. Here are some of the questions and answers I recorded:

Q. *Munendelidi?*
(What have you come for?)
A. *Etu tunenzi nakutala eyi nkaka wunenzi lelu.*
(We have come to look at you, grandfather, who have come today.)
Q. *Nkaka yenu wazatang'adi? Wayilang'ang'ahi?*
(What is your grandfather working at? What is he doing?)
A. *Etu twakata.*
(We are sick.)
Q. *Komana chachiwahi. Munenzi nakuntala. Komana, dinu chachiwahi. Nkaka yenu ijina dindi hinyi?*
(Really, that's good! You have come to look at me. Really, really, that's good! What is your grandfather's name?)

Muchona commented:

Wakwatang'a nukumukwashaku kukola kukwendaku chachiwahi. Hikutaza nakuyambashana jejina akutena muna.
(He catches in order to help someone here to be strong, to walk well. He [the adept] talks loudly and disputatiously; he tells the names and mentions them there.)

It would seem as if the senior male adepts who did the questioning identified themselves with *Kavula* ("You have come to look at me"). Muchona said that "*Kavula* himself is the one who sends the big adepts to ask questions." Thus each has *Kavula*'s mandate. The adepts were probing to see if the candidates knew the secret names of *Chihamba*,—*Kavula*, *Samaseng'a*, and *Samasoli*. In my hearing only Masondi, Muchona's wife, gave any correct answers, and she did not mention the name *Kavula*. Whenever a candidate failed to answer, or answered incorrectly, a great cry of derision arose from the adepts. Sakutoha, who took an active part in the questioning, told me in his usual frank and obliging way, "If candidates answer well, the spirit is glad, but they do not receive a reward, a big *Chihamba* name, for instance. People who failed to answer correctly in the past were called 'failures' [*akwakukang'anya*]. They were allowed to greet *Kavula*, but *Kavula* was not pleased with them. The big adepts tried to help them to answer properly. Indeed, if the people answered quickly, they would come early to *isoli*. Unless one person who was asked a question answered correctly, the whole group of candidates could not go beyond a certain place on the way to *isoli*. Today they are not keeping the custom. Only Masondi knows anything. But they will all get *Chihamba* names. The senior candidate, Nyamukola and Zuliyana, will be healed all right, but they will have to go to many other *Chihamba* drums before they will learn anything."

Fiddling prohibition. Candidates were forbidden to play with twigs or bits of grass while they answered. Nyamukola herself was told off for doing this. The prohibition recalls that in *Mukanda*, where novices in the circumcision lodge are punished for such "childishness." To have grass in the hands is described as "things of sin" (*yuma yanshidi*). It is like "displeasing your spirit." I have heard the act of fiddling with grass jocularly compared with masturbation (*kudihemisha*, literally "to play with oneself") by young men.

Muchona's account of chasing and questioning

"A big adept (the one who acts *Kavula*) instructs some of the adepts to ask the candidates why they came there. Then those adepts go to the candidates and stand asking them, 'Why have you come here?' Then the adepts begin to tell them to go back quickly and run to the village. They chase them, singing and reviling one another and the candidates. Sometimes they lift candidates by their shoulders. The song is '*Owenu owenoye, muyeji wesoli, owenoye muyeji wesoli owenoye muyeji waChihamba owenoye?* ('O that candidate of *isoli*, that candidate of *Chihamba*'). Then all of them enter the hut of the principal candidate. The candidates then lean on their hands on the side of the hut for a rest. The adepts move about in the hut, cursing each other and the candidates, swearing sexually, '*ilomu deyi, mpang'a jeyi, mwitaku deyi*' and so on. They can revile distant in-laws or classificatory mothers, fathers, mothers' brothers, fathers' sisters, and so on, but not close kin, such as sister, mother, father, child, or their own parents- and children-in-law. After a short while, the adepts tell their candidates to go running to *isoli*. They chase them singing and swearing. They stop some distance from *isoli*, and adepts question candidates again. Again they reply, 'We have come to the spirit of *Chihamba*.' Adepts say, 'You have failed. You must return again quickly. You must consider matters well.' Then they chase them back to the hut. Next time back they come a little nearer *isoli*. They do this about forty times. If a candidate tries to explain one of the mysteries [*jipang'u*] or riddles, the doctors trill with pleasure. After a while they come in sight of *isoli*. Now the doctors bring *mpanda*, a forked branch of *mudyi* wood, and tie an *mpanda* to each candidate's neck, for they were formerly slaves with *mpanda*. Then they chase them to the hut in the village, singing and reviling. In the hut the *mpanda* yokes are taken off. The adepts carry the yokes as they chase the candidates back. This chasing lasts from about 8 A.M. until about 5 P.M. They go with *mpanda* three or four times."

5. Greeting Kavula

Shortly before sunset the candidates were washed with medicine at the *musoli* tree chosen as *ishikenu*. Then they were led to a place about fifteen yards from the *isoli* where *Kavula* was made. They were in a line, in order of sex and of capture. This time they sat facing *Kavula*. Once more adepts stood on their right and asked them questions—about the identity of *"Samasoli," "Samaseng'a," "Nkaka yawantu ejima"* ("everyone's grandfather"), and so on.

Once more, with the exception of Masondi, they failed to answer correctly. Headman Itota, a fierce old hunter, who enacted *Kavula*, looked disgusted. He had given instructions to the other adepts not to mention the sacred name of *Kavula*. A woman adept, Manyosa, told us that it was now too late to perform all the details of the ritual properly. The sun was sinking fast. *Kavula*, concealed nearby in the bush, should have asked questions and reviled the candidates. It was too late for all that. About an hour before, Itota had danced magnificently before the madly but rhythmically shaking white image of *Kavula*, his muscled shoulders and limbs and his flat belly jerking in time to three drums. Itota was an old man from the wild lands in the south of Ndembu country in Angola. He had hunted all his life and had climbed many a tree to collect honey from the wild bees, not the least dangerous of tasks. His voice was hoarse and deep, from years of drinking warm *kasolu*, the heady mead loved by hunters. His natural way of speaking was *Kavula*'s. No one ever knew where Itota would be at any given hour, for he lived few of his days in his village and many alone in deep bush or river plain, stalking duiker, roan and sable antelope, and eland with his ancient Tower musket. He was a hard and savage old man, but nevertheless courteous and generous to his guests, should any surprise him at home. His bold wife was also a senior adept in this *Chihamba*. Now he shrugged his indifference at what was happening, for everything was being telescoped into too brief a time.

Instruction of candidates. First Muchona, to show the candidates how to perform their role, hit the image of *Kavula* "on the head," that is, on the blanket-shrouded mortar, with his rattle-butt. Then he ran, miming extreme terror, to the principal patient Nyamukola, and went through a pantomime of having his head cut off, showing her the ghastly things that might happen to her. This, he told me afterward, was to frighten and impress candidates with the difficulty of visiting *Kavula*. Then he demonstrated to the male candidates how to greet *Kavula*, "just like greeting Mwantiyanvwa, for *Kavula* is a relative [*kawusoku windi*] of Mwantiyanvwa," as he put it. He rolled toward the *isoli* tabernacle with its strange god, rolled in the dirt, banging his head on the ground, first to the right and then to the left, as he slowly advanced. When he reached *Kavula* he made an address:

Kalombu Chinyaweji! nkaka eyi aweni Samaseng'a, tunenzi dehi nakukuwana. Antu eyi anenzi dehi, ayeji eyi kukamwihi akumoni akwimushi alembi kudi eyi Samaseng'a. Kalombu Chinyaweji! Tukwashi eyi aweni nkaka; antu anenzi dehi. Velei!

(Kalombu Chinyaweji! [formula of address to a great chief]. Grandfather, you yourself [are] Samaseng'a ["Father of Increase"] we have already come to find you. Your people have already come, your candidates are near that they may see you, that they may greet you, that they may be penitent to you, O Samaseng'a. Ka-lombu Chinyaweji! Help us, O grandfather, yourself; the people have already come. *Velei!* [formula of address].)

He described to the male candidates what should be done next:

Kutapula maseki hikuwaya hamakasa hihevumu nukumesu hikusakilila nakudibulola hamaseki.

(Earth [should be] collected to be smeared on the arms, on the stomach, and on the face [as a sign] of thankfulness and [one should] wallow on the earth.)

Form of greeting women. Then he made Nyamukola crawl forward to *Kavula* to greet him. She rolled slowly along on her belly, twisting from left to right and from right to left. As she went she squeezed her breasts, "to give milk to the chief," as Manyosa explained. Her address was as follows:

Velei kalombu nkaka, nalembi, eyi aweni. Tunenzi nakukutala. Etu twakata·wutwanakenuku tukoli, eyi aweni Samaseng'a. Velei Chinyaweji!

(*Velei kalombu*, grandfather! I am sorry, you yourself. We have come to look upon you. We are sick, please feel pity for us that we may be strong, you yourself *Samaseng'a. Velei Chinyaweji!*)

Muchona told me: "The words of *Kavula* are that I like a woman to thank me with milk" (or "with breasts" for *mayeli* means both).

This was not the normal way in which women greeted Mwantiyanvwa, most informants told me, but their specific way of greeting *Kavula.* After Nyamukola, the other adult candidates greeted *Kavula,* the women first, then the men. After addressing the god, each candidate clapped his or her feet together from a sitting position, "because the legs are strong" as Nyaluwema said. In fact, she went on, one of the reasons for chasing was to test the legs. When women approached *Kavula*, in addition to squeezing their breasts, they beat their arms alternately on the ground. When each candidate or adept had greeted *Kavula* they remained near *isoli*. The children did not approach the tabernacle. Ultimately, the whole company of adult candidates and adepts stood before *isoli* and saw the white *Kavula* within.

6. *The killing of* Kavula

Now three adepts advanced the drums and began to play them. Each candidate in serial order, Nyamukola first, then struck *Kavula* on the head with the butt of a *chileng'a* rattle given to him or her by an adept who henceforth would have a special relationship of ritual friendship (*wubwambu waChihamba*) to the candidate. Actually, such ritual friendships were predetermined by discussion among the adepts, and an adept helped his or her *ibwambu* to answer the questions correctly if he could do so without being noticed.

After each stroke *Kavula* began to shiver and shake convulsively, "like a person who is dying," in time with the drumming and the singing of the adepts. The blanket was not withdrawn from the framework at this *Chihamba* (as described below by Muchona). When the last candidate had struck *Kavula*, Headman Itota declared that the ritual of *isoli* was at an end. Handfuls of meal were then taken from *Kavula*'s "body" and put on each candidate's head. The meal on the heads is known as *chibuwa chamutu* (from *ku-buwa*, "to steal," *mutu*, "head"). They were also anointed with oil brought from the village.

The whole crowd, in no set order, now began to return to the village, at first in silence, then, after they had passed the *mukoleku*, singing. A glint of silver from the new moon, as well as the sun's afterglow, lit their way back. Just before the procession entered Mukanza Village, Lambakasa halted them with a firebrand taken from the sacred fire now burning before Nyamukola's hut, struck it violently on the ground, and let out a great shout, "He is dead." Then they entered the village.

Before giving indigenous interpretations at this point as I have usually done, I now insert Muchona's account of the rites of greeting and killing *Kavula*. I do this in view of the statements of Mukanza adepts and of Headman Itota that "the customs were not being properly carried out." Muchona's account is much richer in detail than the events I observed. I found his accounts of other rituals I have seen so reliable in every respect that I am inclined to believe that his version of these esoteric rites corresponds more closely to traditional Ndembu practice than those I saw performed at Mukanza. It will be remembered that Sandombu, officially in charge of the arrangements, earlier had been accused of having made many errors. During this whole day of chasing and questioning he had been very reserved and had left the direction of affairs to others. The plurality of "bosses" probably helped to account for a number of anomalies and omissions in the ritual form. Muchona himself was for a long time occupied in the construction of the *Kavula* image and could not give much advice, although, as we have seen, he showed adepts how to perform the *mpanda* rite and how to greet *Kavula* correctly. In any case, he was too tactful a man to usurp another's function, especially when the latter was a headstrong character like Sandombu—many of whose violent acts I have chronicled in *Schism and Continuity*.

Muchona's account of greeting and killing Kavula

"*Chisolu* is an ordinary fence, *isoli* is a sacred enclosure. The last time the candidates are chased beyond *mukoleku*, the adepts tell them to sit down. All the adepts sit down beside *chisolu*, the candidates sit on the path. The male adepts sit apart from the women. *Kavula* has by now thrown cassava meal on his body. Then the adepts begin to shout, 'Come and look on him [*twayenu mutali*].' Then they sing:

Lelu mayaku eyeyeye mangoma eye eyeye lelu mayaku eyeye mangoma twakamutaluku nkaka Samalembola hakulembuli watiyang'a.

(Today, not far away, drums, today, not far away, drums, we shall look upon him, grandfather Samalembola, who makes penitent, he is listening.)

"Then all the people begin to look inside *isoli*. They are terrified, they are terrified, they shiver [*ku-zala*] for fear. They are astonished to see something moving about. *Kavula* is covered with skins or with a blanket which is completely whitened with cassava meal. He carries many *yileng'a* rattles in his hands. He curses them in *Kavula* speech. He makes a big noise with *yileng'a*.

"He asks the candidates, 'What have you come for?' They answer, 'We have come for you, that we may be cured by you of our sickness.' Then *Kavula* says, 'Approach.' All the adepts then enter the *chisolu*. [Muchona said that the *chisolu* should have been a circular fence much wider than the one I saw.] All this was about half an hour before sunset.

"*Kavula* begins to ask the adepts questions: 'What have those candidates come here for? What has brought them here? Those people have been running from here to the village. What has caused them to do so?' The adepts answer for the candidates: 'They have come here to be cured by you.' *Kavula* now speaks to the candidates: 'I am going to instruct you. What is my name?' The candidates say, 'Your name is *Chihamba.*' *Kavula* says, 'Yes, I know you have mentioned my name *Chihamba*, but what is my other name?' They always fail to mention his other name. Then *Kavula* is angry, he reviles the candidates and everyone present. He shakes his rattles noisily. He speaks in an angry, thick voice. He tells the older adepts to chase the candidates back, as a punishment. Adepts and candidates run singing as follows:

> *Wanwa mpanda shokoye, wanwa mpanda shoku.*
> (He wears a yoke, get along, wears a yoke, get along.)

"They enter the principal candidate's hut. Then they do as they have done before. They have been tied with the yoke again. But when they return the yokes are not untied until they reach *isoli*. When they are there they remove the yokes and put them in the *chisolu* enclosure. The candidates are now close to *Kavula* again. The adepts sit around the sides of *chisolu*. No one must go near *Kavula*'s *isoli* tabernacle. *Kavula* now asks: 'You call me *Chihamba*. Do you think that I have excreted [*nahambuki—ku-hambuka* means the excreting of children, "making stool"] here? What is my other name?' Now the candidates are secretly told by some adepts, 'When *Kavula* asks you about his other name, you must tell him his name is *Samaseng'a.*' When they tell him this, he expresses great pleasure and agreement. The people begin to shake with fear when he does this. *Kavula* says, 'Please come close to me, candidates, with your *yileng'a.*' The adepts have just given them these rattles. The adepts ask the patients to kill the *Chihamba* spirit 'so that we may see how you kill it.' "

The killing of Kavula. The whole of the meal mortar is covered with a blanket and *Kavula* is under it. *Kavula*'s head touches the mortar. The candidate is told to hit the projection where the mortar is. Then the candidate hits it with the *chileng'a* rattle, saying, '*pa-a!!*' She is followed by the second candidate, and by others, if there are any. The doctors weep and say:

Iyaye anamujahe-e, mwanta Samaseng'a nafwi, anamujahi!!

(Alas, alas, they have killed him, Chief Samaseng'a, they have killed him!!)

"Then *Kavula* pretends to die, shivering like someone about to die. Then some of the big adepts tell the candidates to run back, 'because you have killed *Samaseng'a Chihamba*.' The patients are chased by the adepts, singing:

Wakunyakishang'a, itang'wa dineli eye eyeyeyeye. Wahamikileng'a itang'wa dineli neyi muKavula mwayang'a muntu e eyeyeye mwayili hinyi? yehanda-a? eye yeyeye.

(You must be quick, the sun has set. You used to argue [the sun has set] that into *Kavula* goes a person. Who went into it? Is he alive?)

"They go running, singing this song to the village and back. They return to *isoli*. While they are away the big adepts cut off the red cock's head. They sprinkle its blood round the mortar. Then *Kavula* leaves that place and goes to his own place. He is in hiding. Then the big adepts make a frame of sticks and string and cover it with a blanket again to pretend that *Kavula* is still inside. An adept ties a long string to one stick in the frame. The string is hidden with leaves and extends into the bush. A big doctor or adept holds the string in his hand there. The frame is in *isoli*.

"Now the candidates return to *Kavula*. One of the candidates is given a *chileng'a* rattle and told to repeat the killing of *Kavula*. Then the adept holding the string begins to shake

6. *Kavula*—candidate's view.

it about as though someone is dying. After *Kavula* has been 'killed,' the candidates come close to the blanket. They are told to take it off, to uncover it from the place of the head. Suddenly they see only a mortar. The whole blanket is then removed. One of the big adepts asks them, 'You used to say that a person goes into *Kavula,* have you seen a person here?' The candidates reply, 'No, we have not seen a person here.' The adept asks, 'Have you not seen this blood?' They answer, 'We have seen some blood.' The adept says, 'This is *Kavula*'s blood. The blood of *Kavula* whom you killed a short time ago. You have killed the chief [*mwanta*].' The candidates are told to be patient in their hearts, in order to see it care-

7. *Kavula*—adept's view.

fully. The candidates say, 'This is a real mortar.' Then the people shout with joy. Then the candidates are again asked, 'What is that inside the mortar?' For the mortar was put in upside down. The base is called the 'head of *Kavula*' and is sprinkled with blood. Then they begin to guess what is inside. Some say, 'It is a *mupuchi* tree,' others say, 'There are portions of someone's hair.' When they make a mistake they are laughed at by the adepts. Luckily the candidates are later told by their friends among the older adepts to mention an ax, a hoe, a needle, a razor, and white beads. When they have mentioned these things the adepts say, 'They have been acquitted [*anaying'i*].' The people trill joyfully, then bring cassava meal and put some on each candidate's head, saying, 'You are now innocent.' The cock has already been taken by the adepts to be eaten by them. Then the string of white beads is cut into lengths and each candidate is given a piece to wear round the neck and under an arm [to wear beads in this way is *kupakata;* one *Chihamba* name for women is *Nyaka-pakata*, she who wears a bead-sash, and this was the name my wife received in *Chihamba*].

"Now *isoli* is finished. Adepts tell the candidates to return to the village. Both groups now have *yileng'a* rattles. As they go all sing:

Waying'eye-e waying'eye, waying'eye muyeji wesoli, waying'eye ng'unda wayili nayu kwisoli waying'eye yakufuma nayu mukalung'a waying'eye.

(She has been acquitted [there is no case against her], the candidate of *isoli*, she has been acquitted, she went with cries to *isoli*, she has been acquitted, she went with cries into the grave, she has been acquitted.)

"Some of the adepts are in front of the candidates, some are behind them."

Exegesis of events observed at *Mukanza* performance

Greeting. With regard to the greeting (*kwimusha*) of *Kavula*, Nyaluwema said: "*Kavula* is the greatest in all the world. Chief Kanongesha, and even Mwantiyanvwa himself, would greet *Kavula* in the same way as the male adepts and candidates." She went on to say, "They greet him first, while he is still alive, then they take up their rattles and kill him *pa-pa!* The people feel very sad after this.[13] But they laugh later when the names are called, '*Na Kaluswiko-o, wo-wo-wo, Na Nyakantemba, wo-wo-wo,*' there is great happiness." Nyalu-

[13] Nevertheless, I noticed that when Zuliyana and Makanjila were striking *Kavula*, they were smiling with obvious pleasure.

wema told us that women greeted *Kavula* first, and "killed" him first, "because women made the first *Chihamba* long, long ago, and then the men caught it and caught it." Women used to be the big adepts, nowadays the men are.

Sakutoha disagreed with Muchona's view that the candidates should have been allowed to see *Kavula*, that is, the framework of sticks and mortar. He said that candidates "must not see *Kavula* at their own *isoli*, only at the second *isoli*, when they are small adepts. At the Mukanza performance, only the big adepts saw it. Those who attended *Chihamba* when they were children, like Wankie, Spider, and Musona, were prevented from seeing *Kavula*. They were just like candidates." He added a few remarks about the child candidates: "They will not be caught and chased again when *Chihamba* is next made; they will be thought of as children who have been to *Chihamba*, but know nothing of the mystery [*mpang'u*] of *Chihamba*." Adult candidates, however, like Yana (the first woman caught during the chasing), Masondi (Muchona's wife), Makanjila, and Chilayi (two men) could become full adepts, if they were taught the medicines by a senior adept.

Muchona's comments

Killing. In discussing the killing of *Kavula* with me after the performance, Muchona said: "*Kavula* is killed to frighten the candidate [*kutiyisha muyeji woma*]. For he believes he is really killing *Kavula*. He has been instructed by the adepts that 'if you see the spirit of *Kavula*, you must consider that this is a spirit which helps people.' *Kavula* is *Chihamba*. He is not really the lightning, that is just a name. The adepts are just deceiving the candidates at *isoli*."

Muchona then said, rather enigmatically, "*Kavula* takes all powers [*ng'ovu jejima*]." He would give no further explanation of this. Perhaps it was to offset the impression that the whole affair at *isoli* was just trickery, for he went on to remark that if a person inadvertently entered an *isoli* abandoned in the bush after *Chihamba*, he would be attacked by "a spirit which had come out in *Chihamba*." In other words, the *isoli* was pervaded by authentic mystical power.

Nyaluwema's comments

Nyaluwema told us that if a woman wanted to go to *Chihamba* and had not previously been divined as having been caught by a spirit "in *Chihamba*," she told an adept and the adept had to catch her quickly and run her to the group of candidates. The child adepts did not have *akishi* (spirits) of their own, though it was said that Makanjila had been caught by the same spirit as Nyamukola. Masondi was believed to have a spirit.

She said that it was "*Kavula*'s back that we saw in *isoli*." When *Kavula* was killed, she went on, the spirit flew away into the sky, not to Nzambi (the High God), but "into the wind" (*mumpepela*). It could come again.

In her opinion, people do feel pleased to be candidates and learn the *mpang'u* of *Chihamba*. Mungongu, however, had felt that it was too hard for him and had run away after being chased a few times.

The correct posture for candidates when they sat at the *ishikenu* waiting to come to *Kavula* was to have their hands turned up on their knees, like beggars, said Nyaluwema.

7. Concluding oration at the village

At the village a big fire was burning at the sacred site where the arrow was first planted, outside Nyamukola's hut.

Beans had been cooked and stood in a pot near the fire. All danced around the fire singing *"Naying'i,"* and so on, on arrival. Then the candidates were seated in two semicircles around the fire with their backs to Nyamukola's hut. The child candidates formed the inner group near the fire; Nyamukola was nearest to her hut. Lambakasa, a senior male adept, standing on the opposite side of the fire, nearest to the men's forum (*chota*), then addressed his remarks in the direction of Headman Mukanza, who stood behind the candidates.

He spoke as follows:

Ilang'a twaya kuChihamba lelu, ayeji amavulu nankashi tunenzi dehi. Twayitwala kwisang'a kwisolu hanu. Anaying'i dehi, dichu tunenzi dehi. Yowu wudi nandumba jindi atenteki. Enu amayala neyi mwapanda malomba hela makishi hela tutotoji, tentekenu. Ayeji awa tunenzi dehi nawa hosi wakataku, ejima ngu akola. Wakukotoka mwendu hosi, wakukotoka chikasa hosi. Ching'a akoli ayeji, mwakendakatwamba nenu kwiji ayijaha kuChihamba nehi.

(And so we went to *Chihamba* today, there were very many candidates, we have come already. We carried them away into the bush to *isoli* there. They are now innocent, and so we have come already. If any woman has her familiars let her put them down. You men, if you magically prepare snake-familiars or *makishi* familiars or familiars from *Katotoji* masks, put them down. Those candidates we have come already [with], not one is sick, all are completely well. No one has a broken leg, no one a broken arm. All of them must be strong, or perhaps you might say [some day] "they did not kill them at *Chihamba*.")

Lambakasa went on to say that the adepts would sleep outside to guard the candidates and that they were giving the candidates medicines to strengthen them. He warned them all to turn up next morning "for the planting of *kantong'a*."

He told them to sleep in the open on mats. Even those from other villages than Mukanza had to do this.

Medicines. Near the fire were a number of pots containing herbal medicines. These were being prepared to poultice (*kukanda*) the candidates. They were also to be drunk by them during the night. Nyaluwema had gone out on her own, while the chasing and questioning had been going on, to collect leaves from the following trees for this medicine: *mwang'ala*, *muntung'ulu*, *mukombukombu*, *mukula*. These were added to the ingredients collected on the previous day, *mucheki*, *munkalampoli*, *musoli*, *mucha*, *museng'u*, and *mutuhu*. Nyaluwema said the medicines she collected had been "forgotten" by Sandombu.

The candidates and adepts put their *yileng'a* rattles under the rafters in the roof of Nyamukola's hut. After Lambakasa's harangue, the people dispersed to their villages, except for the candidates who remained to be treated with medicine and to sleep by the fire, and the adepts who had been told to look after them.

Exegesis

Ilomba. The *ilomba* is a human-headed snake, believed by Ndembu to have the same face as its owner. It is always owned by men; chiefs and great hunters are thought to have exceptionally powerful *malomba* and they share the emotions of their owners. The *ilomba* both protects its owner against sorcery and witchcraft and uses mystical power against others on his behalf. Some believe that an *ilomba* feeds on people's shadows (*nyevulu*), conceived as vital principles, and so drains their strength. Other Ndembu think that an *ilomba* and its owner feast together on the actual flesh of their victim. If an *ilomba* is killed by magical means, it is believed that its owner will die with it.[14]

Portions of the masks and costumes worn by masked dancers at *Mukanda* are used as ingredients in the preparation (*ku-panda*) of male sorcery medicine. Like the masks, the familiars prepared or made in this way are called *makishi. Tutotoji* is the plural of *katotoji* and refers to one type of mask.

Andumba. Andumba (literally, "lions"), often called *tuyebela* or *tushipa*, are women's familiars, inherited matrilineally, and have the variable forms of little men with reversed feet, hyenas, jackals, owls, or small rodents.

Lambakasa in his harangue follows a traditional form when he exhorts sorcerers and witches not to practice their evil magic against *Chihamba* candidates. The latter are believed to be in a vulnerable state during ritual and while they are in seclusion. Whenever large crowds of people are assembled Ndembu fear sorcery or witchcraft, for such "bad people" are thought to be secretly present with their bands of invisible familiars.

The expression "killing the candidates at Chihamba" refers to the ritual slaying of the candidates on the following day.

Mwang'ala. The use of the medicine *mwang'ala*, sometimes called *mwang'azembi* (in hunting cults) and *muhang'andumba* (in antiwitchcraft ritual), is derived by Ndembu from its

[14] The belief in the existence of *ilomba* is widespread in central Africa. In a most interesting exhibition of African paintings from northern Rhodesia (The Ernest Knight Collection), held in July 1958 at the Commonwealth Institute in South Kensington, several African patients in the hospital at Lusaka painted *malomba*. One patient came from a village in the Kasai country of the Belgian Congo, others from the Tonga tribe of Mazabuka in northern Rhodesia. The Kasai patient gave his *ilomba* the same face as its owner and showed it, quite horrifically, capturing a child to eat it.

homonymy with *kumwang'a*, "to scatter." Muchona said that it "means to chase away the familiars [*andumba*] of envious witches." *Another old man, Ihembi, told me that it means "the scattering of diseases [yikatu]"* from an afflicted person. It is used, apparently without mystical reference, as an ingredient in medicine to treat pyorrhea, "because it is bitter and hot." Where a disease (*musong'u*) is believed to be at work without the intervention of a spirit, medicines are often used because of their bitterness (*wukawu*) or heat (*ku-yeya*), which can "kill" or "drive off" the disease. A disease is regarded as a living creature, rather like an animal, which "moves about" in the patient's body, and can be "driven away."

Muntung'ulu. Muntung'ulu has many rootlets; in the same way a woman should have many children.

Mukombukombu. Mukombukombu is regularly used as an ingredient in a leaf broom (*musampu*) employed to sprinkle or sweep medicine over a patient in several kinds of ritual. Ndembu derive its meaning from *ku-komba*, "to sweep" and say that it "sweeps diseases from the patient."

Mukula. On page 64 I gave some of the connotations ascribed to *mukula*. Ndembu derive *mukula* from *ku-kula*, "to mature or grow up." The central reference is to a girl's first menstruation. The tree exudes a red gum and this is likened, among other things, to menstrual blood (*kanyanda* or *mbayi*). It is also likened to the blood of birth (*mashi akusema*). Indeed, when a woman has successfully borne her first child, Ndembu say *"wunakuli dehi,"* "she has matured." The common pseudoetymological derivation is here related to a natural property of the plant. As we have seen, this is not always the case. *Mutuhu*, for example, has no natural characteristic that associates it with *kutuhuka*, "to leap out." Other medicine plants, like *mucha*, are used because of their properties and not because of their names.

Finally, a word on moonlight. According to Muchona, most rituals having nocturnal episodes are performed in bright moonlight. "If a ritual is performed in the dark [*mwidima*]," he said, "it meant that there was no time for waiting. The patient was very sick and would soon get worse. Moonlight is chosen because when the moon [*mweji*] is shining, everything is seen, is clear. The moon is white, clearly seen, like *mpemba*, white clay, like good health [*wukolu*]. The moon and the sun [*mutena, itang'wa*, or *mwana*] are symbols [*yijikijilu*] of *mpeza* [another term for white clay], which is a symbol for whiteness or purity. The darkness is a symbol of blackness or bad luck [*malwa*] or death [*ku-fwa*]. The sun and moon are also symbols of God [Nzambi]. The moon is a revelation [*chimwekeshu*]."

The Fourth Day

Since the first episodes on this day form a dynamic unity, I will describe them serially without interpolating Ndembu exegesis. I will, however, insert Muchona's accounts.

1. The cutting of the ikamba daChihamba *root and collection of components of* kantong'a *and medicines*

Early in the morning Lambakasa led the candidates and adepts into the bush in the opposite direction to the site of *isoli*. They found a large *ikamba daChihamba* tree about a hundred yards from the village. The name of this tree means cassava root of *Chihamba*. The candidates were left about ten yards away from the tree, while the doctors circled it (*kubola*) thoroughly. Then Lambakasa squatted down before the main trunk of the tree—a well-grown one—and prayed to the afflicting spirit of Nyamakang'a. After he had finished praying he struck the trunk with his *chileng'a* rattle.

Then Itota's wife—the wife of *Kavula* in fact—took a hoe and dug up the ground to expose the thick, cassavalike taproot. First she inspected the main trunk, then guessed where the root would be. Her first hoe stroke revealed the beginning of a very large root. This good guess was thought to be lucky. She quickly but carefully exposed the dorsal portion of the root for about eight feet. While doing so she accidentally cut the root, and the whole company of adepts gasped, then began to sing "he is wounded, he is wounded." Lambakasa, brother of Itota's wife, quickly took his *isaku* pouch, put medicine from it on the "wound," then rubbed in castor oil with the handle of his rattle. Nyaluwema said, "You must not wound the root for it is the spirit." She then observed to me that the oil was "to please and heal the spirit." The rattle was used, she said, "because this is the important tree of *Chihamba*." She whispered that "the *mukishi* is in the ground at the foot of the tree." After that they left the taproot in the ground; they were forbidden to cut and remove it. They took a smaller root branching off from it. Any such root would do, said the adepts. This root was also "wounded"—perhaps not accidentally. The "wound" was treated like that in the taproot. Then Sakutoha prepared to cut out a section of the smaller root. First he knocked on it with his rattle-butt, then with his ax he neatly cut out a section of root about a foot long. The adepts approached and with their rattles, which they pushed under the section, they carefully and solemnly lifted it out and conveyed it into the *lwalu* medicine basket. The adepts had all been marked with medicine from *isaku* pouches—by the outer orbits. The candidates waiting at the

path ten yards away were also marked by Lambakasa with
isaku medicine. They were then dressed in clean clothes and
adorned with white beads, which "represented the spirit,"
according to Lambakasa. Meanwhile the adepts quickly and
unceremoniously collected leaves and chipped off bark from
mukombukombu, *mudyi*, and *nununa* shrubs in a rough circle
around the *ikamba daChihamba* tree. Then they collected
twigs and bark scrapings from each of the following trees:
mukula, *musoli*, *muhotuhotu*, *mututambululu*, *mukombukombu*,
mudyi, and *ikamba daChihamba*. Nyaluwema had brought a
cassava cutting (*ndimbu*) from her own garden.

Muchona's account

I give here Muchona's account of this episode, told me several months before I observed the rites:

*Kutachika kuya kwikamba daChihamba, embang'a kumuzaji nakuwu-
ketula muzaji diyu mukishi. Anateti dehi muzaji ahung'unwinang'ahu
tumanji, ashang'ahu nawa luseng'a lwesaku. Ayiputang'a yejima nakudo-
monayu hamesu nihehama nihamuchima. Hikuteta dinu nyitondu ya-
kantong'a, ayang'a kumusoli, atetang'aku mutondu nikumukombukombu
nikumututambululu nikumuhotuhotu nikumudyi nikumukula.*

(First they go to [an] *ikamba daChihamba* [tree], they sing at the
root [while] cutting it—the root is the spirit. [When] they have already cut the root, they pour in drops of oil, then they put on medicine from the *isaku* skin. They mix everything up and put it on the
eyes, on the forehead, and on the liver. They cut then the trees of
kantong'a, they go to *musoli*, they cut at the tree, and at *mukombukombu* and at *mututambululu* and at *muhotuhotu* and at *mudyi* and at
mukula.)

2. *The* yibi *episode*

After leaving the bush, the adepts lined up the candidates
along the path leading past Mukanza Village. On the side

nearer the village, the adepts hoed up a mound of earth about eighteen inches long and six inches high. Then they smoothed it with great care, trimming the edges. On top they sketched in with white *isaku* medicine the outline of a man. The head was circular and the arms and legs were at right angles to the straight line of the body. This was said by Muchona to stand for *Kavula*. The cross-markings in white clay on the arms of adepts noticed previously (see page 51) also symbolized *Kavula*, according to Muchona. At the foot of this cross-shaped figure, the big adepts set a split sapling of *musoli*. Each cleft portion was then bent away from the other, and its head was inserted into the ground. In this way a double arch was formed. Then the adepts placed the *lwalu* medicine basket, emptied of its contents, the right way up, on top of the figure of *Kavula*. Next they made the line of candidates advance a few paces. Now Nyamukola, the principal candidate, was ordered to crawl by herself on elbows and knees, with lowered head, to the mound, figure, and arch, which were collectively termed *yibi*. Some adepts guided her to the right place with their hands. A medicine broom (*chisampu*) was laid near *yibi*. The *yibi* was still covered by the *lwalu* basket. The head of the figure lay toward Nyamukola, and the sapling arch beyond the figure. She greeted *yibi* in the same way she had greeted *Kavula* the previous day. She was then questioned once more about the secret names of *Chihamba*. After the interrogation she was splashed with medicine made from bark scrapings from the trees mentioned on page 121. Then Lambakasa made passes with a knife over each of her shoulders and her head and finally shaved along the hairline over her brow and at the back of her head.

Muchona told me while this was going on:

Yibi kuyikosa Chihamba hamujimba kulonda atooki, amwilu ki dimu Chihamba chachiwahi nakumutena dinu nawu Kavula.
(*Yibi* [is] to wash them [the candidates] [with] *Chihamba* on the body in order that they might be white [or pure], that they might know him well there in *Chihamba*, and to mention him as *Kavula*.)

Nyamukola was then anointed with *isaku* medicine. After that she had to slink away down the path in an attitude of shame (*wusonyi*), to the derisive laughter of the adepts, who called out "*nshimba!*" (genet cat). According to Nyaluwema, "*Nshimba* is an animal that goes secretly [*chakujinda*]. The adepts mean that the candidate should go away from this *yibi* place now to leave room for another candidate."

After Nyamukola, all the other candidates, including Wankie, Mungongu, and Spider, had to greet *yibi* and undergo questioning, ceremonial killing, shaving, anointment with *isaku* medicine, and jeers.

According to Nyaluwema, the passes made over the head and shoulders with the knife meant "wherein the spirit passed" (*mwahitilayi mukishi*). The arched sticks were "for the spirit to pass along the path." Muchona said, "The candidates were deceived, for adepts tell them 'they kill you—when you go to *Chihamba*, you will die.' " In his view the passes with the knife meant "feigning to kill them [*ku-dimba kuyitapa*]."

After all the candidates had been dealt with, the *lwalu* basket was inverted over the figure of Kavula and the split sapling was driven through it to peg it down over the mound. It was then declared taboo to touch the basket, and it was left to moulder away.

8. Doctor applies castor oil with the butt of his rattle to the exposed taproot of an *ikamba daChihamba* tree, identified with *Kavula*.

3. The making of kantong'a *shrines*

After *yibi*, a personal shrine, known as *kantong'a*, was set up for each adult candidate, near his or her own hut. Most of these shrines were set up simultaneously in the villages of the different candidates. Nyamukola's was the first to be erected.

When the adepts came from *yibi* they brought a mat and put it outside Nyamukola's hut. Then they encircled the hut singing and holding aloft their axes, hoes, medicine basket, and medicines. They sang the *waying'e-e* song, "she is innocent." After that they put the *lwalu* basket on the mat and Nyaluwema slipped a cassava cutting (*ndimbu*) into it. Then

9. Doctor anoints the wounds of the white spirit.

Sakutoha picked up all the twigs collected before *yibi*, one by one, starting with the *ishikenu, ikamba daChihamba*, the others in no set order. Then he put them in a bundle, adding the cassava cutting to them. The bundle was called *mukanji wayi-tumbu* or "bundle of medicines" and tied about with a wisp of tough grass.

Next the adepts made a hole (*ikela*) in the ground, close to where the arrow of *Chihamba* had originally been inserted, with a round opening. One adept had gone to fetch black mud (*malowa*) from the bottom of a stream. Some of this was placed in the hole, which was about six inches deep. Then Sakutoha began to address the *Chihamba* spirit as follows:

10. Doctor "sings at the root" of *ikamba daChihamba.*

Neyi yeyi Chihamba wayikatishang'a ching'a lelu akoli.

(If you, *Chihamba,* are the one who is making them sick, today they must be well.)

After invoking he poured white maize beer into the hole. Then he put the bundle of twigs upright into the hole, using more *malowa* to make it stand up firmly. *Malowa* was also tamped around the base of the bundle. When completed the upright bundle was called *kantong'a*—according to Muchona, from *ku-tong'ashana,* "to think about." It is, therefore, a me-

11. Preparation of *yibi* shrine; image of *Kavula* painted in white *isaku* "medicine"; note split sapling of *musoli* at base of image.

morial to the *Chihamba* spirit and a mnemonic of the *Chihamba* ritual. A clay pot called *izawu* was placed next to *kantong'a*, and black mud was pressed around its base.

4. Beheading of a white hen

Next Sakutoha killed a white hen in the usual Ndembu fashion by cutting off its head with a knife, and let its blood gush into the *izawu* pot. He sprinkled blood over the *kantong'a* bundle and the sides of the pot. Then he pressed

12. Preparation of candidate for his symbolic execution at *yibi*.

the head of the fowl, gaping beak first, over the top of the *kantong'a*. The rest of the fowl was given to the candidate to eat at leisure. The intestines were removed by disemboweling (*ku-busa*, see pages 82–83) and draped over the forked branches of twigs in the *kantong'a*. Other pots were

13. The *yibi* shrine is left as a memorial of the rites.

14. A candidate's personal *kantong'a* shrine surrounded by a fence to keep dogs away from the head and intestines of a hen—to be later impaled on the "medicine" branches.

brought and beer calabashes were placed near the base of *kantong'a*.

5. *Cutting medicines for the pots* (ku-teta mazawu)

The candidates present at this time were Nyamukola, the child-candidates from Mukanza Village, and child-candidates from distant villages who were staying at Mukanza Village during *Chihamba*. The other adult candidates, as we have said, were in their own villages, where *tuntong'a* were being made for them. A *kantong'a* was erected for me and my wife during the rite, and we missed some of the *ku-teta mazawu* episode at Nyamukang'a's hut. We did not have this episode at our *kantong'a*. Lambakasa officiated at our *kantong'a* rite, much to the irritation of Sandombu, who by this time had been quietly but effectively elbowed out of the role of general organizer. Sakutoha and Lambakasa had taken over most of the ritual tasks.

I was told that Sakutoha had first made invocation, then poured out maize beer at the base of *kantong'a*. A large clay pot had been brought and Mukanza Village adepts, such as Nyaluwema, Mangaleshi, Mika, and Sandombu, took bark and leaves from the medicine plants collected and began to cut (*ku-teta*) them up in small pieces, putting them in the *izawu* pot. Water and beer were also poured into the pot. The large section of root from *ikamba daChihamba* was then half buried close to the pot.

When we arrived Sakutoha was just about to pour beer in the pot. He held a mug in his hand and prayed to the afflicting ancestress Nyamukang'a that the candidates "should be strong." Before he poured the beer out another adept took hold of his arm, another grasped that adept's shoulder, and so on, until a human chain of adepts stretched out behind Sakutoha. This was "to add power" (*ng'ovu*) to the act of pouring. Next little chips of *ikamba daChihamba* bark (*yibalu*), about half an inch square, were cut with the small knives used by the adepts. These were placed on the backs of adepts' and candidates' hands. When all were ready, each person crossed his or her hands at the wrists, and at a signal from Sakutoha all threw the chips up, over, and backward, with a hooting sound.

6. *Planting beans and maize round* kantong'a

Sakutoha took his rattle and dug a circle in the earth round the pot and *kantong'a*, using the butt for this purpose. He also used the head of his medicine ax. When a groove about two inches deep had been made all round, he took some beans and grains of maize from a bowl and gave a few to each candidate and adept present. Adepts and candidates all leaned forward together and put the beans in the trench, chanting in unison. Then they spoke over the beans, but I did not record what they said. After this all collaborated in covering the beans and grain by hand. As mentioned, the section of *ikamba daChihamba* root had been partially buried near the *izawu* pot on the side facing Nyamukola's hut. Beer was poured as a libation to *Chihamba* at each end of the root section.

Each of the collective acts mentioned, throwing the chips and sowing seeds, was done in a single coordinated movement, as though by one person. Lines were then drawn in cassava meal from the *kantong'a* and medicine pot to Nyamukola's hut, then to the village muyombu tree ancestor shrines.

A fence of stout sticks was afterward put round *kantong'a* and *izawu* to protect them from dogs who might have tried to drag off the head and intestines of the hen on the *kantong'a*.

The medicine in the large *izawu* was for the candidate's use during the succeeding period of partial seclusion. She was obliged to wash in it and to drink it occasionally.

At the *kantong'a* rite the special cult name of the candidate was used by the adept when he invoked. Afterward the *Chi-*

hamba "friend" (*mulunda*) of the candidate mentioned the fact of their friendship (*wulunda* or *wubwambu waChihamba*) and expressed her pleasure at it.

7. "*Stopping up* Chihamba" (ku-jika Chihamba)

After all the adult candidates' *ku-teta mazawu* rites were concluded, all the adepts and candidates gathered near Nyamukola's hut and started to revile and jeer at one another. Then they started a mock battle, snatching up brands of firewood and cindered logs from the sacred fire to throw them at one another. Sakutoha threatened people with the meal mortar that had not been used for pounding medicine. This behavior was called *wusensi waChihamba*, the joking of *Chihamba*. During this joking, Sandombu and a woman adept danced, facing one another with a long pole stretched from the shoulder of one to that of the other, making the suggestive movements of the *danse du ventre*.

Everyone was in an extraordinary good humor. After a final crescendo of badinage and horseplay, all rushed away in different directions.

Exegesis

The cutting of the ikamba daChihamba root, etc. It is clear from the adepts' behavior and comments that the *ikamba daChihamba* root is identified either with *Kavula* or with the afflicting ancestress—or perhaps with both. The wounding (*ku-tapa*, which also means in different contexts, "to kill," "to behead," "to stab," "to execute") of the root parallels the killing of *Kavula*. The wounding of the root also immediately foreshadows the ritual killing of the candidates—also described as *ku-tapa* or *ku-tapana*—as does the anointing of the root with *isaku* medicine, for the candidates are also anointed.

Tapping with a rattle-butt is frequently done in *Chihamba*—the principal candidate's hut door was banged thus on the day of chasing; the mortar was tapped with an adept's rattle at the making of *isoli;* and more important *Kavula* was "killed" (*ku-tapa* again) by the rattles of the candidates. All I could get in the way of interpretation from most adepts was a series of vague statements by Nyaluwema, Sandombu, and Sakutoha that it meant "making a person or thing strong." Muchona disagreed, saying that it meant "to kill" and that it was also "just a sign" (*chinjikijilu hohu*) of *Chihamba*. He meant presumably that in esoteric contexts the action meant to kill—and here one is tempted to regard it as the lethal power of the lightning (see page 49)—and in others it was taken as a shorthand or metonym for the ritual as a whole, which of course was aimed at making people strong or well.

Yibi. [15] Before discussing the components of the *kantong'a* I cite Nyaluwema's interpretation of the *yibi*. No one knew what the name meant; they merely said that "it came from Mwantiyanvwa long ago." Nyaluwema told us that "the *yibi* is for killing the candidates. It takes some of their hair. They are not really wounded but the spirit is angry with them. The image of *Kavula* on the mound is like an animal's skin stretched out (*ku-tanda*) to dry. *Chihamba* passes through the split and arched stick."

Making kantong'a. Muchona discussed the *kantong'a* episode with me not long after I saw the rites performed. He told me that "the *ikela* hole was made to cause the *kantong'a* bundle to stand upright, for standing up means strength. *Malowa*, black

[15] The only reference I have come across in the central Africa literature which might have a possible connection with *yibi* is the name of a Lala clan in Mkushi District, the *Ibi* clan, which means "anus." See Munday 1961: xv.

mud, is cool, for it comes from water. It is put in the hole in order that all the diseases in the bundle should rest peacefully for ever after. For the bundle is a collection of every disease that attacked the candidate into one form [*yuma yejima yatiyang'amu muyeji anayi kaseli hamu, nyisong'u nawa yidikung'ili hamu yiwundi*]."

"The *izawu* pot," he went on, "contains everything. If a woman was very sick, she must become better from *izawu*. If there are witches [*aloji*] present they are now made cool [*kuyifomona*], are prevented [*kuyilekesha*] from bewitching, in *izawu*, for in it is every kind of medicine. The *izawu* contains a root of *ikamba daChihamba*, there is also a portion of each twig. Then cold water is added.

"The candidate must go on washing in *izawu* at dawn and sunset every day. She stops when the seeds planted around the *kantong'a* have grown up."

Beheading of a white hen. Muchona told me that "they sacrificed [literally, *aketwili*, 'they cut' the white hen so that the candidate's body 'should be white' [*mujimba atooki*]. The sprinkling [*ku-sansa*] of blood is for the *Chihamba* spirit, who is given blood. The head of the hen is food for the spirit. In the same way a hunter keeps an animal's head for himself—it is the most important part. At the *Nkula* ritual the head of the red cock killed at *isoli* is put in the small spirit-hut for the spirit that has come out in *Nkula*. The head [*mutu*] is the place of life [*wumi*]."

Muchona then began to talk about *wumi* in more general terms. But since beheading plays such an important role in *Chihamba*, it is worth giving some of his views.

He said: "When a man's head is cut off he is dead. Mwantiyanvwa had two men, Kambanji and Nswanakayanda, who used to behead people. So did other great chiefs.

"Life [*wumi*] is in a living person, the shadow [*mwevulu*] comes from a dead person. You can dream of a *mwevulu*, for when a person is asleep, his *mwevulu* can wander about, he is 'dead' [*nafwi*]. But your *wumi* is in your blood even when you are asleep. *Wumi* is also in the heart, the lungs, and the intestines."

According to Nyaluwema, the *kantong'a* fowl could be of any color, but had to be a hen. Its head was food for the spirit, in this case for the spirit Nyamakang'a. She said that invocations were made to Nyamakang'a, while *Kavula* was the spirit which gave names. The intestines (*nyijing'wa*) stood for procreative power (*lusemu*) and helped to make the beans and grain planted grow more quickly.

Cutting medicines for the pots. Nyaluwema said that when the water is poured into the *izawu* "people say that *Chihamba* is visible [*Chihamba wamwekana*]." She went on to say that the back of the hand is used to throw the chips of *ikamba daChihamba* "because it is forbidden to throw them as people usually do." She then told us that "good things are put into the pot and bad things are thrown away."

Muchona suggested that the chips might be for the spirits of mischievous or sterile persons, the *ayikodjikodji*.

Planting beans and maize around kantong'a. Nyaluwema explained that *Kavula* likes new beans and new maize "because they are white." The beans and maize that grow around *kantong'a* are not cooked and eaten when grown. They are "separate for the spirit." "If you go away to live in another village," she said, "you don't eat up your *Chihamba* cassava [the roots that eventually grow from the cassava cutting in *kantong'a*], but, you take a cutting from the plant with you."

She said that "they start to dig the ground with their *yileng'a* rattles, because it is a thing from the elders." Both adepts and candidates sow beans "because both are of the *mukishi.*" "When the seeds grow high up in the air, the candidates are innocent and happy. The spirit has already gone away from the *kantong'a,* and the people are glad of this, but it might come back. A *kantong'a* is put in because the people are crying that *Kavula* is dead. A *kantong'a* is like a *muyombu* tree, a village tree-shrine, it is for your ancestor spirit."

The components of kantong'a and izawu medicine. The twigs composing the *kantong'a* bundle are, in fact, taken from just those species of trees that are used most often in Ndembu ritual, either as ingredients of medicines or as components of physical structures, such as shrines, seclusion huts, symbolic bows, slave yokes, and the like. The *kantong'a* is a sort of abridgement or compendium of Ndembu curative ritual. When Muchona said that "the *izawu* pot [containing bark scrapings and leaves from the species of trees used in *kantong'a*] contains everything," he meant just that. When he called *kantong'a* "a bundle of diseases," he meant more than that. He was saying elliptically that the trees used represented the total system of rituals of affliction.

I list these trees once more: *ikamba daChihamba, mudyi, mukula, musoli, mukombukombu, mututambululu,* and *muhotuhotu.* The first has important uses in the *Chihamba* ritual, the second is the dominant symbol of *Nkang'a,* the girls' puberty ritual, the third is the dominant symbol of the *Nkula* ritual, while *musoli* is dominant in certain hunting cults. The last three must be considered together, for their leaves constitute the traditional medicine broom as a set used in many kinds of ritual.

With the exception of *ikamba daChihamba,* all these trees are used in many kinds of ritual. If one considers the full range of meanings allocated to them by Ndembu, one sees that they represent the highest and most pervasive values explicitly recognized in Ndembu ritual as well as the lowest common denominators of biological experience and economic life.

Since Muchona—and other adepts corroborated his statement—regarded the *kantong'a* as epitomizing Ndembu curative ritual, I believe that it is legitimate to inquire into what each of the components is said to mean by Ndembu informants in kinds of ritual other than *Chihamba*. One is then in a position to see just what sorts of things and meanings are concentrated into the single form of *kantong'a*.

Ikamba daChihamba. Although *ikamba daChihamba* is not used in any ritual of affliction other than *Chihamba*, and does not appear in any life-crisis ritual, it was formerly used as a war medicine to render warriors invulnerable to spears or musket balls. In this context it was known as *musambanjita* and was derived by Muchona from *ku-samba*, "to acquit oneself" or as Windson Kashinakaji translated it, "to be free from," and *njita*, "war" or "raid." This meant that those who used it would be free from injuries sustained during fighting.

In *Chihamba* itself, as we have seen, its root is compared to a cassava root, which is known by the same term *ikamba*. Lambakasa explained that it resembled a soaked cassava root, not a fresh one. A soaked root is white, he explained, like that of the plant. It meant all the things signified by cassava root, said Muchona. Thus when a diviner was asking people why they had come to consult him he would say, "Why have you assembled here? Is it for a cassava root? A cassava root is important—is it the cassava root of living people, or of dead people?" (*Chalema mukamba: mukamba wawantu akahanda indi wawantu afwa?*)

He explained that *mukamba* was a white cassava root and

stood for the destiny of the person to be divined about. The root was the luck or fate of a human being. Sometimes, he went on, a cassava root means "a person's body" (*mujimba wamuntu*) because it is thick and round like a body. So the *ikamba daChihamba* would be the body of the *Chihamba* (spirit). When it was half buried near the *kantong'a*, it represented *Kavula*, said Muchona, "for you only saw the back of *Kavula* as he came out of the ground."

Finally, most adepts I asked said that *ikamba daChihamba* was a very strong tree, and it was used in medicine to make people strong.

Mudyi. I have mentioned *mudyi* before, in connection with the *mpanda* yokes. It will be convenient to present various informants' interpretations here.

Muchona consulted Manyosa, an expert in the field of *Nkang'a* customs, and gave my wife a text which, to my mind, presents the best point of departure for the interpretation of *mudyi* symbolism:

Mudyi diku kwakaminiyi nkakulula hakumutembwisha ninkakulula mukwawu ni mukwawu ni kudi nkaka ni kudi mama ninetu anyana diku kumuchidi wetu kutwatachikili ni amayala nawa chochu hamu.

(*Mudyi* is the place where slept the [founding] ancestress, where they caused her to be initiated, and an ancestress, another one, and another, and [down] to the grandmother, and to the mother, and to us the children, it is the place of our tribal custom where we began, and also the men in just the same way.)

Manyosa and Muchona explained this by saying that "*mudyi* is the place of all mothers; it is the ancestress of women and men. *Kutembwisha*, 'to cause to be initiated,' means to dance round and round the *mudyi* tree where the novice lies. The *mudyi* is the place where our ancestress slept, to be initiated there means to become pure or white [*ku-tooka*]. Men, too, are initiated there for they are circumcised at *Mukanda* under a *mudyi* tree. When we are thinking of a particular novice [*kankang'a*] we say that *mudyi* is 'their lineage' [*mwevumu dawu*]" (that is, it represents the novice's own matrilineage).

Women interviewed during the girls' puberty ritual said that the *mudyi* tree represented a mother and her child (*mama namwanindi*). Others described the leaves of the *mudyi* taken at one stage of the ritual and thrust into the thatch of the mother's hut as the novice's "children."

Muchona told me that *mudyi*, because of its white gum, represents that part of a woman "from which everyone comes—the breasts. A novice in *Nkang'a* will bear children, and some of them will be hunters. A woman who goes to sleep at *mudyi* [a euphemism for the ordeal undergone by a girl novice who has to lie motionless throughout the whole of a hot and noisy day at the foot of a *mudyi* tree] will bear hunters and men of sexual desire. *Mudyi* stands for all mothers."

Mudyi is also regarded in *Nkang'a* as a symbol for learning (*ku-diza*). Just as a child drinks milk from its mother and grows strong, so does the novice learn tribal customs, say many informants, during *Nkang'a*.

Outside *Nkang'a*, *mudyi* has many uses and interpretations. For example, it is used in a medicine for inducing a flow of milk in women's breasts. If a baby's mother dies, or if a mother has refused to nurse her child, it is said that a grandmother's teats may be washed with *mudyi* latex and water. After that she is believed to be able to feed the baby. If a mother of twins has insufficient milk she is said to be similarly treated.

If a baby dies it is buried beneath a *mudyi* tree. An abortion receives the same treatment. Manyosa said that *mudyi* leaves are also put in the grave. "If such a body," she went on, "were buried in the ordinary 'red grave' [*kalung'a kachinana*], deep in the subsoil, the mother would never bear another child. But if it is buried beside a *mudyi*, the mother will bear another baby quickly."

At the antiwitchcraft ritual of *Kaneng'a*, curative medicine is collected in the form of sticks from the trees near which dead children are buried. According to Muchona, these *mudyi* trees are "where the life of dead children is [*diku kudi wumi wawanyana afwa dehi*]. The spirits of dead people are there."

"Doctors go there for medicines," he continued, "because witches rely on people's graves as places where they get their meat quickly. But when they find that the doctors know those places well, by having *mudyi* sticks from the graves there, they become afraid. They understand that they are well-known themselves."

According to Mungwayanga, a senior adept, in the *Wubwang'u* cult performed for mothers of twins, at one phase of *Wubwang'u* two kinds of trees make up a ritual arch over a stream. One is of *muhotuhotu* and means a man, and the other is of *mudyi* and represents a woman.

Their union represents marital intercourse, and a chunk of *malowa* taken from the streambed directly under the arch, represents marital peace (*wuluwi*).

Finally, a baby's placenta is buried under a frame of about a dozen sticks of *mudyi* wood. The mother's husband collects these sticks and gives them to the midwife, who digs a small hole a yard or two behind the parents' hut. The navel cord is

also buried under the *mudyi* frame with one of its ends pro-
truding from the ground. It is said that if the cord is completely buried the mother will not bear another child.

A word should be said here about the regular association
of the *mudyi tree* and initiation ritual with ordeal, suffering,
and death, as well as with nurturance and rebirth. Boys are
circumcised beneath a *mudyi* tree, girls have to lie under one
all day without so much as stirring, during the first phase of
Nkang'a. The site of circumcision and the site of endurance
are both known as *ifwilu* or *chifwilu*, "the place of dying,"
from *ku-fwa*, "to die."

Another term used for these sites is *ihung'u* or *chihung'u*,
which Windson Kashinakaji translated as "the place of suffering." The term *ihung'u* also refers to a hut where a woman is
in labor. And indeed it is applied to the hut of the principal
candidate at *Chihamba*. Another interpretation of *yihung'u*
(plural of *chihung'u*) was given to me by Muchona. He said
that "*Yihung'u* is any kind of trouble or sickness given by a
spirit because a candidate has only passed the *ku-lembeka*
phase of a ritual and not the full *ku-tumbuka*. The same word
also means a person caught by a spirit. The spirit becomes
angry because he has not been given beer, food, or blood,
signs that he has been forgotten."

These links between *mudyi* and terms like *ifwilu* and
ihung'u, which are themselves knots in associative networks,
make *mudyi* a symbol for suffering and rebirth through suffering as well as a symbol for motherhood, nurturance, and
fertility. The pains, as well as the pleasures and profits of
womanhood, are represented by this symbol.

Mukula. Mukula (see p. 64) is a tree that secretes a red
gum. This gum in the *Nkula* cult ritual symbolizes maternal
blood (*mashi amama*). This gum quickly coagulates (*ku-*

zemuka), and part of its use in medicine is to make a woman's maternal blood coagulate to form around the fetus. For *Nkula* is most frequently performed for women with menstrual disorders, in some of which (such as menorrhagia) there is an excessive flow of blood. In connection with blood, *mukula* is also used at boys' circumcision. Just after each novice has been circumcised he is taken to sit with his companions on a log of *mukula* wood. The belief is that the boys' cuts will speedily stop bleeding, in sympathy with the coagulative properties of *mukula*. Like menstruating girls the novices are said to have matured, *anakuli dehi*, at this point in the circumcision ritual.

In all the hunting cults *mukula* represents blood, in particular the blood of animals (*mashi atunyama*). It also stands for their meat (*mbiji*). Here its referents are to pleasurable things and activities—food, eating, and hunting. Nevertheless, the notion of killing (*ku-tapa*) pervades these meanings.

Mukula, too, is connected with rituals of affliction, with suffering and death, real and symbolic.

Musoli. Musoli has been discussed on pages 57–58. We have seen how it denoted the process of making visible (*ku-solola*) or of revelation. It summarizes and condenses in a single formation a number of related ideas: (1) making the invisible (i.e., hidden game in the bush, spirits afflicting a patient with disease or misfortune, secret witches and sorcerers) visible in real or symbolic form; (2) making the forgotten remembered, such as the name of an ancestor spirit, whose anger is caused by his or her having been forgotten (*kumwanuka nehi*); (3) making the unspoken spoken, as in the *Ihamba* ritual, where a *musoli* root is the principal medicine, when the patients' kin are obliged to confess their private grudges against him; if they do not confess, the doctor will be unable to effect a cure; (4) making the hidden known to all, as when it is used to bring about a successful pregnancy and birth. It is used in almost every cult of affliction and also in life-crisis ritual. For example, at *Mukanda*, circumcision medicine is during one episode placed in the fork of a big *musoli* branch at a public gathering so that it may be seen by many people. Thus they can see for themselves that it is bona fide medicine.

Because of its association with all these contexts of situation it is considered representative of curative ritual in general. Wherever it is thus used representatively, it carries the value that making things plain and open is good.

Mukombukombu, mututambululu, and *muhotuhotu.* These three medicines must be treated as a group, for they are literally bound together in many kinds of ritual to form a broom (*chisampu*), which is used for splashing or sweeping the patient with medicine prepared from pounded leaves. In discussing *mukombukombu* I pointed out that one aspect of the broom's meaning was sweeping away diseases or ridding the patient of familiars of witchcraft. But it also has the implication of something swept on as well as away. All three trees have large nectar-filled flowers attractive to bees. One informant, a hunter called Nswanandong'a, explained: "In the same way the medicines prepared from them are believed by Ndembu to attract many people to the ritual where they will hear the name of the afflicting spirit mentioned and so remember that spirit. And so the spirit will be pleased and will help the patient." Sweeping with the broom is also thought to make the patient himself or herself attractive. Women so swept will have many children, many animals will be drawn toward a hunter, many people will assemble to praise the patient. The term *mututambululu* is associated by Nswanandong'a with *ambululu,* a species of a small bee that hovers in clouds around its flowers.

The etymology of *muhotuhotu,* on the other hand, is connected with the repellent, and not with the attractive aspects of the *chisampu* trio of species. Muchona derived its name from *ku-hotumuna,* "to fall quickly." [16] In the same way, he said, "people trust that the disease or bad luck will fall away from the patient." *Ku-hotumuna* properly refers to the falling leaves, and Muchona said that *muhotuhotu* leaves fell all together if the tree was shaken.

The *chisampu* medicines, then, mean to sweep away bad qualities and confer beneficial ones. As part of *kantong'a* they remind candidates of trouble, diseases, and misfortunes and suggest that these have been swept away.

8. Ceremonial payment of adepts

The last episode of the Fourth Day of *Chihamba* was the payment of the adepts. These sat in an old kitchen on the opposite side of the village from Nyamukola's hut. For the purposes of making payment, adepts from Mukanza Village were regarded as village members, and were therefore liable to pay. Men sat in the village meeting hut (*chota*) and women just outside it. The adepts sent representatives at intervals to the Mukanza group and bargained over payment. The representatives carried bits of maize or grass stalks twisted into symbolic shapes. Each shape had a traditional name and was supposed to correspond with a particular kind of reward.

---

[16] Another informant, when discussing the *Wubwang'u* ritual, in which *muhotuhotu* is used as a medicine, derived the word from *ku-hotumuka,* "to slip and fall"—"like a windfallen tree lodged on another one, a disease lies on a person's body; they want to make it slip off."

The bargaining contained a great deal of fooling about as adepts expressed their surprise or indignation at the amount of reward offered.

Exegesis

Interpretation of the objects was provided by Lambakasa and Muchona. The first symbolic object sent was an imitation feather crown representing those worn by great chiefs, made from the wing or tail feathers of a red fowl. This object was called *nsala yakalong'u*, "gray parrot crown," because chiefs used to wear—and still wear on state occasions—the red tail feathers of the gray parrot (*nsala*). In the past the adepts were rewarded for this by a fowl; today they receive from 2s. to 3s.

Next, the adepts sent two pieces of twisted grass or maize stalk, called and roughly resembling a hoe (*itemwa*) and an ax (*kazemba*). Formerly a real hoe and ax were returned; today these are commuted into cash payments of 1s. each.

The next symbol sent was *ndehu yamung'wa*, "a pot of salt," consisting of a hollowed-out hank of grass or a whittled bit of wood. Formerly a real pot of salt, today 3s. to 5s. is returned. Sometimes a small calabash spoon with a few grains of salt is sent by adepts to the sponsoring village.

Other twisted stalks represented a basket of cassava (*mutong'a wamakamba*), meat (*mbiji*), and fish (*inshi*). At Mukanza Village, these were returned in kind and shared among the women adepts. Another stalk represented a mat (*chikang'a*). They gave 6d. for it. Then a large stick was sent. It was called *mutondu wekumi*, "the stick of ten (things)." Formerly ten small articles might have been returned or preferably a goat (*mpembi*). Today a wealthy sponsor might give 30s. or more. At Mukanza Village only 15s. was returned. There was a good deal of grumbling among the adepts at this.

The same objects are made by adepts and rewarded as described at *Nkula, Kayong'u, Mukanda, Mung'ong'i*, and *Nkang'a* ("where the sticks represent the money paid by the bridegroom-to-be," said Muchona) but not at hunting ritual or at *Isoma* or *Wubwang'u* (both rituals performed in connection with female reproduction). The custom, say all Ndembu I have asked, "came with us from Mwantiyanvwa."

9. Taboos

Earlier, I mentioned some of the food taboos of *Chihamba* and gave Muchona's explanation of them. These prohibitions concerned the meat of the hippo, the *musonji* catfish, and the yellow-backed duiker. Nyaluwema gave us a more extensive list that included the species mentioned and named in addition the *mbing'a* fish, guinea fowl (*mbang'ala*), bushbuck (*mbala*), zebra (*ng'ala*), or any striped or spotted animal, fish, or bird. "Eating striped and spotted things," she explained, "caused leprosy [*mbumba yalozang'a*]." This should be compared with the list of taboos at *Mukanda* (Turner 1967:226–228, 234). White beans were also tabooed.

These taboos were operative from the beginning of *ku-tumbuka* until the *ku-jilola* (lifting of taboos) rites which took place when the cassava cutting, the beans, and maize at the *kantong'a* shrines had reached a reasonable height. In Mukanza Village the taboos were lifted exactly four weeks after the first day of *ku-tumbuka*, on April 3, 1954.

Sexual intercourse between a candidate and his or her spouse was also forbidden for a week after the *kantong'a* rites.

Candidates were forbidden to eat with uninitiated persons during the month before *ku-jilola*.

On the positive side, candidates were enjoined to wash in

the medicine in the *izawu* pot by *kantong'a* every day at dawn and sunset. Also they were frequently given *mucheki wa-luseng'a* [17] medicine (collected on the second day of *ku-tumbuka*) to eat, mixed with salt, and administered from the butt of an adept's *chileng'a* rattle. One had to lick it off the butt. Nyaluwema gave my wife and me some *mucheki* medicine every evening, rather like a nurse administering cod liver oil to potentially recalcitrant charges.

Four Weeks after *Ku-tumbuka* (April 3, 1954)
Lifting of taboos (ku-jilola)

At about 9 A.M., cassava was pounded by Zuliyana, the second candidate in importance, in a mortar beside the *kantong'a* shrine of the principal candidate Nyamukola. A fire had been lit and as many of the forbidden meats and varieties of fish as could be obtained (yellow-backed duiker, bush-buck, *musonji* fish) were cooking on it. Nyaluwema, the principal female adept, sifted the cassava meal, while another female adept helped with the cooking. Adepts kept arriving from other villages. Soon they began to argue whether *isaku* medicine should be applied to the fence around the *kantong'a* shrine. At last this was done, and *yileng'a* rattles were also placed on the fence, after having been vigorously shaken by both male and female adepts.

Greetings. Next all the adepts, male and female, formally greeted one another by the dual handshake and clapping deemed appropriate between equals. Then the adepts all went behind Nyamukola's kitchen and returned at once. Sakutoha, the principal male adept at many episodes, brought white beer in a cup from Nyamukola's hut and poured it down the *kantong'a* bundle of medicine sticks.

[17] *Luseng'a* means powdered medicine.

An argument broke out between representatives of Mukanza Village, headed by Sakazao, Nyamukola's brother and second-in-command to Mukanza, and several senior adepts about payment. Sakazao was eventually led aside by a female adept and harangued until he quieted.

Shaving. Nyauwema came up with a store razor blade, the same one, adepts said, that had been buried in the meal mortar that did service for *Kavula*'s "head" at the *isoli* rite. Water was put in a pan lid near the *kantong'a*. Now all the candidates were lined up and made to sit in a row on mats, in the order in which they had greeted *Kavula* at *isoli*. Several male adepts then shaved them all the way round the hairline. The child patients kept swapping places to get shaved before their companions.

Prayer and communion beer drink. A calabash of maize beer was now brought. Nyaluwema poured out some as a libation to Nyamakang'a, the afflicting spirit, and prayed to her that all the candidates would be strong, mentioning each one present by name. Then all the adult candidates, but not the adepts, drank beer—called the beer of the ancestor spirit. Next the white beads originally tied round the arrow in Nyamukola's hut were tied round an adept's rattle, untied again, and taken away by Nyaluwema to her hut.

Feast. A female adept stirred the cassava mush (*nshima*). An uninitiated woman (Makanjila's wife—he was a candidate) cooked the beans. But she was promptly told off by adepts and forced to pay a small fine, grumbling and fuming.

The adepts approached the candidates who still sat drinking. Lambakasa and Nyaluwema washed their hands in the water in the pan lid. Lambakasa now prayed to Nyamakang'a and other ancestors of the Mukanza Village lineage, to which he was patrilaterally linked. Now all the adepts and candidates took pellets of cassava mush and threw them into the enclosure around *kantong'a*. Afterward they threw pellets beyond *kantong'a*, mentioning that these were for the *ayikodjikodji*, the spirits of the mischievous dead.

Next Lambakasa put pieces of all the tabooed foods available, together with some cassava mush, on the butt of a *chileng'a* rattle. He gave this to Nyaluwema who ate it, then spat to the left and to the right. Lambakasa anointed her on the brow and temples with *isaku* medicine. Then he struck her on the head and on the joints of all her limbs with his *chileng'a* rattle. Makanjila, representing the male candidates, and Nyamukola, the women candidates, were then treated by Lambakasa in the same way. Then all the adepts and candidates were anointed with *isaku* medicine on the brow and temples and licked a little off rattle-butts.

Finally, a line of white *mpemba* was drawn down one arm of each candidate. *Ku-tumbuka* was over.

Muchona's account of *ku-lembeka*

Ku-lembeka, it will be remembered, is the first and less elaborate phase of a cult ritual. It relates to a specific patient-candidate, the one whose sickness or misfortune led her relatives to consult a diviner. I mention this because minor and junior candidates may have their first experience of a given cult ritual at the *ku-tumbuka* or more elaborate phase. Such candidates have been chosen or seized by adepts, not (as it is believed) caught by an ancestor spirit in a certain mode of manifestation.

Muchona described to me two variants of the *ku-lembeka* rites of *Chihamba:* the river and bush types, known as *ng'uvu* (hippo) and *katala matung'a* (lourie) or *kalendu* (lightning) respectives.

Ng'uvu or river Chihamba. I present Muchona's account as a literal translation: "A person begins by being sick—in the neck so that the neck cannot move, or sometimes she suffers cold in the whole body [*watiyang'a mumujimba mashika*]. Her relatives go to a diviner. He divines that she has been caught by *Chihamba* [*anamukwati kudi Chihamba*]. The *Chihamba* spirit moves about in the air like other spirits. Then her relatives go to a big *Chihamba* adept who will make *Kavula*.

"In the *ng'uvu* rites the adepts first go to the streamside forest [*itu*] and collect the *ishikenu* [or greeting] medicine *katochi*, one root and some leaves. Then they collect *musojisoji*, a root and some leaves. Then they enter the water and take some *ntotu*, leaf flotsam of any species under the water. Then they take a decayed piece of stick from under the water [*kamutondu katookela hameji*, a little stick whitened on the water] of any length or kind. After that they collect *kabwititeng'i* root and leaves, then *musombu* root and leaves, then *muleng'u* root and leaves. They also bring *malowa*, black river mud. That is all for the river. In the bush they collect roots, a piece of the stem, and some leaves from *mutung'ulu*. Sometimes they take *mukeketi*, root and leaves."

Exegesis of river rites. Muchona explained these medicines as follows:

"*Katochi* grows near rivers, it is an elder in these rites. It has a very large white root. Its bark is used for bark string in the making of snares.

"*Musojisoji* has red gum like blood. Its gum adds blood to the patient.

"Leaf-flotsam [*ntotu*] is used because the hippo sleeps under the water and flotsam in this way resembles the hippo.

"The decayed stick represents the decay of seeds. If a patient planted maize or beans in her garden and failed to play the *Chihamba* drum, such seeds would be found to be decaying.

"*Mukeketi* is used because of the whiteness of its root and its sweet juice.

"*Kabwititeng'i* and *musombu* are used because their leaves are gathered by women as stoppers for calabashes when they go to draw water. When they reach their huts they throw the leaves away quickly. In the same way diseases or misfortunes will be thrown away. *Kabwititeng'i* is used as medicine in *Nkula* too. Here it means that the patient will give birth quickly without a long labor. *Kabwititeng'i* leaves and flowers have a pleasant odor which makes them suitable calabash stoppers.

"*Muleng'u* is used because it has many fruits. The patient should have many children.

"*Wutotu* has white gum, this represents a person who is suffering from *Chihamba*—for often a patient has boils on the body which exude white pus [*mashina*].

"*Mutung'ulu* has many branching roots of a red color. It is used so that the patient will have many children, and many people will help her.

"*Malowa* will cool diseases. But it is also used because of its blackness, which means trouble or bad luck [*malwa*]. It stands for the bad luck that will go away with its blackness. If there is blackness on the body it must become white [*neyi hamujimba heyila hakatooki*]."

Muchona went on to explain that of the two kinds of *kulembeka* rites, *ng'uvu* was the man [*iyala*] or husband [*mfumu*] and *katala matung'a* was the woman [*mumbanda*] or wife [*ng'oda*]. He meant by this that the riverside rites were more important and for more serious illness and misfortune than the bush rites. He then discussed the medicines collected for the bush rites.

Bush rites. "When the patient's relatives consult a diviner, he may say 'it is *Chihamba* of the lourie or of the lightning [*Chihamba chakatala matung'a hela kalendu*].' *Kalendu* means lightning, for in it people go to a lightning-struck tree and cut laths [*mbalu*] from it, which are cut up small to be put into *nzenzi* rattles.

"Then the adepts go into the bush to the tree of greeting, which is here the *mukula* tree. They pray at the *mukula* with *ku-pandula*. *Ku-pandula* is to awaken [*ku-tonisha*] spirits. Some-times [in the *Kaneng'a* ritual, for example] it is to make witches realize that they are known. It is done as follows:

"A leaf is taken by an adept. He places it on his half-clenched fist. He puts the leaf bottom upward on his fingers over the hole. The adept takes his right hand and slaps down the *mpandula* of spirits and sorcerers, in order to wake up the spirits and all the sorcerers [and witches] that they may stop making the person sick from now on; [it is] in order that the spirits should stay well and that sorcerers should hide them-selves somewhere else and go away." [When a number of people *pandula* together the smacking noise as they all bring down their flat palms on the leaves is like the report of a gun.]

"The principal adept puts *mpemba* [white clay] at the foot of the *mukula* tree and addresses [*wasansa*] the spirit: 'If per-haps you are *Chihamba Chakalendu* help this person today that she may sleep soundly.'

"Then they take leaves for *nsompu* washing medicine.

"Next they take leaves from *ikamba daChihamba*, then from *musoli*, then from *mwang'ala*, then from *munkalampoli*, then from *mukombukombu* and from *mututambululu*, and finally *mukeketi* leaves."

Exegesis of bush rites. Muchona interpreted the meanings of these medicines as follows: "*Mukula* means blood. *Ikamba daChihamba* is used because of its white root resembling cassava root. *Mwang'ala* is used because of its bitterness [*wukawu*] and its name [*ijina dindi*] which means the spilling away [*ku-mwang'a*] of diseases.

"*Munkalampoli* has thorns which catch people. If *Chihamba* catches a person it must release her today.

"*Mukombukombu* and *mututambululu* are used for the leaf-broom [see above].

"*Mukeketi* is the *isolu* of the bush; it makes spirits appear [*kusolola wakishi*]. It has a white root with no fruits."

Washing with medicine. Muchona next described how the patient was washed with medicine. Here the *ng'uvu* and *katala matung'a* rites were identical.

"When the adepts come back from the bush, the patient is waiting in the doorway of her hut facing inside. They pound the leaves into *nsompu* medicine and add cold water. The patient then sits on the pounding-pole and a big doctor washes her whole body with *nsompu*. After washing the remaining medicine is poured on the threshold of the hut.

"For many days the patient must stay near the fire in her kitchen."

General discussion on *ku-lembeka* with Muchona

Muchona told me that *ku-lembeka* was by no means finished after the patient had been washed with *nsompu*. He said that if the patient seemed to be recovering after washing, the adepts agreed that *Chihamba* had caught her. They then went once more to the bush, went to the *mukula* tree, and addressed it (*ku-sansa*): "If that woman was washed with *nsompu*, we have come again to collect more medicine from you, o *mukula*, in order to *lembeka* her truly [*nakumulembeka chalala*]."

Here I interpolated with the query: "Does an adept address the tree itself or an ancestor in the tree?" Muchona replied that "the words are addressed to the tree so that the spirit may hear them. But the spirit is separate from the tree. A doctor adept does not give power to medicine himself, but he knows how to address words [*ku-sansa*]. Such words cause the tree to listen and the spirit to help. Both tree and spirit give power to the medicine." These remarks directly contradict others I heard made at the *Nkula* ritual, where the *mukula* tree was identified with the *Nkula* spirit by adepts. Muchona's view is also opposed to those adepts at the *Chihamba* ritual I observed who identified the *ikamba daChihamba* root with *Kavula*, and with "the *mukishi* ancestor spirit." It must have become clear to the reader that Muchona had a highly independent and thoughtful approach to his religion. Moreover, he had moments of devastating common sense, as his next remarks exemplify. Most of his interpretations are based on analogies and sympathies between the form and meanings of symbols. But when I asked him why certain medicines were regarded appropriate in certain kinds of rituals and not in others, he replied: "In the beginning when *Chihamba* was first started, they found its medicines by trying a person first with one sort of medicine, then with another. If they tried *ikamba daChihamba* and *mukula* and found that the patient recovered from sickness, they agreed that, yes, these medicines can help someone in this ritual for a spirit. If they found that a medicine was worthless, they did not use it." In other words, if Muchona is correct, the Ndembu proceeded on strictly empirical lines by testing a medicine for its effects on the patient. If this were, indeed, the case then most of the interpretations offered were fallacious rationalizations. The medicine was interpreted in terms of the beliefs and values guiding and expressed by the total ritual, subsequent to its incorporation in that ritual on empirical grounds. Muchona could see no discrepancy between the notion that a medicine was good because experience had demonstrated its beneficial qualities and the notion that it was good because the plant it was derived from had an association in name, appearance, or thought with the supposed attributes of afflicting spirits or witches, with Ndembu values and cultural goals, and with the physical condition of the patient. In his view the reason why a medicine helped the patient was precisely because it had a mystical connection with spirit, patient, and tribal values, and this connection was made visible in certain aspects of its outward form, physical properties, or traditional name. The process of testing the efficacy of the medicine was for him at the same time a process of finding out what were its special mystical affinities—were they with the *Nkula*, *Chihamba*, *Wubwang'u*, or other modes of spirit-manifestation?

Reverting to the *ku-lembeka* rites (which in this case were bush *Chihamba* rites), we find that roots as well as leaves of *mukula* were collected this time, as were roots and leaves of *ikamba daChihamba*, *mwang'ala*, *mukombukombu*, *mututam-bululu*, *munkalampoli*, and *mukeketi*. *Nzenzi* rattles were then made from slivers of *kata wubwang'u* wood. At sunset the adepts returned to the patient's hut, where a fire had been lit. After that a similar rite was performed to the one I witnessed—and described on pages 66–72, where an adept impersonated *Kavula* inside the patient's hut. The patient was washed with the medicines just collected. In many respects *ku-lembeka* appears to be a truncated or abridged version of *ku-tumbuka* without the important episodes of chasing, questioning, and killing *Kavula*.

Muchona told me that at this second medicine gathering at *ku-lembeka*, the patient-candidate accompanied the adepts into the bush. He may, however, have been confusing this episode with the chasing and questioning episodes of *ku-tumbuka*. At any rate he first cited, then interpreted, the following song in such a way as to indicate that a patient was at the medicine-collecting:

Ng'undo ye eyeye ng'unda yakuya eyeye yakuya nayu mwisang'a eyeyeye yakuya nayu mukalung'a eye yeyeye yakuya nayu mwisang'a.

(Cries made by beating the lips, *ng'unda* cries go, go into the bush going with [*ng'unda*] into the grave, going with [*ng'unda*] into the bush.)

Muchona said: "The *ng'unda* sounds, *owe-e-e*, wake up the spirit and the patient too. The *ngu'nda* of going to the bush means a sound to awaken the spirit while the adepts go to the bush. The other song, 'going with it into the grave,' means that when the patient thought she knew what the medicines were she was 'in the grave,' that is, she had failed. When she returned to the village, this meant that she was taken from the grave, she had been helped by the adepts, she was now alive. Coming back, they sang *waying'e*, 'she has been acquitted' [18]; she has been acquitted because she has now seen all the medicines. The doctors have been asking her to name all the medicines correctly. When she returned to the village they put cassava meal on her head, as a sign that she was acquitted. Long ago diviners put cassava meal, and not

---

[18] See page 112. This was the song I heard when the candidates returned after "killing *Kavula*."

mpemba, on the heads of those who had not used witchcraft. Cassava meal means that the patient was pure or white."

After *Ku-jilola*

What persists after a great ritual is over are the ties of friendship (*wulunda*) established by it. *Chihamba* friends have the obligation to offer one another hospitality and must exchange gifts periodically. My own *mulunda* was Sandombu, declared to me as such when my *kantong'a* was set up. I received the name Ndumba Samlozang'a, a hunter's name but also a *Chihamba* name. By having it I also became a namesake of the headman of Kafumbu Village, an offshoot of Mukanza Village, from which several of the adepts and candidates came. The headman gave me a present of beer, a chicken, and cassava "because we were namesakes [*majinda*]," and I reciprocated in cash. Sandombu and I had been in the habit of exchanging presents since I first arrived in Mwinilung'a over three years previously, but we had a ceremonial interchange of gifts after *Chihamba*. The principal candidate Nyamukola entered on *Chihamba* friendship with Headman Kafumbu's mother, from whom practically all the Kafumbu villagers were descended. My wife became *mulunda waChihamba* with Manyosa, already her friend of long standing.

CHAPTER 2

Some Notes on the Symbolism of *Chihamba*

Perhaps the simplest way of classifying the symbols of *Chihamba*, and of other Ndembu rites, would be under two main heads: symbolic articles [1] and symbolic actions. The former would include, for example, powdered white clay, the *isaku* medicine, each of its ingredients—*mucheki* root-scrapings and *ibanda* salt—the representations of *Kavula*, the *kantong'a* shrine and each of its components, and so on. The latter would include blowing *mpemba* on the sacred *Chihamba* rattles, inserting an arrow into the thatch of the senior candidate's hut, anointing arms with *mpemba*, rousing the candidates at dawn with red cock's feathers, the "killing" of *Kavula*, the cutting of the *ikamba daChihamba* root, and so on. They would also include taboos on certain actions, for example, ritual interdictions on food, sexual intercourse, inter-dining with uninitiated persons.

I have selected these examples at random to indicate the wide range of articles and actions covered by this loose dual classification. We must now examine symbols from each class more closely, (1) with a view to finding out whether further subclassification is necessary, (2) in order to say something

---

[1] I use the term "article" in preference to "object," since I later use "object" as "what a symbol signifies."

about the relations between a ritual symbol and what it signifies, and (3) to discuss the relationship between symbolic
articles and symbolic actions.

Symbolic Articles

Symbolic articles (*yinjikijilu*) may be simple or composite.
An example of a simple symbolic article would be the *mucheki*
tree used in the preparation of *isaku* medicine, which would
constitute a composite symbol. Some composite symbols,
like *isaku* medicine, are made up of only a few parts, others
are made up of many parts. Let us then distinguish between
these orders of complexity by calling the former a compound
symbol and the latter a complex symbol. The representation
of *Kavula* and the *kantong'a* shrine would exemplify complex
symbols, while *isaku* medicine would be better defined as a
compound symbol. Among the simple symbols which represent the constituent parts of compound and complex symbols, one is usually singled out by Ndembu for special
emphasis, such as *mucheki* in *isaku* medicine and *ikamba
daChihamba* in *kantong'a*. The overturned meal mortar in the
representation of *Kavula* might also be considered such a
symbol. Usually this symbol is the object of elaborate and
exceptional ritual action before it is united with other symbols. For example, the *mucheki* tree, which tends to grow on
the precipitous slopes of damboes, was declared to be the
ishikenu or point of initial contact between the profane and
sacred realms or between lesser and greater sacredness or between different sorts of sacredness. Then petitions to the
afflicting ancestress were made at *mucheki*, but not at any
trees from which other ingredients were collected. Finally,
the root of the tree was cut off to the accompaniment of elaborate ceremonial, and the trunk was then replaced in an

upright position. The *ikamba daChihamba* tree was also the
scene of an address to the afflicting spirit, and its root was
treated just as though it was a person's body, vulnerable to
ax wounds. The meal mortar which later became the "head"
of *Kavula* and was struck by the candidate's "death-dealing"
rattles was also given special ritual treatment, for it was
passed under a tunnel of adepts' legs and then dragged from
the fork between old and new paths to the *isoli* "tabernacle."
Such symbols I would be inclined to call dominant symbols
or dominant elements of a compound or complex symbol. It
must be stressed, however, that dominance is situational. A
symbol that is dominant in one situation may in another be
secondary or instrumental.

The concept of dominance is also applicable to compound
and complex symbols in the wider ritual contexts. For example, it might be cogently argued that the *nfunda* medicine
bundle, a complex symbol discussed by C. M. N. White
(1961) and by me (1953) is the dominant symbol of the *Mukanda* boys' circumcision rites of the Ndembu and Lovale, in
view of the protective influence it is believed to emanate over
everyone involved in them. Dominance may also be episodic
and not total. For example, the *kantong'a* is dominant over
the final episodes of the *ku-tumbuka* phase of *Chihamba*, but
does not appear at all in the *ku-lembeka* phase, and must be
regarded as secondary to the representation of *Kavula* in *ku-
tumbuka*, since it is set up for individuals and not for the
whole cult group. In relation to the total rite of *ku-tumbuka* it
is secondary to *Kavula*.

Thus a preliminary typology of Ndembu symbolic articles, according to their degree of composition, gives us a
division between simple, compound, and complex symbols.
In compound and complex symbols we find dominant simple

symbols. In ritual episodes we find dominant compound and complex symbols, which, however, may be secondary to other compound and complex symbols when wider ritual contexts, such as total rites, and even classes of rites, are taken into account. And in the frame of the total system of rites, symbols that are dominant in one situation may be secondary in another.

The Semantics of Ndembu Ritual Symbolism

So far we have dealt with symbols. Now we have to take into account their meaning. As Susanne Langer, following Ernst Cassirer, pointed out in her *Philosophy in a New Key* (1958), the word "meaning" has at least three aspects: signification, denotation, and connotation. These aspects must be seen as related to the four essential terms of the "symbol-function." These are: subject, symbol, conception, and object. Signification is concerned with the relation between a symbol (or sign) and its object. The two terms, symbol and object, would be interchangeable, were it not for the subject for whom they constitute a pair. It is the subject who finds one member of the pair—the object—more interesting than the other, and the other member—the symbol—more easily available (Langer 1958:59). Thus a ring around the moon is not important in itself; but as a present, visible item coupled with something more important but not yet present, such as a change in the weather, it has significance for a subject. Denotation is "the complex relationship which a name has to an object which bears it." Proper names are the best instances of denotation. They stand for something substantial and concrete. "James" may represent a conception but it names a certain person. There is a very close connection here between conceptions and the concrete world. The more

direct relation of the name, or symbol, to its associated concept is its connotation. The connotation of a word is the concept it conveys. "Because the connotation remains with the
symbol when the object of its denotation is neither present
nor looked for, we are able to *think about* the object without
reacting to it overtly at all" (Langer 1958:64).

These remarks are pertinent to the analysis of Ndembu ritual symbolism. But an examination of some actual examples
will show us that some modifications have to be made in
Langer's model of the symbol-function. Let us take the case
of *Kavula*, for example. *Kavula* is a secret name which denotes a specific demi-god or nature spirit. At once we are
confronted with something not of the sensory order, with the
realm of ultrahuman or mystical beings and powers, with
belief rather than knowledge. *Kavula*, moreover, has far more
than a single connotation: he is, to take a few at random,
lightning, fertility, chiefly authority, masculinity, grandfa-
therhood, a divine victim. Furthermore, *Kavula* is a summa-
tion of all the senses of all the simple symbols that constitute
it—the roots, razors, axes, white clay, white meal, white
crosses, *musoli* and *mucheki* trees, and so on. There is quite
often an inverse relation between a symbol and its meaning,
such that a complex symbol has an essentially simple meaning and a simple symbol a complex meaning. Thus *Kavula*, a
complex symbol, denotes quite simply a spiritual being,
while the white clay which in certain situations represents
Kavula, has additionally a plurality of referents: health,
strength, purity, good rapport with the ancestors, chiefly authority, and many other things. This may be because sym-
-bols are mobilized in Gestälten under the influence of a few
major aims which impose a unitary pattern on many diverse
components. For example, the *kantong'a* shrine is basically a

mnemonic (from *ku-tong'ashana*, "to think about") or memorial of *Kavula*. Yet looked at as an assemblage of simple symbols, each with a fan of referents, a full interpretation of *kantong'a* would fill a fair-sized volume. A simple symbol, standing alone, like the *mudyi* tree around which women dance at a girl's puberty rite, may be attributed by Ndembu with a multitude of senses. The same species of tree, become a mere component of a *kantong'a*, is stripped of all these precise connotations and rather vaguely represents female fertility and its vicissitudes, or motherhood. In other words, when a symbol, possessing a spread of connotations, becomes, under the influence of a culturally standardized leading purpose or emotion, a member of a configuration of symbols, a selection is made among its connotations for that one or those few compatible with the "telos" of the situation. In this instance the distinction between manifest and latent senses might be apposite. In addition to the senses manifestly allocated to the elements of a complex symbol, such as *kantong'a*, there must be, for the participants who belong to the same tribal community and share the same values and similar experiences, a subliminal perception of latent senses. These must charge the complex symbol with an affective glow. Certainly, many of the persons I have observed taking part in the *kantong'a* rites were known to me as adepts in and interpreters of other kinds of ritual in which the symbols employed in the *kantong'a* bundles appeared as dominant symbols with wider ranges of reference. Perhaps it is this preconscious perception of the latent meaning of a complex symbol that causes the sensation of fear (*woma*), or awe, often associated with its presentation. Manifestly simple it is latently rich in the texture of its meaning. For example, no Ndembu could be unaware of the implications of *muhotuhotu*, *mututambululu,* and *mukombukombu,* used as components of the *kantong'a* medicine-bundle, in the dark field of witchcraft-sorcery. Nor could he fail to recall, at some level of the psyche, the joyous bustle and tense ordeal of the girls' puberty rite (*Nkang'a*), when he (or still more poignantly she) notices the frond of *mudyi.* And the *mukula* brings into the situation its overtones of hunting and circumcision rites and the remembered tang of blood. It has further implications of parturition and menstruation. Bisexual, ambivalent, multidimensional, personal as well as social, a symbol like *kantong'a* must be apprehended by Ndembu as a momentary embodiment, or perhaps container, of the generic power underlying the cyclical, repetitive orders of nature and society that frame their experience.

The Semantic Paradigm of the Ritual Symbol

Ritual symbols are, as we have seen, polysemous, that is, they have many referents, some of which may be denotata, others connotata. The Oxford Dictionary, as is well-known, defines a symbol as "a thing regarded by general consent as naturally typifying or representing or recalling something by possession of analogous qualities or by association in fact or thought." The term "naturally" is, of course, confusing in the present context where linguistic factors play so prominent a part. Here what is natural is only so by cultural definition and not necessarily by physical or biological character. But the rest of the definition is most pertinent to this discussion. Analogy and association are principles that govern the chains of connotata making up the meaning of most kinds of symbols. In the general case of the ritual symbol, there is not a single chain but several chains, for several links of analogy or association are utilized, based on the natural or culturally

defined properties of each thing used as a symbol. Furthermore, in such a symbol there is often a reference to the mystical beliefs of its users at some point in one of its chains.
Perhaps the terms "reticulation" or "network" (of referents or
senses) are preferable to "chains," since the chains often in-
tersect.

In the specific case of the Ndembu ritual symbol, and in
other central African systems of ritual as well, there are three
main points of departure for analogy and association. The
first of these is the name of the symbol, the second is its substance—by which I denote its essential character, including
its physical and biological character; the species of tree which
wholly or in part becomes a symbol would, for example, be
an aspect of its substance—and the third is its appearance as
an artifact, as the product of human fashioning, in short, as
an object of culture. In other words, we have nominal, substantial, and artifactual sources of meaning.

Now let us consider an actual example, the *ikamba daChihamba* tree, viewed first as a simple symbol, then as a component of the complex symbol *kantong'a*. Immediately we are
confronted by the fact that this tree has an additional name,
musambanjita.[2] Duality of names for a symbol is not uncom-
mon in Ndembu ritual.[3] Sometimes the second name is an
esoteric one, but in this case both names are widely applied
outside the ritual context. *Musambanjita* stands for freedom
from attack and was formerly used as a medicine for confer-
ring invulnerability on warriors in battle. The hardness of
the tree's wood and the thickness of its root were probably
responsible for this belief. But the name *ikamba daChihamba*
(also mentioned in Frank Melland's book [1923:178] on the

---

[2] Mentioned by Melland (1923:178), under the name of *musambazhita*.

[3] See Turner 1961:27, 36.

basis of observations made by W. Bruce-Miller) is clearly appropriated to the *Chihamba* rites and stands for "cassava root of *Chihamba*." I have reported the Ndembu exegesis of this identification earlier and will here merely point out that this root, which resembles a peeled or soaked cassava root, is regarded as a kind of materialization of *Kavula*. One could argue from these interpretations that *Kavula*, a storm demigod, descends in the rains, enters the crops, and after his mystical death at the hands of women and men (here the accumulation of symbols connoting aspects of the cultivation and preparation of food—ax, hoe, meal mortar—becomes important) is born again as a multitude (*ku-seng'uka* and *Samuseng'u* symbolism) of crops of which cassava is paramount and representative. I am unable to say whether the term *ikamba* was applied to the root of the *musambanjita* tree before cassava was introduced among the Ndembu, or whether it received this name from its likeness to the cassava root. Several features in *Chihamba* indicate that the rites may have been influenced by contact with Europeans, probably Portuguese, or with Europeanized Africans from western Angola. The miming of capture and of the slave caravans—with symbolic slave yokes, the recurrent cross motif, and the ritual importance of cassava (a plant of comparatively recent introduction into central Africa)—all suggest that borrowing has occurred, though probably not later than the period of Chokwe slave raids (see, the song on page 89, "she has been caught by the Chokwe") in the 1880's. The use of *musambanjita* as a war medicine probably became prevalent at this epoch.

I mention these possible connections to indicate that history is very often crystallized in dominant ritual symbols, either as part of their denotation or of their standardized interpretation. Unfortunately, in a society without written documents, it is often impossible to establish connections between ritual symbols and historical events, but it must never be forgotten that the semantics of such symbols are influenced by the historical process.

We will now consider more closely what has already been hinted at—the physical properties or substance of *ikamba daChihamba*. The whiteness of the root is of the first importance and connects it with other white things typical of these rites. Let me list them in order of their appearance: white beads, white clay, lightning, white cross, *mucheki* root-scrapings, white beer, *musoli* wood, white *ibanda* salt, cassava meal, white shelled beans, avoidance of persons who are "lacking in whiteness," the white representation of *Kavula*, yokes of *mudyi* ("milk") wood, moonlight, *ikamba daChihamba* root, white hen, *katochi* root, *mukeketi* root, *wutotu* (has white gum). *Chihamba*, then, may be regarded in terms of its symbolism, as a concentration of white symbols. *Ikamba daChihamba*, regarded as "the body of Kavula," who is "a white spirit" (as is *Chihamba*), may fairly be considered an outstanding expression of the principle of whiteness (*wutooka*). I have collected numerous interpretations of whiteness from Ndembu informants, of which the following list is a summary: Whiteness (or *mpemba*, white clay, with which it is interchangeable) is goodness (*ku-waha*), which is:

1. making strong and healthy (*ku-koleka*),
2. purity or good luck (*ku-tooka* has both senses to be contextually determined),
3. being without bad luck (*ku-bula ku-halwa*),
4. having power (*kw-ikala nang'ovu*),
5. being without death (*ku-bula ku-fwa*),

6. being without tears (*ku-bula madilu*)—having no occasion to mourn the death of kin,
7. chieftainship or headmanship (*wanta*),
8. (it is when people) meet together with ancestor spirits (*adibomba niakishi*),
9. life (*wumi*),
10. health (*ku-handa*),
11. procreative capacity (*lusemu*),
12. huntsmanship (*wubinda*),
13. giving (*kw-inka*),
14. eating (*ku-dya*),
15. remembering (*kw-anuka*)—to reverence the ancestor spirits,
16. laughing (*ku-seha*)—to laugh and show one's white teeth is a sign of openness—one has nothing to hide,
17. multiplying and increasing (*ku-seng'uka*),
18. making visible or revealing (*ku-solola*),
19. becoming mature or attaining elderhood (*ku-kula*),
20. sweeping clean (*ku-komba*), mainly in ritual contexts,
21. washing oneself (*ku-wela*), mainly referring to ritual ablution.

This catalogue of virtues (goodness, generosity, piety), the fruits of virtue (health, strength, headmanship, fertility, food) and ritual activities (sweeping, washing, assembling to venerate the ancestor spirits) is exemplified in the rites of *Chihamba*. Some white things are qualities, not material objects, others are activities. Nearly all these connotations of whiteness may be connected with features of *Chihamba*. Take, for example, *ku-koleka*, "making healthy or strong": this theme is represented in Sakutoha's invocation to the spirit of *Nyamakang'a:* "You must give her strength." It also appears in Lambakasa's invocation to the same spirit and in the interrogation of the candidates by *Kavula*. The theme is further expressed by the *mukoleku* frame and in the greetings to the representation of *Kavula. Ku-tooka,* "purity," is represented by the placing of white cassava meal on a candidate's head after she had learned the medicines of *Chihamba. Wanta,* "chieftainship," is portrayed by the mode of greeting *Kavula* at the *isoli,* and in several of his titles.

I need not cite further instances; they abound in the account of the rites. Here I merely suggest that among the latent senses of *ikamba daChihamba,* deriving from its classification among white symbols, are those listed above. The shape and thickness of the root, like those of cassava root, are thought by Ndembu to resemble and in ritual to represent the trunk of a human body. Thus *ikamba daChihamba,* by reticulation of the association chains stemming from its name and from its physical properties, stands for "the body of *Kavula.*"

Once this sense has been allocated to it, it is not difficult to see why the taproot should be treated with such solicitude. Indeed, the identification between root and spirit has become more than symbolic representation; it has acquired the character of a primitive sacrament. (See Nyaluwema's remark: "You must not wound the root for it is the spirit," and the anointing of its cuts with medicine and castor oil.

This process of exposure of the taproot is one of the tree's artifactual sources of meaning. As a finished product of human action *ikamba daChihamba* displays additional senses. Not the main root but a branch root is taken and some chips of its bark, though the branch root is also "wounded," perhaps deliberately to emphasize its identification with the *mukishi,* "the spirit." The severed root then becomes the pri-

mary component in a *kantong'a* shrine. As such it may be
viewed as a dominant simple symbol in a complex symbol,
dictating the primary sense of the latter while the other simple symbols stand to it as qualificatives. *Ikamba daChihamba*,
half buried as it is, represents *Kavula* and all that *Kavula* is
and stands for, while the bundle of medicines is, as I have
stated, "a sort of abridgement or compendium of Ndembu
curative ritual." It is this dominance of the *Chihamba* spirit
over other manifestations of ancestor spirits that makes *Chihamba* what Melland, following J. L. Keith's account, called
"the most remarkable of the purely tribal spirits." Keith, incidentally, recognized a connection between the modes of
manifestation, which he calls "tribal spirits" (distinguishing
them thus from the "family spirits") and the High God, for
he writes, "The Alunda say that [these tribal spirits] were
made by Nzambi [God] and will always be a trouble to the
tribe." (1923:173).

Each dominant simple symbol then has nominal, substantial, and artifactual sources of meaning, and from each source
there extends a chain or chains of association, some of which
reticulate with chains deriving from other sources. A complex symbol may be less polysemous than a simple symbol,
for, although it is made up of many such symbols, only certain senses of each are stressed—those that refer to the aim or
intention of the manipulators of the complex symbol.

Symbolic Actions

Here we enter the field of symbolic actions. It will be
remembered that Langer defined the symbol-function as a
structural relation between subject, symbol, conception, and
object. In discussing symbols as articles we have hitherto
paid little attention to the role of the subject who finds the

object of the symbol's reference more interesting than the symbol itself. Now we have to inquire into the intentions of the subject or subjects, as revealed by their behavior, including verbal behavior. In a previously published work,[4] I have distinguished between the exegetical level of meaning possessed by a ritual symbol and its operational level of meaning. The former represents the interpretations of indigenous informants, but the latter results from equating a symbol's meaning with its use, by noting what Ndembu do with it, and not only what they say about it. The operational level also has a sociological aspect because it is here that we examine who uses the symbol, what groups and categories of persons are involved and how they behave toward one another. Symbolic actions, more directly than symbolic things, refer to or imply social relationships. Often they mime behavior expected or desired between occupants of social positions, such as the obsequious respect shown to the representation of *Kavula*, held to be a model of the chief-subject situation. Sometimes they represent inversions of standardized secular patterns, as when women candidates precede men to greet *Kavula*. In any event, such symbolic actions afford the clearest evidence of the purposes of the rites and the intentions of the participants. If the study of symbolic articles gives us a picture of the cognitive structure of the rites and emphasizes the symbol-object-conception aspect of the symbol-function, we must concede that the study of symbolic actions helps us to understand more fully the orectic structure of the rites, the standardized purposes and emotions, and emphasizes the subject-symbol aspect.

Here the anthropologist's analysis of the structure of the

[4] Turner (1967:Chapter 2), given originally as a paper at the Third International African Seminar, 1960.

social system is indispensable, for he must be able to relate such symbolic actions as the "greeting of *Kavula*" to what he knows about the articulating principles of the social order if he is to appreciate their full meaning. Thus in the case mentioned, it is significant that *Kavula* should be regarded as masculine, as a great chief, as a "grandfather of everyone," as associated with the whole country, with such general values as fertility, abundant and timely rainfall, with cultivation, and with hunting. It is significant, too, that the "great adepts," including those who manipulate the representation of *Kavula*, should be male, while the senior candidates, including those who are actually ill and who greet *Kavula* first, should be female. It is also significant that *Kavula* should be regarded as "nourished" by the breasts of the female candidates. For in this matrilineal society, masculine authority is dependent on matrilineal descent, while the women through whom such descent is traced are politically subordinated to male chiefs, headmen, and, in village affairs, to their husbands. Masculinity, in the symbolism of the "greeting of *Kavula*," seems to be equated with the widest territorial unity of people of Lunda stock—here the symbolic connections between *Kavula* and the great Lunda chief Mwantiyanvwa are significant—while femininity—represented by the afflicting ancestress who belongs to a known and specific matrilineage, as well as by the senior candidates who are her living descendants—seems to be equated with specific components of Ndembu social structure which demand narrow and localized loyalties. Many ritual symbols appear to cover up disparities of reference and conjoin contrary senses under the rubric of a single representation. For in so doing they are bringing into relation with one another principles of social structure, roles, and groups that are normally situationally segregated. It must be remembered, too, that for Ndembu the ritual symbol is not a mere system of referents but a source of power—dangerous if misused but capable of domestication. Harnessed, it may be used to bring blessing, avert catastrophe, reconcile the moody dead with the living and the angry living with one another. I have suggested that subjectively at least the power of such symbols may be related to their multiplicity of referents. A. N. Whitehead has drawn attention to the fact that for members of Western industrial society few of a symbol's referents are present to consciousness at the moment it is employed. He writes:

The particular direction of individual action is directly correlated to the particular sharply defined symbols presented to him at the moment. The response of action to the symbol may be so direct as to cut out any effective reference to the ultimate thing symbolized. This elimination of meaning is termed reflex action. Sometimes there does intervene some effective reference to the meaning of the symbol. But this meaning is not recalled with the particularity and definiteness which would yield any rational enlightenment as to the specific action required to secure the final end. The meaning is vague but insistent. Its insistence plays the part of hypnotizing the individual to complete the specific action associated with the symbol. In the whole transaction, the elements which are clear-cut and definite are the specific symbols and the actions which should issue from the symbols . . . but in fact the symbol evokes loyalties to vaguely conceived notions, fundamental for our spiritual nature. The result is that our natures are stirred to suspend all antagonistic impulses, so that the symbol procures its required response in action. Thus the social symbolism has a double meaning. It means pragmatically the direction of individuals to specific actions; it also means theoretically the vague ultimate reasons with their emotional accompaniments, whereby the symbols acquire their power to organize the miscellaneous crowd into a smoothly running community. [1928:86]

Ritual symbols, more than other kinds of symbols with the possible exception of poetic symbols, exhibit this penumbral power, expressed in "vague ultimate reasons with their emotional accompaniments," and this is a major factor in their socially cohesive efficacy. Consider, for example, the gigantic shadow of meaning cast by *kantong'a*, ostensibly a simple memorial of *Chihamba*. It reaches over many sectors of Ndembu social life (represented by the tree symbols, the cultivated crops, the sacrificed white hen, the *ku-teta mazawu* rite), cooling (the *malowa* symbolism) and unifying them (the bundle of *kantong'a* symbols). C. S. Jung has suggested that a symbol is "alive" insofar as those who employ it are not fully aware of its significance (1949:602). "A symbol is pregnant with meaning." When the meaning is "born out of it," much of the efficacy is lost. Jung is, of course, discussing symbols in connection with his hypotheses about the existence of a "collective unconscious" and "archetypes." It is because his symbols dip deep into the collective unconscious and because their appearance stirs inherited memories of archetypal forms that they are "alive." Without accepting Jung's views about archetypes we are nevertheless prepared to accept that Ndembu symbols may well affect the unconscious layers of the psyche. But we must distinguish the meaning a symbol has for the unconscious psyche from that which it possesses for the preconscious psyche. In the latter case the subject is capable not only of bringing to consciousness and listing the situationally manifest senses of a ritual symbol, but also many of its situationally latent senses—which may be dominant in other kinds of rites or other episodes of the same kind. Whitehead seems to have in mind this penumbra of preconscious senses when he talks about "vague ultimate reasons." These are the senses which one may perhaps associate with the "social function" of a ritual symbol, for in one situation of collaborative activity, involving symbolic action, other collaborative activities, both symbolic and pragmatic, are preconsciously recalled, through the latent senses, and the ties between persons in those activities are presumably strengthened.

It would seem, therefore, that in any given instance of a symbol's use, we have to take into account three orders of reference: (1) its manifest sense(s), of which the subject is fully conscious and which is (are) related to the explicit aims of the ritual (to remove sterility, bring on rain, remove a dead hunter's incisor tooth from the body of his living kinsman, and so on); (2) its latent sense(s), of which the subject is only marginally aware but could have become fully aware and which is (are) related to other ritual and pragmatic contexts of social action; and (3) its hidden sense(s), of which the subject is completely unconscious and which is (are) related to infantile (and possibly prenatal) experiences shared with most other members of his society, and perhaps with most other human beings. I have argued elsewhere (1967:Chapter 1) that this third order of reference falls outside the anthropologist's analytical scope and is best left to the various and by no means unanimous schools of depth psychologists. For example, the killing of *Kavula* is undoubtedly connected in some way with the Oedipus complex, but the anthropologist is not so much interested in how it is so connected as in the modes of relationship between social categories such as men and women, old and young, adepts and candidates, chiefs and subjects, grandfathers and grandchildren, displayed during this critical episode. He is also interested in such cultural aspects of the ritual pattern as the values, norms, ideals, and attitudes therein presented.

Most symbolic actions are directed by culturally standardized purposes, though they may also express unconscious wishes, fears, and anxieties. Among the Ndembu there seem to be two main categories of such actions. First, there are actions which may be regarded principally as preparing, mobilizing, or constructing symbolic articles for ritual use. Such, for example, are the collection and preparation of *isaku* medicine and the preparation of the *isoli* tabernacle. Second, there are symbolic actions which together constitute a ritual drama, with plot, role-enactment, and audience. The greeting and killing of *Kavula* and the *yibi* episode exemplify this category. This rather than the pragmatic and instrumental first category is symbolic action proper, and each of its component gestures and mimetic acts is redolent with meaning. Often such symbolic action portrays a death, a killing, or a sacrifice. In the *Nkula* rites of the Ndembu, for example, the most esoteric episode consists of the veneration of a *mukula* tree, which is said to be the afflicting ancestress and is then cut down and carved into figurines, while a red cock is beheaded nearby. The key symbolic action of *Mukanda*, boys' initiation, is the violent and bloody act of circumcision with ritual concomitants. Death, in these cases, may be real or symbolic—in either case it represents a major, qualitative change in the status and state of being of the subject. Sometimes this ritual drama has a mythological charter, as have both *Nkula* and *Mukanda*. More often, in Ndembu ritual, they have not. If *Chihamba* has a foundation myth I have been unable to find it, or it has been forgotten.

The killing of *Kavula* is clearly one of Jung's "living" symbols of whose full meaning those who enact it are unaware. An analysis of Ndembu social structure helps the non-Ndembu reader little toward an understanding of the complex personality of *Kavula*. I have a suspicion that *Kavula* may also be a living symbol for the reader. At any rate, my reading in literature and comparative religion has suggested to me that among the hidden senses of a dominant symbol some may fall within the province of the ontologist rather than the depth psychologist. Certain features of the *Kavula* symbolism, notably its whiteness, and the connection between whiteness and killing, seem to be of wide, if not universal distribution. At random I can think of a number of these in addition to those discussed below—Melville's white whale and the white symbolism in Judaism and Christianity. There are Coleridge's albatross and Mallarmé's swan, the Unicorn and Virgin myths of the Middle Ages, the sacrifice of white or unblemished beasts in many societies. This wide spread of white symbolism, and its importance for those reared in the Judeo-Christian tradition, poses a problem for cross-cultural comparison. What follows is an attempt to solve it.

CHAPTER 3

Some White Symbols in Literature and Religion

An Experiment in Cross-cultural Comparison

What are we to make of the character of *Kavula?* He is an ambiguous and self-contradictory being who both conceals and reveals himself, who is a god and not a god, a man and not a man, an ancestor spirit and not an ancestor spirit. He brings misfortune on the Ndembu and brings benefits to them. He reviles his adepts and promises to help them. He is likened to a great chief but is slain like a slave. His being is an enigma, nay, a paradox. He is at once the lightning of destruction and the fertility of rain. He is in the sky and the air, and yet, like a root or a seed, he is in the earth. It is impossible to catch his vital life, to characterize him adequately, in any of the terms or definitions Ndembu employ about him. Nevertheless, one gets the strong impression that he is a personality, a unified and complete individual.

When one attempts to say what *Kavula* is, one is experiencing the same difficulty felt by the Ndembu, a difficulty indissociable from the very structure of language and conceptualization. What the Ndembu are trying to do, when they use this profound symbol and attempt to interpret it, is to express the act-of-being itself rather than the concept of being. For, as Etienne Gilson writes, in his book on Aquinas:

"It is quite impossible to come to the act-of-being by an intellectual intuition which grasps it directly, and grasps nothing more. To think is to conceive. But the proper object of a concept is always an *essence*, or something presenting itself to thought as an essence; in brief, an object. An act-of-being is an *act*. It can only be grasped by or in the essence whose act it is. A pure *est* is unthinkable; but an *id quod est* can be thought. But every *id quod est* is first a being" (1956:368). This formulation of Gilson's exposes for us a vital function of religious symbolism. A nuclear symbol or a symbolic personality like *Kavula*, is an inexhaustible matrix of concepts, a fount of definitions. Its dynamic wealth is inexhaustible precisely because such a symbol is an attempt to give visible form to the invisible act-of-being. Here, too, we find the inner significance of a semantic cluster of Ndembu terms associated with the verb *ku-solola*, "to reveal," "to make visible." It is no accident that the supreme representation of *Kavula* takes place in an *isoli*, "a place of revelation," near a *musoli*, "a revelatory tree." It is no accident that this revelation of *Kavula* possesses the attribute of sheer whiteness, or candor. *Kavula* is here the embodiment, or, better still, the personification of all that Ndembu mean by whiteness. Whiteness is wholeness, or even holiness. Moreover, the adverb *chalala*, "truly" or "really" (from the radical *-alala*, "true" or "real") is frequently used in conversation as a synonym for *to-o*, "in a white manner." The esoteric representation of *Kavula* may well be said to represent the act-of-being itself as the ultimate truth and as a personal act-of-being. There is an uncanny similarity between the rite at *isoli* and the episode recorded in the third chapter of Exodus when the Lord appeared to Moses "in a flame of fire out of the midst of a bush: and he saw that the bush was on fire and was not burnt."

There is a parallel here with the dazzling whiteness of *Kavula* in its fence of broken bushes. It will be remembered that Moses asked God: "If they should say to me: What is his name? What shall I say to them?" And God replied: "I AM WHO AM." He said: "Thus shalt thou say to the children of Israel: 'HE WHO IS hath sent me to you.'"

One might argue with some point that *Kavula* represents the ultimate unity of Ndembu society, transcending all its contradictions of principle and value. He is, for example, the "grandfather" of his cult members, he is a "chief," he is a "slaveowner," he is the "husband" of the afflicting ancestress, he clearly typifies virility and huntsmanship. But such a sociological explanation would not adequately account for many of his characteristics: his connection with meterorological phenomena, such as thunder and lightning and the rains. It would not cover his patronage of the fertility of crops and game. It would not explain his power over human health and other biological processes. Nor would it account for his intensely personal relationship with his worshipers, nor for his mystical death and rebirth. The ethical and spiritual values he represents and sanctions are no mere product of the social process. Indeed, Ndembu religion has its own set of ends, which clearly transcend the social category. Each candidate and adept in *Chihamba* has his or her own personal relationship with *Kavula*, a relationship involving a specific set of behavioral norms and a specific mode of behavior unlike those found in any other form of relationship. Many kinds of repetitive social behavior and many kinds of natural regularity are associated with *Kavula*, but what he is in himself transcends all these and yet is immanent in all of them. Each of these regularities has its own formal principle. None of them can be reduced to or substituted for any other. But they share a common act-of-being, a very *Esse*. To say that everything represented by or personified in *Kavula* has a bearing on the social life of the Ndembu is to say very little. In general form and in detail, *Chihamba* enjoys a wide measure of autonomy from secular Ndembu society. There is here no necessary causal nexus between the social and ritual structures. The latter is certainly not monocausally determined by the former. If economists operate successfully with the concept of "the economic man" and judges with the concept of "the reasonable man," we might find it fruitful to use the concept of "the ritual man." This concept would involve a sense of dependence on a primary act-of-being, whether this act-of-being is regarded as personal or not. Herman Melville, of whom we shall say much more, vividly expresses the notion of a generic ritual man in *Moby Dick* (Melville 1952:93). Ishmael in that story argues to Captain Bildad that the Polynesian idol-worshiper, Queequeg, is a "born member of the First Congregational Church." "What Church dost thee mean?" asks the Quaker captain. Ishmael replies: "I mean, Sir, the same ancient Catholic Church to which you and I, and Captain Peleg there, and Queequeg here, and all of us, and every mother's son and soul of us belong: the great and everlasting First Congregation of this whole worshipping world; we all belong to that: only some of us cherish some queer crotchets no ways touching the grand belief; in *that* we all join hands."

But if *Kavula* represents one of man's manifold attempts to depict act-of-being, why do Ndembu enact the drama of his symbolic slaying? The fact is, however, that it is only the candidates who believe that they have "killed the chief." The adepts know that *Kavula* has merely changed his mode of manifestation. They know that on the following day he will become the life of germinating grain and sprouting roots in the *kantong'a* shrines. They know, too, that the supposed killing is a piece of mystification, aimed at bemusing and exhilarating the candidates. How perplexed must these people be, when, after having been taught to greet the great chief with humble ceremony, and having been assured of his blessing, they are then commanded to strike him on the head with their "thunder rattles." And how bewildered they must be when the white covering has been removed and they are told that there was no one concealed under the blanket, but that the blood upon the mortar was *Kavula's* own. This series of paradoxical situations is the nearest Ndembu can get to the expression of a total act-of-being which transcends both life and death in the material sense. In the total context of *Chihamba*, *Kavula*, at the point of his apparent killing, changes what may be termed the appearances of his existence. Before he was a person; afterward he becomes a potency for growth. No longer is he depicted as a boisterous demigod conversing with the candidates. Now he is, by a species of transubstantiation, a root of *ikamba daChihamba*. He has become the cruciform figure, drawn in white clay, of the *yibi* shrine. He is also the principle of growth in the crops, which form a component of the *kantong'a* shrine.

Kavula has undergone yet another kind of change. Before the *isoli* rite he has a unitary nature—the unity of a personality. Afterward he is, as it were, distributed among many persons and objects. He is in a certain sense identified with each of the candidates who are symbolically beheaded at the *yibi* shrine, for each of them has entered into *Kavula's* "death." He is also in the roots, crops, and trees of the *kantong'a*. In this change the ubiquity of the spiritual order is represented. Again, it may be said that from being transcendental, he becomes immanent in many persons and objects. Clearly his "death" is no more than a metaphor for radical change in his mode of manifestation. Such a metaphor is perfectly consistent with the idiom of Ndembu ritual belief. Boys and girls are said to "die" during initiation, but this merely means that they pass symbolically from childhood to adulthood. Furthermore, for Ndembu, physical death does not mean extinction: it means the passage from a visible to an invisible mode of existence. As we have seen, ancestor spirits interfere in the most lively way in the affairs of their living kin. There is also a vague and imprecise belief in reincarnation or rather in the return of certain of the physical and mental attributes of dead persons to descendants named after them. Indeed, Ndembu believe that it is exceedingly difficult to prevent the return of the spirits of the dead to their former associates and haunts, and these returns are usually accompanied by misfortune to the living. Both life and death depend upon and are permeated by the ineradicable act-of-being, which, represented most nakedly by *Kavula*, is the very soul of paradox and represents the ultimate unity of creation and destruction.

Here, then, we have another instance of ritual paradox. We find that death is not death. This paradox is only one among several, for the candidates are called "innocent" in the song sung *after* the symbolic killing. After killing their cult deity they are innocent. Before, as the song says, they were guilty: a reversal of the secular order. Moreover, before they kill *Kavula* they are treated in a humiliating manner and are said to be in a state of shame (*nsonyi*). From the extremity of abasement they are elevated through an enjoined act of symbolic execution to a state of innocence, in which they receive the chanted praise of the adepts: "She has been acquitted, the candidate of *isoli*." Again let us listen to Nyaluwema: "They greet *Kavula* first, while he is still alive, then they take up their rattles and kill him, *pa-a, pa-a!* The people feel very sad after this, but they laugh later when the names are called, there is great happiness."

Thus the events in *Chihamba* do not follow a normal order. Things are not what they seem. As Muchona said, "The candidate has been instructed that *Kavula* is a beneficent spirit, and is later told that he has killed *Kavula.*" He is awed and terrified by this deliberate disordering and disorienting of his mental habits. The whole process is reminiscent of Arthur Rimbaud's formula for the obtaining of vision: *"Un derègle-ment raisonné de tous les sens"* (a reasoned disordering of all the senses). The aim appears to be, both for poet and for Ndembu ritual man, to break through the habitual patterns formed by secular custom, rational thinking, and common sense, to a condition where the pure act-of-being is directly apprehended. The candidate is in a world where nothing follows its expected sequence. He is mocked for being unable to answer what he could not reasonably be expected to know and praised for doing what he might well consider to be a criminal and even impious deed. There is more in this than crude chicanery or mere mystagogy. The fact that adepts themselves believe that an abandoned *isoli* is fraught with dangerous mystical power does not support the view that they are skeptics. No, there lies behind the cumulative dis-play of symbols, and the series of paradoxical actions, the implicit intention of putting the candidates "beside them-selves," or even above themselves, literally in a state of ec-stasy, but conceived not so much as a prophetic frenzy as a mild beatitude. It is believed at the therapeutic level at least that the candidates have been made whole. As Lambakasa, the senior adept, said during his oration after the killing of

Kavula: "Not one of those candidates whom we have brought is sick, all are completely well. No one has a broken leg or arm. All of them must be strong or perhaps you might say some day, 'They were not killed at *Chihamba*.' " But they have also been made spiritually whole. Our own observations confirm this impression of an atmosphere of mild diffused happiness. As we returned from the *isoli* to the village all the participants spoke gently together when they had finished singing, as though something great and difficult had been brought to a successful conclusion. Subjectively, the nearest one can get to it is to say that the feeling tone resembled that among a group of Christians just after the Easter Vigil service which ends the tragic drama of Passiontide.

In *Schism and Continuity* I sketched out a preliminary attempt at a sociological analysis of *Chihamba*. Since finishing that book I have tried to analyze its symbolism and its plot in many different frames of reference. At one time I employed a method of analysis derived essentially from Durkheim via A. R. Radcliffe-Brown. I considered the social function of *Chihamba* with reference to the structural form of Ndembu society. But this method did not enable me to handle the complexity, asymmetry, and antinomy that characterize real social processes, of which ritual performances may be said to constitute phases or stages. I found that ritual action tended thereby to be reduced to a mere species of social action, and the qualitative distinctions between religious and secular custom and behavior came to be obliterated. The ritual symbol, I found, had its own formal principle. It could be no more reduced to, or explained by, any particular category of secular behavior or be regarded as the resultant of many kinds of secular behavior, than an amino-acid molecular chain could be explained by the properties of the atoms interlinked by it.

The symbol, particularly the nuclear symbol, and also the plot of a ritual, had somehow to be grasped in their specific essences. In other words, the central approach to the problem of ritual has to be intuitive, although the initial intuition may then be developed in a logical series of concepts.

I have already taken up the position in this book that we have in *Chihamba* the local expression of a universal human problem, that of expressing what cannot be thought of, in view of thought's subjugation to essences. It is a problem that has engaged the passionate attention of the ritual man in all places and ages. It is a problem, furthermore, that has confronted artists, musicians, and poets whenever these have gone beyond the consideration of aesthetic form and social manners. But I am not going to make a comparative study, in a wide range of religions and works of art, of human attempts to grapple with this problem. I shall content myself with examining a narrow sphere of comparative data, and then only with regard to two aspects. My point of departure is the *isoli* episode of *Chihamba*. From this episode I take two elements: whiteness and violent death. Next I shall examine the Biblical narrative of the finding of the empty tomb of Jesus. Finally, I shall analyze the central motifs of Herman Melville's classic novel *Moby Dick*, the whiteness of the great whale and its last encounter with the *Pequod*.

The Empty Tomb

The basic text for this analysis is Matthew 28:1–6: "And in the end of the sabbath, when it began to dawn towards the first day of the week, came Mary Magdalen and the other Mary, to see the sepulchre. And, behold, there was a great earthquake, for an angel of the Lord descended from heaven and rolled back the stone and sat upon it. And his countenance was as lightning and his raiment as snow. And for fear of him the guards were struck with terror and became as dead men. And the angel, answering, said to the women: Fear not you; for I know that you seek Jesus who was crucified. He is not here: for he is risen, as he said. Come, and see the place where the Lord was laid." Luke 24:4 mentions two men in the sepulchre "in shining apparel." John 20:12 writes of "two angels in white" sitting one at the head and one at the feet, where the body of Jesus had been laid. Mark 16:5 writes that the two Marys "saw a young man clothed with a white robe" sitting in the sepulchre, who told them that Jesus "is risen; he is not here. Behold the place where they laid him." He further mentioned that "a trembling and fear . . . seized them."

I draw attention to the following similarities between *isoli* and the empty tomb. *Kavula* was described to me as a *mufu*, a dead person; he is believed by the candidates to have suffered a violent death, and when the covering blanket is removed, the candidates see no one under it. The name *Kavula* means lightning, and the angels, according to St. Matthew, have faces "like lightning." *Kavula*'s covering is dazzling white; all the gospel writers agree that the angels wore white garments—"like snow." *Kavula* is described as "a chief"; Jesus was called "the King of the Jews." The senior candidates at *isoli* were women; women were the first to visit the empty tomb. In the song sung after the *isoli* episode occur the words "she went with cries of rejoicing into the grave, she has been acquitted." This song refers to the senior candidate, the one whose behavior brought on affliction by *Kavula*. It will be remembered that Mary Magdalen, before her conversion, had the reputation of being "a great sinner." It is perhaps worth mentioning here that *Kavula* is represented on two separate occasions in *Chihamba* by a white cross. It is also worth mentioning that Jesus himself was associated with whiteness at his transfiguration: "And whilst he prayed the shape of his countenance was altered and his raiment became white and glittering" (Luke 9:29). "And his garments became shining and exceeding white, as snow, so that no fuller upon earth can make white" (Mark 9:2). "And his face did shine as the sun and his garments became white as snow" (Matthew 17:2).

Finally, it will be noted that both the disclosure of *Kavula*'s absence and the finding of the empty tomb take place at "liminal" times: between day and night in the former case and between night and day in the latter.

Moby Dick

Most people are familiar with this great novel by Herman Melville. Its theme is simple: Captain Ahab's relentless pursuit of the white whale Moby Dick that had bitten off his leg. The book is steeped in symbolism, and many writers and critics have attempted to interpret it. Sherman Paul, for example, writes that "the symbolic method of the book is one of its primary meanings: where ambiguity is of the nature of things, and inscrutability a divine attribute, man's search for absolute truth will necessarily end in disaster. The truth glimpsed in moments of intuition can never be permanently fixed. The whale is, indeed, 'the ungraspable phantom of life'—the 'one grand hooded phantom, like a snow hill in the air' that swims through the narrator Ishmael's dreams."

My attention was drawn to this book, not because of its literary qualities, but because of the remarkable similarity between its symbolism and that of the *Chihamba* ritual of the Ndembu. In fact, it was the very unlikelihood of this resemblance that arrested my attention, for there could be no connection at all between the ritual customs of an obscure African tribe and the imaginative writings of a New England author. Some might argue that elements of *Chihamba* might have been borrowed directly from Christianity since Catholic missionaries had begun their work in Angola and the Congo more than four centuries before I saw *Chihamba*. But I never heard of an Ndembu tribesman who had read *Moby Dick*.

The episode I wish to consider is the final chase of the white whale, in the course of which Ahab harpoons Moby Dick three times. The third time is on the third day: "Now when three days flow together in one continuous intense pursuit; be sure the first is the morning, the second the noon, and third the evening and the end of that thing—be that end what it may." The stricken whale turns on the whaling ship and breaches its side. The ship sinks, and the whole crew is lost with it, except for Ishmael who is saved by clinging to a coffin. That is the bare narrative of events; I now wish to draw attention to some of the crucial details.

First there is the "whiteness of the whale." In a chapter with this name Melville attempts to set down the major referents of whitness in past and present European culture. Sherman Paul (1950) writes: "He heaps up historical and timeless associations, narrowing their meanings as he proceeds, but creating their intensity out of the vast penumbra." To begin with, Melville lists, just as Ndembu do, the beneficent associations of whiteness. He shows how this color represents "dominion," "pre-eminence," and "mastership," quoting examples from Hanover, Siam, and the Austrian and Roman empires. It will be recalled that Ndembu describe chiefly rule (*wanta*) as "white."

Melville writes: "Whiteness has been even made significant

of gladness, for among the Romans a white stone marked a joyful day!" For Ndembu whiteness also stands for joy; they anoint themselves with white clay at the festive phases marking the end of initiation ceremonies. Further attributes of whiteness given by Melville may be compared with the Ndembu interpretations on pages 168–170: "the innocence of brides," "the benignancy of age," "the divine spotlessness and power," "Great Jove himself incarnate in a snow-white bull," "the Passion of Our Lord," "whatever is sweet, and honourable, and sublime."

But beneath these beneficent associations Melville detects "an elusive something in the innermost idea of this hue, which strikes more panic to the soul than that redness which affrights in blood." He cites as examples the white polar bear, the white tropical shark, and the albatross, "that white phantom." Worse than these is "the White Squall, the gauntleted ghost of the Southern Seas." Then he mentions "the marble pallor of the dead" and "all ghosts rising in a milk-white fog." He adds to these white terrors "the muffled rollings of the milky sea; the bleak rustlings of the festooned frosts of mountains; the desolate shiftings of the windowed snows of prairies." Melville then seeks "to solve the incantation of this whiteness" and "to learn why it appeals with such power to the soul" and "why it is at once the most meaning symbol of spiritual things, nay, the very veil of the Christian's piety; and yet should be as it is, the intensifying agent in things the most appalling to mankind."

He attempts to answer his questions by suggesting that "by its indefiniteness [whiteness] shadows forth the heartless voids and immensities of the universe, and thus stabs us from behind with the thought of annihilation." "Or is it," he asks, "that as in essence whiteness is not so much a colour as the visible absence of colour, and at the same time the concrete of all colours; is it for these reasons that there is such a dumb blankness, full of meaning, in a wide landscape of snows—a colourless, all-colour of atheism from which we shrink?" He uses other explanatory metaphors: "the palsied universe . . . like a leper," "the monumental white shroud that wraps all the prospect around," and concludes by saying, "And of all these things the Albino whale was the symbol. Wonder ye then at the fiery hunt?"

The Ndembu, like Melville, have an ambivalent attitude toward whiteness. For example, in their herbal therapy for leprosy, the white-spotted bark of a certain tree is used as a sympathetic cure for the white spots made by that dreaded disease. The white gum of the *kapumbwa* tree and certain white roots represent the pus produced by venereal infections. Whiteness also represents the destructiveness of lightning. In hunting rituals, too, whiteness has terrifying and lethal associations. *Mundeli*, for example, is said to be a mode of spirit affliction that appears in dreams in the form of a European. It was formerly believed that Europeans lived under the South Atlantic and that their skin color got its corpselike bleach from long immersion in the salt water. Another spirit, believed to persecute hunters, *Mukala*, is represented in the ritual of that name by such white symbols as white clay and white beads, because it takes the form of marsh lights (described as "white") which lead hunters to their destruction in morasses. As lightning and as will-o-the-wisp, light has its malevolent manifestations. Here another affinity with *Moby Dick* should be noted, see Chapter CXVIII, the candles where the ominous corpusants burn on the lightning rods of the *Pequod*: "Three tapering white flowers; God's burning finger laid on the ship," "the white flame but lights the way

to the white whale." It is significant, too, that only *Chihamba*
and *Mukala*, among modes of spirit manifestation, are believed to have the power of causing death and not merely
misfortune. It should be noted also that such "white" beings
as chiefs and ancestor spirits have the power to punish those
who disobey them. They are feared by their juniors and infe-
riors. No less than Ishmael do the Ndembu find white things
"appalling."

The second point of comparison between *Chihamba* and
Moby Dick is that in both there is a chase, and in both a
semidivine being undergoes death, symbolic in the first case,
real in the second. In *Chihamba* the candidates are symbolically slain; in *Moby Dick* the crew of the *Pequod* are drowned.
But there is the important difference that in *Chihamba* both
the demigod and his cult adepts are believed to have renewed
life, symbolized by the sprouting grain and cassava of the
kantong'a shrine. In this respect, *Chihamba* has closer affinities
with the Christian resurrection. In Christianity, too, many of
the disciples atoned for their desertion of Jesus by suffering
martyrs' deaths. Just as Jesus' death prepared the way for the
resurrection, so were these apostle martyrs regarded as having become saints in heaven, as having eternal life. But in
Moby Dick there is no resurrection, unless Ishmael's escape, a
mere literary device, be regarded as such. It is not made clear
whether the whale himself is slain, but the implication is that
this white leviathan is somehow indestructible. In Melville's
modern view, proud will encounters proud will; there is no
question of any conscious being voluntarily surrendering his
life out of charity, and because charity is immortalizing,
thereby regaining it. Of course, the killing of *Kavula* is
hardly cognate with Jesus' sacrifice, but nevertheless
Ndembu do have a feeling that rebirth and renewal of the

personality imply an acceptance that one must pass through ordeal and death.

I do not want to discuss the philosophical and theological aspects of this comparison between pagan, Christian, and neopagan attitudes toward the supernatural. My principal aim is to point out that whiteness in all three examples represents pure act-of-being. It is everything that cannot be conceptualized, and whenever people attempt to interpret it they are forced to give a long inventory of referents, many of which clearly represent the human standpoint adopted toward the *ipsum esse* (the act-of-being itself). Melville, identified with Ahab, proud and modern, emphasized the hateful and terrifying aspects of that whiteness which transcends mortality. The Ndembu lay stress rather on the social and communal aspects of being, since their social system is basically structured by kinship ties. The Christian interpretation of whiteness makes paramount the qualities of innocence and charity exemplified by "the Lamb of God who taketh away the sins of the world." But in all of them whiteness represents an attempt to grasp the ungraspable, to embody the invisible. The symbolism of hunting and killing, and indeed the real crucifixion of Christ, would seem to represent human attempts to capture or nail down the elusive and pure act which is creating the universe. Man wills to have what he mistakenly conceives to be this "power" for himself or even to destroy it, but somehow the awesome innocence, without attributes or with all attributes, which he covets, slips through his grasp. There is nothing under the brilliant white covering of the supposedly slain *Kavula*. The stone was rolled away from Christ's tomb and it was empty. Melville does not record the death of Moby Dick. But *Kavula* has somehow gone into the air; he will return first to persecute, then to bless other elect. And "the Lord is risen," "Lo, I shall be with you, even unto the end of the world." It seems that Melville wishes us to suspect that the white whale is deathless, for he writes: "Some whalemen . . . declared Moby Dick not only ubiquitous, but immortal (for immortality is but ubiquity in time)"; "that though groves of spears should be planted in his flanks, he would still swim away unharmed; or if indeed he should ever be made to spout thick blood, such a sight would be but a ghastly deception; for again in unensanguined billows hundreds of leagues away, his unsullied jet would once more be seen."

The point I am trying to make by this comparison is that a strictly sociological explanation of the white symbolism we have been discussing would appear to be inadequate. One has to consider religious phenomena in terms of religious ideas and doctrines, not only, or principally, in terms of disciplines which have arisen in connection with the study of secular institutions and processes. White symbolism is but one genus of religious symbolism, which gives us actual clues to the nature of realities we cannot perceive by means of the senses alone. It is not a question of setting the intellect to work at reducing the religious symbol to sensory terms. Our task is rather, like T. H. Huxley's in quite a different context, to sit down before facts as a little child, be prepared to give up every preconceived notion, follow humbly wherever and to whatever abysses nature leads, or we will learn nothing. We must likewise learn of the pagan and Christian "ritual man," whither his symbols, like landmarks or blazes of a trail, point and guide. It was truly said by H. Butterfield (1959:151) "that it might well be required of any religion that its truth should be open to the vision of the humble and poor, of those who can be as little children, though that truth might be hidden from the wise by those intellectual systems which they have built for themselves, and which can be a screen between oneself and reality." In studying religious symbols, the product of humble vision, we must ourselves be humble if we are to glimpse, if not fully to comprehend, the spiritual truths represented by them. In this realm of data only innocence can hope to attain understanding. That is the reason why the attempts of such scholars and philosophers as James Fraser and Durkheim to explain away religious phenomena in naturalistic terms have been so obviously unsuccessful. Like Captain Ahab, such scholars seek to destroy that which centrally menaces and wounds their self-sufficiency—the belief in a Deity—and like Ahab they suffer shipwreck without transfixing the quick of their intended victim.

We must go to school with the Ndembu, learn of Queequeg, and seek to understand the teaching of the carpenter's humble disciples, if we would discover religious truths. If we would be "full of light" (whiteness), then our "eye must be single." That is to say, we must be prepared to accept the fruits of simple wisdom with gratitude and not try to reduce them to their chemical constituents, thereby destroying their essential quality as fruits and their virtue as food.

I have drawn attention to the remarkable parallels both in theme and detail between these three episodes. It would appear that men in very different times and lands tend to use the same kind of symbolism to express act-of-being and the dangerous task of giving expression to it. D. H. Lawrence once wrote that analysis presupposes a corpse. Here conceptualization requires a corpse. Ahab, for example, wanted to kill the great eternal beast. Pilate tried to limit and identify

Christ as "the King of the Jews," and his crucifiers denied him all movement. But the empty tomb betokened that the ungraspable godhead had escaped human categorization. Even for the Ndembu, *Kavula* could not be definitely linked with any of his particular manifestations and symbols. He evaded total definition, and just when the candidates thought that the mystery of his existence would be finally known by them, he became an emptiness, or something that had passed into the air.

But if there are many points of resemblance, there is a crucial difference between the Christian and pagan examples. For the Christian, the resurrection is a historical event; fact and symbol are one. The holy women really did see shining white beings. For the Christian, the supernatural erupted, as it were, into the natural at a specific time and place; the spiritual order became visible to the senses in the most "spiritual" of sensuous experiences, that of white light. It is quite possible that Melville, brought up a Calvinist, was influenced in some way by the Christian white symbolism, but the attribution of whiteness to a whale was his personal mythopoeic addition. It is also conceivable that some of the symbols in *Chihamba*, such as the white cross, have been borrowed from Christian sources. But white symbolism is so intrinsic to Ndembu ritual and plays such a major role in the ritual of so many African tribes, that one must regard it as indigenous. Both Ndembu rite and Melville's myths use whiteness to represent what appears to underlie the order of nature; in Christianity whiteness helps to reveal the order of grace. Each "white" manifestation of God or Spirit to the Israelites and to the followers of Jesus (the burning bush, the lightning on Sinai, the Transfiguration, and the angels in the tomb) represents the divine initiative toward man. The fashioner of these events is a personal God who freely wills to manifest himself to mankind. Melville and the Ndembu, on the other hand, seem to be trying to impose their will on what they feel to be the power in and behind the natural order. Here the initiative is taken by man. In both the primitive African and capitalist American probings of the unknown God we find a fatalistic attitude. Melville writes about Moby Dick's "predestinating forehead" as the whale is about to send the *Pequod* to its doom. The Ndembu, in their employment of the symbolism of the slave yoke, appear to indicate that men are subjugated to the repetitive social order. Besides, *Kavula*, as we have seen, stands for many kinds of natural regularity. In *Chihamba* and *Moby Dick*, the white beings, since they are human creations, do not transcend the symbolic category: they can never be more than symbols. In the biblical narrative, the white beings and phenomena do not stand for something else, they are what they are. The difference may also be expressed by saying that in the Christian revelation men see the growing evidence of God's love for man, whereas in the fatalistic examples we have considered we see rather man's awe of God not untinged with fear and hatred and emulous pride.

But whereas it could be argued that *Chihamba* is some kind of primitive revelation of godhead, logically if not chronologically prior to God's historical incarnation, this cannot be said of *Moby Dick*, which is written with full consciousness not only of Christianity, but also of primitive Polynesian religions of a not widely dissimilar general type from that of the Ndembu. What we have here seems to be a "dehumanizing" of God, with the consequent reduction of his typically Judeo-Christian attributes of love and compassion. The act-of-being is not seen as an act-of-loving, but as an act-of-punishing. The great white whale punishes human presumption, but its victims remain impenitent and even, Melville would suggest, somehow justified in their pride. We are presented with the picture of a pitiless central principle in the universe which resents being challenged by its own conscious creation, man, represented principally by Ahab, who resembles that principle in his own pitiless and unyielding spirit. It is a universe emptied of the Christian Trinity, ruled by pride, the monism of a monomaniac. It is also the picture of our materialist civilization of the West, in which we have developed an almost superstitious fear of a judgment, that will be brought upon us by the forces of nature which we have in our pride sought to subdue to our vainglorious ends in the pursuit of power, wealth, and material prosperity. In seeking to usurp the prerogatives of the Creator we have only succeeded in making manifest the ultimate physical energies of destruction. It is not altogether fanciful to see in *Moby Dick* a remarkable prophecy of the discovery of nuclear fission. Man has pushed his exploration of externality to an ultimate conclusion, and from the depths comes churning the great white punishing beast. Melville sees no way out, in *Moby Dick* at least, of this fatal dénouement, for he does not believe in Providence.

The fatalism implicit in *Chihamba* is of quite a different kind. It is not the anguished anticipation of an inevitable doom brought upon man by his own *hubris*. It is rather a resignation to what is, patience under trial and misfortune, and trust in the cyclical regenerative power of the cosmos. *Kavula* is a terrifying being; but he is terrifying in a human way, like a chief or a village elder in the eyes of a small child. Although he threatens, he also promises to cure and benefit those who undergo his rites with good will and decorum.

Ndembu know, if they are prepared to suffer and endure to the ultimate degree, even to symbolic death (a feature of many kinds of ritual), that restorative processes will the sooner come into operation. Like all primitive and peasant communities they have a sensitive awareness of cyclicality, of successive phases of drought and rain, of heat and cold, of hunger and plenty. Because they trust in the supersession of phases inimical to human welfare by phases of prosperity, they can in ritual feel emboldened to represent in symbols the humiliation, poverty, and death of their ritual subjects. And precisely through plumbing the depths they expect to regain the heights. In one sense *Kavula* represents simultaneously, in a lightning flash, so to speak, the whole cycle. That is why his attributes are so ambivalent. In another sense he is beyond the cycle, the formless energy which maintains it in being, the pure act which is not acted upon but is present in every event of the turning year and the social cycle. Yet *Kavula* is clearly a personality and an individual. In other words the Ndembu perceive will and consciousness as attributes of what is at the same time creative energy. These human characteristics of *Kavula* account for the unexpectedness and irregularity of his interventions, both as an afflicter of wrongdoers and from the point of view of the candidates in *Chihamba*. Although he is in some sense identifiable with cosmic regularities and more or less predictable kinds of events, he is the very essence of the unpredictable and unexpected. It might almost be said that he represents the freedom of the creator with regard to his creation. He keeps it going, but he need not if he does not want to. From one point of view *Chihamba* is a long plea for the restoration of the normative order and an act of penance by and on behalf of those who have transgressed moral norms which are believed to have the same validity as natural regularities. Thus *Chihamba*, unlike *Moby Dick*, represents a humble submission to the act-of-being of and behind all phenomena. It emphasizes dependence, whereas *Moby Dick* asserts a suicidal independence.

The Resurrection symbolism, perhaps most aptly expressed for comparative purposes in the Easter liturgy of the Catholic church, may also be described as regenerative. It does not deal with regeneration within the natural order, but with the quickening of man's spiritual faculties deadened by original sin: the resurrection inaugurated the order of grace, thus redeeming man's nature from sin. In the liturgy of passiontide the priest vests in white stole and cape, incenses the paschal candle, and announces Christ's "glorious resurrection" to all the people, who hold lighted candles. "As the apostle teaches, we are baptized into his death, and buried together with Christ: and as Christ rose again from the dead, so we, too, must walk in newness of life; knowing that our old man hath been crucified together with Christ, so that we shall no longer be in servitude to sin. Let us look to ourselves, therefore, as dead indeed to sin, but living to God in Christ Jesus our Lord" (standard Catholic liturgy before Vatican II). Here we have white symbolism quite clearly associated with God's self-sacrifice for man's spiritual regeneration. The act-of-being, so despotic in the other examples we have been considering, here reveals itself as an infinite self-giving, which is the same as forgiving. And what is marked is not a transition from one phase to another within the order of natural necessity, but an incorporation of that order into a higher order, that of spiritual freedom. Necessity is not abolished or superseded, but men's eyes are opened to its role as a mere means to sanctification. Its very hardships and perils become of more avail than its material benefits, as means of preparing the human soul for union with the act-of-being, now apprehended as the divine mercy. We have in this yet another example of the way in which Christianity reverses the values of natural religion. This is no fertility ritual, although it includes some of the symbols of pagan fertility cults. The triumphal aggregation of white symbols, such as the paschal candle, baptismal water, and white vestments, does not primarily represent the wished-for prosperity of a peasant community. It represents the regeneration, through grace, and assenting free will, of each individual soul, a regeneration made possible and exemplified by Christ's passion and resurrection.

In these high mysteries of religion and poetic insight we have seen as direct presentations of the act-of-being as it is possible for human beings to grasp. The long, slow process of converting "sensibles into intelligibles" is here dispensed with in favor of a direct confrontation of man with mystery. White symbolism is most appropriate here because in an important aspect it represents, as Melville suggested, the absence of all sensuous phenomena. It is absence presented, invisibility made visible. It is as though, whenever men attempt to represent the act-of-being, they have an innate propensity to use the same symbolic form, unsullied whiteness. On the other hand, depending on whether their attitude toward the act-of-being is one of humility or of pride, of love or of hate, they will qualify whiteness by associating it with other symbols and with various ritual plots. Or whiteness may itself be regarded as contingent; it may appear as the mere attribute of a more prominent symbol. For example, Moby Dick is a murderous beast primarily; his whiteness is subsidiary to his murderousness. In associating himself with whiteness, Jesus conveyed on the act-of-being the supereminent quality of sacrificial love. In Ndembu society the whiteness of *Kavula* became associated with the principle of gerontocratic authority, for *Kavula*, the white being, typically appears as a brow-beating but genial grandfather or chief. There is a certain engaging innocence about the Ndembu interpretation of whiteness which one feels to be lacking in that of Melville and indeed of many of his nineteenth-century literary contemporaries. It is this which gives point to G. K. Chesterton's remark that the next best thing to being really inside Christendom was to be really outside it.

PART TWO

NDEMBU DIVINATION: ITS SYMBOLISM AND TECHNIQUES

A Preliminary
Analysis of Ndembu
Divinatory Symbolism [1]

Before presenting the ethnographic data, I wish to comment briefly on the structure and properties of symbolic objects used in Ndembu divination. This class of symbols exhibits marked differences from most of the symbols employed in curative cults and life-crisis rituals. The major difference between the two classes is that the objects of divination have many of the characteristics of signs. C. S. Jung (1949:602) stated the familiar distinction between signs and symbols in a new way when he wrote that "a sign is an anal-

[1] The first chapter of Part Two, "A Preliminary Analysis of Ndembu Divinatory Symbolism," was read to the Intercollegiate Seminar of Departments of Anthropology at London University in February 1958. Some of the facts mentioned in it are duplicated in the ethnographic section which follows. I have not removed them, however, since in Chapter 4 they appear in a frame of analysis and in Chapter 5 in a frame of ethnographic description. It is methodologically desirable to keep these frames separate.

I would like to express my appreciation to the Rhodes-Livingstone Institute for financing my field research, to my colleagues at the University of Manchester, notably Professor Max Gluckman, for helpful criticisms, to the London Intercollegiate Seminar members for their stimulating comments, and I remember with gratitude the help of the late professor Daryll Forde. I an also grateful to C. M. N. White for comments on the vernacular texts.

ogous or abbreviated expression of a *known* thing. But a symbol is always the best possible expression of a relatively *unknown* fact, a fact, however, which is none the less recognized or postulated as existing." Although some may dislike his addiction to metaphor, Jung makes the telling point that a symbol is "alive" insofar as those who employ it are not fully aware of its significance. "A symbol," he says, "is pregnant with meaning." When the meaning is "born out of it" much of its efficacy is lost. Many objects, relationships, events, and items of behavior exhibited in ritual contexts among the Ndembu are symbols in this sense. Although both experts and laymen are able to verbalize some of the senses of important symbols, exegesis of others is blocked (see Turner, 1967:22–41). Some blockages, I have argued, are situational; in certain ritual contexts no meaning can be allocated to a symbol which can be interpreted by Ndembu in other contexts; other blockages are complete. In both cases, the presence of the symbol appears to be related to recurrent kinds of unconscious conflicts, both social and endopsychic, accompanied by powerful, and often illicit, emotions.

Jung's distinction implies that a single item may be both a symbol and a sign in the same society, and even in the same social situation, for different categories of persons. The more esoteric a man's knowledge, the more he will tend to regard that item as a sign, and the more readily he will be able to allocate meanings to it. This association certainly holds good for Ndembu diviners. The experienced diviner can allocate more meanings to the items of his divining apparatus than the novice diviner, and the latter can interpret them far more fully than the uninitiated villager. Thus at the esoteric level of indigenous interpretation symbols approximate to the status of signs. They become objects of cognition and cease progressively to be objects of emotion. The more they are known, the more they are mastered; the less they are known, the more they exert mastery. The prestige and influence of the ritual expert depends on this simple fact. Nevertheless, in Ndembu society, even for diviners the figurines and substances they use never become true signs. This is because their meanings rest ultimately on axiomatic beliefs in the existence of mystical beings and forces. Of course, diviners, working within the framework of their beliefs, are extraordinarily shrewd and practical men. As we shall see, the way they interpret their divinatory symbols reveals deep insight both into the structure of their own society and into human nature. But diviners are not charlatans; they believe that they are possessed by spirits when they divine and that their divinatory objects have a certain intrinsic power.

Among Ndembu the diviner regards his task as the practical one of revealing the causes of misfortune or death. These are almost invariably mystical or nonempirical in character, although human wishes, desires, and feelings are involved in their operation.

The diviner's insight is retrospective, not mantic; he discloses what has happened and does not foretell future events. Ndembu diviners are seldom oracular, unlike many southern Bantu diviners. Furthermore, the diviner does not himself inaugurate the divinatory process; clients come to consult him. Modes of divination are regarded as both lie-detecting and truth-discovering instruments, although, since they are operated by fallible men, their verdicts are not always accepted without question. For witches are credited with extraordinary powers of deception and even great diviners fortify themselves with special medicines to combat the deceits and illusions sent by their secret antagonists to baffle them. One such medicine is used at the first stage of a consultation. A clearing is made in the bush about half a mile from the diviner's village. Two poles are inserted in the ground and a third placed on them to make a frame resembling goalposts. On this are placed three headpads (*mbung'a*), similar to those worn by women when they carry heavy loads. These are made of a special kind of grass called *kaswamang'wadyi*. Etymologically, this term is derived from *ku-swama*, "to hide" and *ng'wadyi*, "the bare-throated francolin," a bird like a partridge much prized as a food. Francolins love to conceal themselves in this long, fine grass. In hunting cults this grass is used as a symbol for the desired invisibility of the hunter when he stalks game. Here it stands for the witch's attempts to conceal vital matters from the diviner. I translate a text given me by a diviner explaining the meaning of the headpad: "The headpad is a sign to the diviner not to forget anything, for he must not be ignorant of anything. A witch or sorcerer [*muloji* means both] could use medicine to deceive the diviner [*chitahu* or *mukwakuhong'a*] or hide things from him. The headpad is medicine to prevent this, for it keeps the diviner wide awake, it is a reminder to him. The grass in it is twisted like the witch's attempts to deceive." Under the frame must pass the diviner's clients, who may unwittingly harbor a sorcerer or witch in their ranks. The medicine may expose him to the diviner.

Another medicine used by diviners and kept by them in small calabashes (*malembu*) while they divine is a nerve from the root of an elephant's tusk. In ritual contexts this is called *nsomu*. Because it resembles a limp penis, it often has the meaning of masculine impotence. In divination it has the further meaning of a sorcerer, for sorcerers are believed to be able to blast the fertility of their victims and to kill them. *Nsomu* is also a suitable symbol for death since impotence is regarded as a kind of death. When an impotent man dies a black line is drawn with charcoal from his navel downward and over his genitals, indicating that his name, and with it certain vital elements of his personality, must never be inherited by the children of his kin. This is social death. Known sorcerers are treated in the same fashion.

As a divinatory medicine *nsomu* was interpreted to me as follows by a diviner: "Diviners use it to see secret things which crop up unexpectedly when they are divining, just as a hunter expects to come upon animals by chance when he is hunting. *Nsomu* is like a torch at night whereby he can see witches openly. This is because *nsomu* is a secret thing that has been brought into the open. Let me explain this to you further. A pregnant woman gave birth unexpectedly to a stillborn child. Some old women took that child to bury it in its grave. Before burying it they cut off part of one of its fingers. These women were witches who eat human beings. They use the finger together with *nsomu* to kill people. The child was just like *nsomu*, it came suddenly and unfortunately died."

I have cited these texts at length for two reasons. The first is to demonstrate how readily and explicitly diviners are able to offer interpretations of their symbolic items. The second is to exhibit an important variation on a theme which pervades all Ndembu ritual, that of bringing into the open what is hidden or unknown. This variation has the special sense of exposing deception and secret malice. The main theme of revealing the hidden is exemplified in all cults to cure persons afflicted by ancestor spirits with disease, reproductive disorders, or bad luck at hunting. The process of cure is essentially a process of what Ndembu call "making known and visible" (*ku-solola*) or (*ku-mwekesa*), albeit in symbolic guise, the unknown and invisible agents of affliction. This is brought about in various ways. One way is by mentioning the spirit's name in prayer and invocation (*ku-tena ijina damu-kishi*). The belief is that the spirit is aggrieved because it has been forgotten, not only by the victim, but by many of its other kin. It afflicts its living kinsman, sometimes in his personal capacity, but often in his capacity as representative of a kin group. If, however, it is mentioned and hence remembered by many people, it will cease to afflict but will benefit its victim, who becomes a sort of living memorial to it. Another mode of revelation is through representing the spirit in some material form, either as a figurine, named after it, or as a contraption of branches covered with a blanket whitened with cassava meal (*Kavula*). These representations are made at the end of protracted rituals, in sacred sites which only cult adepts may enter, called *masoli* (from the verb *ku-solola*, "to make visible" or "reveal"). It is said that the spirit, when it is afflicting its victim, is concealed in his or her body. This is thought especially to be the case where women suffer from some reproductive disorder. But when the spirit has been adequately represented in symbolic form, and frequently named, it is believed to emerge from its victim, reconciled with the latter and with the whole kin group.

The Ndembu term for symbol contains the implication of a revelatory process. This term is *chinjikijilu* and is derived from *ku-jikijila*, "to blaze a trail" in the bush. When hunters set out on expeditions into the deep bush (perhaps into thick *Cryptosepalum* forest), they cut marks on trees and also break and bend over their lower branches to indicate the way back. The blaze or landmark, in other words, leads from unknown, and, therefore, in Ndembu experience as well as belief, dangerous territory, to known and familiar surroundings, from the lonely bush to the populated village. Ritual symbols have a similar function, for they give a visible form to unknown things, they express in concrete and familiar terms what is hidden and unpredictable. They enable men to domesticate and manipulate wild and wayward forces.

Now let us return to the diviner's variation on the theme of revealing the hidden or making public what is private. When he confronts witchcraft, the diviner has the aim of exposing secret deceit and malice, of revealing the identity and the motives of sorcerers and witches. This aim shapes much of the symbolism of divination. Independently of the personal acuity and insight possessed by the diviner, the symbols he uses reveal how Ndembu have come to stereotype certain forms of fraudulent and malevolent behavior. Ndembu have many types of divination. I have records of ten, and C. M. N. White (1947) has written of others I did not meet. Here I am concerned with one mode of divination only which brings out most clearly the stereotyping of hidden malice I have mentioned, and with certain other characteristics of divinatory symbolism I shall shortly discuss.

This mode of divination is called by Ndembu *ng'ombu yakusekula*, which means literally, "divination by shaking up or tossing (objects in a basket)." The diviner keeps a set of from twenty to thirty objects of various shapes, sizes, and colors in a round basket with a lid. When he divines he places these objects in a round, flat, open basket (*lwalu*) of the type used by women to winnow millet, shakes them and throws them up so that they form a heap at the far side of the basket. He examines the top three or four objects, individually, in combination, and with reference to their relative height in the heap. Before throwing he asks his apparatus a question. Then he throws three times, after each throw putting the top few objects under the rest of the heap before shaking the basket again. After the third throw, he asks his consultants a question, suggested to him, Ndembu say, by the arrangement of the objects in his basket. If the same object comes uppermost three successive times, one of its various senses is reckoned to be part of the answer the diviner seeks. If a particular combination, stratified in a particular way, comes to the top three times running, the diviner has the greater part of his answer. His skill as an individual consists in the way in which he adapts his general exegesis of the objects to the given circumstances. For he is usually confronted by a group of kin who wish to find out which particular ancestor, sorcerer, or witch is causing the sickness or misfortune of their relative. Ndembu believe that this group itself may contain sorcerers or witches. In reality, as the diviner well knows, it may contain rival factions, one of which may stand to benefit by the death of the sick person if the latter holds office or is wealthy. If his clients wish him to divine into the cause of a death, the situation is still more serious. In the past, before witchcraft and witch-finding were declared illegal by the British administration, such consultations took place near the most important village in the neighborhood cluster of villages where the deceased person lived. Everyone in the neighborhood was expected to attend, and failure to attend was a cause of suspicion. The diviner had to make a sound appraisal of the balance of power between rival factions interested in the death who were present at the public gathering. If he did not, and gave an unpopular verdict, he was likely to be in some danger himself. Many diviners sought the protection of a chief and performed near his capital village. But I have been told of several diviners who despite such protection were speared to death by angry kin of the persons declared to be sorcerers.

The winnowing basket itself stands for the sifting of truth from falsehood. The diviner is believed to be possessed by the spirit of a diviner-ancestor, in a particular manifestation known as *Kayong'u*. *Kayong'u* is also said to be a manslayer (*kambanji*) because people may be slain as a result of a divining decision. The *Kayong'u* spirit causes the diviner to tremble and thus to shake the basket. Before becoming a diviner he must have been afflicted by this spirit, which causes asthmatic shortness of breath and makes him tremble violently while being washed with medicine. He is treated by a cult group, led by a famous diviner. Many of the symbols of the *Kayong'u* ritual stand for the "sharpness" which he must display as a diviner. These include needles and razors, the former being embedded in the hearts of a sacrificed cock and goat. When the diviner trembles and breathes heavily he is said to be feeling the pricking of the needle, which itself symbolizes the *Kayong'u* spirit, in his heart, lungs, and liver. After he has been treated, the novice diviner apprentices himself to an established diviner, who teaches him the meanings of the objects in a diviner's basket. The established diviner encourages the novice to divine himself, criticizes his performance, and gives him some of his own equipment. He enlists the aid of a professional woodcarver to make other objects. In Angola today a novice may pay 40 yards of cloth or a cow for knowledge of how to interpret divining objects. In the past, it is said that a novice would give 40 yards of cloth and a muzzle-loader or even a slave for such knowledge.

I have information on twenty-eight divinatory symbols. Their total range of meaning embraces the whole sorry story of misfortune, loss, and death in Ndembu life and of the mean, selfish and revengeful motives believed to be responsible for these afflictions.[2] Since so few objects have to represent so many things, it is not surprising to find that each of them has many meanings. Furthermore, the links between separate meanings of the same symbol are often of the vaguest sort, indeed, in some instances hardly perceptible to the European observer, unless he can set the symbol in its specific context of Ndembu culture. It is likely that some of the meanings of symbolic items have developed in the course of time as the result of their recurrent appearance in configurations of such items. Such meanings in short are functions of positioning in Gestälten. I consider that the items in a typical diviner's basket have come to possess the property of being easily combined in a wide variety of configurations.

These symbolic items are called by Ndembu *tuponya* (singular: *kaponya*). Some are further designated as *ankishi* (singular: *nkishi*). These are figurines representing generalized human beings in various postures. The root *-kishi* is found in the term for ancestor spirit, *mu-kishi*, and in the term for the masks and costumes used at circumcision and funerary rituals, *makishi* (singular *ikishi*). The general sense underlying these various meanings seems to be some mystical power associated with human beings, alive or dead. In this chapter I will discuss three divinatory figurines, or *ankishi*, and seven other *tuponya*, or divinatory objects. Both classes have reference to human activity and purposiveness. Some represent

[2] Junod 1927:571. "The Diviner's basket is a resumé of their whole social order, of all their institutions." Ndembu divination highlights the seamy side of social life, stresses conflict rather than regularity. Only those aspects and institutions of society which consistently form part of the background of action situations of conflict and disturbance are represented by the symbols.

structural features in human life, aspects of the cultural landscape, principles of social organization and social groups and
categories, and dominant customs regulating economic, sexual, and social life. Others represent forces or dynamic entities, such as motives, wishes, desires, and feelings. Not infrequently the same symbol expresses both an established
custom and a set of stereotyped conflicts and forms of competition that have developed around it. It is roughly true that
the human figurines represent universal psychological types
while many of the other objects refer specifically to Ndembu
structure and culture.

The same *tuponya* are used in different stages of a consultation. The meaning of each *kaponya* may change somewhat at
each stage. In this chapter I will present excerpts from texts
about some *tuponya* and analyze the excerpts that exemplify
their use at some stages and not at others. A consultation
consists of several stages. The diviner first invokes the aid of
ancient chiefs and of his *Kayong'u* spirit. Diviners claim that
already they know all about the case, but that their duty is to
make everything clear to their clients. That is why they use
the method of question and answer. The clients are expected
to try to deceive the diviner by giving incorrect answers to
his questions, feigning to agree with him when they really
disagree and vice versa. Since their answers are of the "yea
and nay" variety, and since they must exhibit spontaneous
unanimity before the diviner makes his next point, it is not
too difficult for an experienced diviner to spot discrepancies.
First he ascertains why they have come: on account of death
or because of sickness or misfortune? If they have come
"about death" he finds out whether the deceased was a man
or a woman. Next he discovers whether the death was
caused by sickness or accident, if by sickness, whether it was

long or short, in what part of the body, and whether it was contracted during the day or at night. He finds out what kinds of bark rope were used for the stretcher to carry the corpse to the grave and whether the body was buried wrapped in mats or nailed in a box. An experienced diviner will then ascertain the name given to the deceased at birth. He does this by classifying all Ndembu names under various rubrics (*nyichidi*, "kinds") in a stepwise increasing specificity. Thus he will ask, "Does the name belong to the ground, to trees, to water, to animals, to fish, where is it?" Step by step he proceeds until he identifies the right category. Under the rubric "animals," for example, fall the subcategories *yikwa* (hoof marks) and *mafumbu* (pad marks). *Chifulu* (Wildebeest) is a personal name belonging to the first of these subcategories. Under water (*menji*) fall the names *malowa* (black mud), *mulumbi* (a torrent), *chifu* (a small bush overhanging rivers), and so on. In all this, he is as logical as Linnaeus himself.

Next he finds out the precise relationship in which each of his clients stood to the deceased person. Then he finds out the relationship to the dead and the name of the sorcerer or witch who killed him. Finally, he finds out the exact nature of the enmity between witch and victim, its history and motivation. Often in the past, the order of the last two inquiries was inverted. The consultation ended with the diviner's assistant putting red clay (*mukundu* or *nkung'u*) as a sign of guilt on the head of the sorcerer or witch. Meanwhile the diviner darted away into the bush to avoid being attacked by the latter's kin and friends.

If the person consulted about was sick, the inquiry would take a different course. The main trend of the divination would be to ascertain the relationship and name of the spirit afflicting the patient, the grounds of its punitive action, its mode of manifestation, and the propitiatory cult ritual appropriate to that mode. Often, of course, sickness is attributed to witchcraft. Both for death and sickness the divinatory process consists in bringing to light, first, matters hidden to the diviner, then matters hidden to the clients. Where sickness was concerned, the curative ritual would complete this process of revelation, and, in the case of spirits, also of commemoration. Each pronouncement made by a diviner after questioning is called a *chidimbu*, "a point" or "statement."

Bearing these phases of interrogation in mind, let us now examine the human figurines or *ankishi*. The most important of these is a group of three, clipped together in a band of horn, representing a man, a woman, and a child. These are called either simply *ankishi*, "figurines" or *Akulumpi*, "the Elders." The prefix *A-* here implies that the figures are invested with some animate quality. They are "elders" in several senses. In the first place, this term signifies that they are the most important of the *tuponya*, the focal point of reference in the whole set. In the second phase, they represent a chief and his kin. The male figurine is compared with Mwantiyanvwa, the title of the great Lunda king in the Congo from whose kingdom the Ndembu, like many other central African tribes, are said to have migrated about two hundred and fifty to three hundred years ago. If a piece of red clay (*mukundu, nkung'u,* or *ng'ula*) in a container of mongoose skin, representing enmity or a grudge (*chitela*) came persistently to the top of the set with the Elders when the diviner was seeking to locate a sorcerer, this would mean that the latter belonged to the close kin of a chief, or might even be a chief himself. In the third place, the Elders might represent a headman and his kin, depending upon the question asked. If a thin circlet of iron, called *lukanu* and representing the bracelet worn among Ndembu only by Senior Chief Kanongesha, repeatedly came to the top with the Elders, this would mean that Kanongesha or his close kin played an important role in the situation divined into. If a lump of white clay (*mpemba* or *mpeza*) rose with them when sorcery was being investigated, this would mean that Kanongesha and his kin were innocent. Again, the diviner might himself specify that the Elders stood for a particular matrilineage (*ivumu*), say, that descended from the dead person's own mother's mother. He might ask, "Did the enmity come from this lineage?" If then the Elders came to the top three times associated, say, with red clay and with another *kaponya*, called *Chanzang'ombi*, in the form of a wooden snake with a human face, representing a sorcery familiar called *ilomba*, this would have been proof that a male member of that lineage was the sorcerer and had killed because he had a grudge against his victim.

In other contexts and phases, the Elders represent sorcerers or witches, in a general sense, without particularizing the mode of bewitching. Thus if a random assortment of *tuponya*, consisting of the Elders, red clay, white clay, a *kaponya* called *Chimbu*, which represents a spotted hyena and often stands for women's necrophagous witchcraft and a witch's familiar, and a piece of wood wrapped round with bark string, representing a corpse tied to a bier, and called *Mufu*, "a dead person," rose to the top of the heap, the diviner might say, addressing his *tuponya*: "Why have you appeared here, piece of white clay? Does this mean that there is no witchcraft here at all?" Then he might put the uppermost set under the other *tuponya* and shake his basket again. If all except the white clay appear again on top, and this

combination is then repeated twice more, he would argue as
follows: "The Elders mean that someone has been bewitched—to death, for *Mufu* can mean a dead person [from
ku-fwa, to die]. The red clay means that enmity or revenge-
fulness [*chitela*] led to witchcraft. And *Chimbu* tells me that
the killer was a woman, a necrophagous witch. Now I must
find out where this woman came from. Perhaps from the
mother's side, perhaps from the father's of the victim? Or
perhaps from a stranger residing in the village, or from a
woman married into it [*kudi ambanda amasumbu*]?"

What is interesting in terms of social structure is that the
man, woman, and child, comprising the Elders are not primarily regarded as an elementary family, although they can
be specified as such, but as comembers of a matrilineage—
not necessarily brother, sister, and sister's child, but interlinked in any way the diviner cares to designate. All kinds
of groups, relationships, and differences of status can be expressed by this symbol, doing all kinds of things. Divinatory
symbols are multireferential, and their referents are highly
autonomous and readily detachable from one another. Ritual
symbols proper are much more highly condensed; their
meanings interpenetrate and fuse, giving them greater emotional resonance.

The second figurine we shall consider is called *Chamutang'a*. It represents a man sitting huddled up with chin on
hands and elbows on knees. *Chamutang'a* means an irresolute,
changeable person. One informant told me a little tale to
bring out the meaning of the term. "Once there was a sick
man in a certain village. One of his relatives said to the
others, 'Let's go to another village to divine for our relative
who is very ill.' They answered, 'Oh but we haven't enough
money to pay a diviner.' Some days passed, but the patient

grew worse. So another relative said, 'Please let's go today to divine for our kinsman, for he seems very, very ill.' The others said, 'Why not ask those two men over there to go with you? For our part we haven't enough money, and besides we're tired today for we drank a lot of beer yesterday and anyway we've just come from working in our gardens. We can't possibly go today. We're exhausted.' Time passed, and still the man grew worse. At last some women asked the patient's relatives, 'What about paying the sick man a visit? After all you do live in the same village.' They replied, 'Oh, is he really ill? Yes, I think we'd better have a look at him.' They entered his hut. They found him on the point of death and cried, 'Oh dear, he must be dead. Well, we can't do anything more for him now.' A few days later the patient really was dead. Now when that matter was taken to a diviner, he divined and saw *Chamutang'a* on top, and said, 'This matter was never properly settled by the patient's relatives. That is why he died.' He went on to find out who the actual sorcerer was. The sorcerer was dealt with, but those hesitating people had their share of the guilt even though they weren't sorcerers or witches themselves. In this case *Chamutang'a* stood for prevaricating people [*antu adilabeka*]."

It is obvious that from one point of view diviners use *Chamutang'a* in their professional interest. They state firmly that people should have speedy recourse to a diviner if someone falls ill. Poverty is no excuse. On the other hand, the employment of this symbol asserts certain pervasive social values. People should put the care of their kin before all selfish considerations. Sins of omission in this respect are almost as bad as sins of commission, such as sorcery. Again, people should make up their minds quickly to do their duty; they should not equivocate.

Chamutang'a also means "the man whom no one knows how to take." His reactions are unnatural. Capriciously, informants say, he will at one time give presents to people, at another time he will act mean. Sometimes he will laugh immoderately with others, sometimes he will keep silent, for no apparent reason. No one can guess when he will be angry or when he will fail to show anger. Ndembu like a man whose behavior is predictable.[3] They praise both openness and consistency. They hate to be misled by a false or counterfeit demeanor. A man whom they feel is not genuine may very likely be a sorcerer. The theme that what is hidden is probably dangerous and malevolent is once again exemplified.

Chamutang'a has the further meaning of "a man who is all things to all men." They put it in this way: "Such a man is like beeswax. If it is taken to the fire, it melts; if it is taken into the cold, it becomes hard." In other words, a man of this sort doesn't ring true. He changes his behavior with his company. The "smooth" man too is likely to be a sorcerer, just as much as the awkward customer. Both are men whom, as Ndembu say, "one fails to know."

Diviners sometimes use *Chamutang'a* to withdraw from the awkward situation that may arise if they cannot enlist the unanimous agreement of their clients to their judgments. One client may deny the diviner's imputation that he is a sorcerer, others may support him, others may say that they are not certain, and others may assert that the divination itself was false, perhaps because of the interference of a witch. In such situations, *Chamutang'a* is likely to come uppermost in the basket. The diviner asks *Chamutang'a*, "What have you come here for? Does this mean that my divination is in error?" If it appears two or three times running, the diviner

[3] A high value is therefore attached to the custom-observing man.

"closes down" the divination (*wajika jing'ombu*), demanding from those who have come to consult him a couple of pieces of cloth for his trouble. The diviner tries to salve his reputation by blaming his clients for the failure and tells them that the witch in their midst is trying to confuse his verdict. This is one of the sanctions against lack of unanimity in response to a diviner's queries and statements (*nyikunyi*).

The other figurine normally used by diviners is an effigy of a man in the traditional posture of grief with both hands clasped to his head. It is called *Katwambimbi*, a name derived from *ku-twa*, "to pound," and *mbimbi*, "weeping." It means the "one who inaugurates the mourning" when someone dies. *Kutwa* is used here with reference to the position of the two hands on the head, analogous to hands on a pounding pole. The primary sense is the one who brings news of death to the relatives of the deceased. Here is an example of its use in divination. When a diviner is trying to ascertain the outcome of a serious illness, if *Katwambimbi* does not come uppermost, or as Ndembu say, "keeps on hiding itself," [4] there is a very good chance that the patient will survive. If, again, the Elders are thrown several times on top of the heap with *Katwambimbi* just below them, it is thought that if the patient is treated by a great doctor he might recover, but that it will be touch-and-go. If, on the other hand, *Katwambimbi* recurrently rests on the Elders, it is believed that the patient will die, do what his relatives will. Here the Elders seem to have the meaning of life and *Katwambimbi* of death.

But *Katwambimbi* has another, and if anything, more sinister meaning than this. In the words of one informant, "*Katwambimbi* is a mischief-maker [*kakobukobu*] who carries tales

[4] Ndembu attribute personal qualities to *tuponya*, which are said to think and will.

from one person to another, claiming that each hates and is trying to bewitch the other. If one of them is induced to kill the other by witchcraft or sorcery, *Katwambimbi* is the one who weeps the loudest at the wake, although he is the one who has the greatest guilt." This behavior reminds one irresistibly of the double-dealing of Mord in the Icelandic saga of *Burnt Njal*. *Katwambimbi* differs from *Chamutang'a* in the realm of perfidy in that his hypocrisy is cold-bloodedly deliberate, whereas *Chamutang'a*'s is rather the result of weakness and default. In Ndembu custom a person divined as a *Katwambimbi* receives the same punishment as a sorcerer or witch—in the past, death by burning or ostracism from Ndembu society with confiscation of property, and today banishment from village and neighborhood.

In discussing these figurines, I have found it impossible to avoid mentioning several of the other *tuponya* or divinatory symbols, such as white and red clay, the Hyena (*Chimbu*), and the Dead (*Mufu*). This is because the dominant unit of divination is not the individual symbol but the symbolic configuration (*kudiwung'a hamu*). I shall now examine three other commonly used *tuponya*, first, three or four oblong fragments of calabash strung together called *Yipwepu*. The word means literally "any part of a calabash used for domestic purposes." One of its meanings is a matrilineage (*ivumu*) and by extension, the principle of matriliny. My best informant on ritual explained this to me as follows: "Before a calabash is used for drawing water, it contains many seeds; these seeds are members of the lineage [literally 'womb']. Those little seeds, when they are planted anywhere, will give rise to more and more calabashes. It is the same with men and women who come to a single lineage. Without a lineage (or, better, a reckoning of descent through the mother's side) a kindred would never become so many." Just as the bits of calabash in the *kaponya* are threaded together, Ndembu would hold, so are matrilineal kin united into a group.[5]

Yipwepu also has the general sense of "a collection of articles" (*ku-long'eja*). One such collection is the set of utensils which a woman brings into a marriage with her, at her first marriage usually given to her by her mother and other female uterine kin. These include a calabash, a clay pot, a round basket, a plate, and a cup. She also brings assorted seeds for planting and cassava cuttings. All these together constitute her collection, called colloquially and on the principle of the part for the whole, *Yipwepu*. From this usage, *Yipwepu* in divination has the further meaning of marriage, or even virilocal marriage, and, by extension, of the vicissitudes of marriage. It can, for example, mean a severe marital quarrel and, indeed, divorce, since a woman takes her collection of things with her when she goes off in a huff (*ku-fundumuka*).

By a further extension *Yipwepu* means traveling on visits, for a traveler takes a collection of food with him, a man, in a cloth bundle, a woman, in a long openwork basket (*mutong'a*). Again, it can stand for any happening on such journeys, usually for misfortunes, such as death, sickness, or violent accident.

Yipwepu also represents a collection of duiker horns (*nyiseng'u*) containing medicines. A collection of *yipwepu*, of broken calabashes containing medicine horns, is known as *yikuyung'ulu*. One term for a man with sorcery familiars is a man with *yikuyung'ulu*, that is, with a set of collections.

Finally, *Yipwepu* represents the liquids water and beer, for these are contained in calabashes. It may also represent cas-

[5] The same principle applies in the girls' puberty ritual (*Nkang'a*) where a string of white beads represents the children of one womb.

sava mush, which is meal boiled in water. For example, if red clay rises to the top of the *tuponya* in association with *Yipwepu*, one interpretation might be that enmity between two women arose over the possession of a calabash. It might also mean that a calabash of beer or a plate of mush had been medicated by a sorcerer. Which reading was correct would depend upon the juxtaposition of other *tuponya* as qualificatives.

Another *kaponya* is the large hard stone of a species of tree called *mucha* (*Parinari mobola*). In divination this is called *Mwaka*, which means literally "a season," as in the expressions "dry season" and "rainy season." It also stands for "a long time" and sometimes for "long ago," "in the distant past." *Mucha* fruits take a long time to mature, and the stones take an even longer time to decay in the ground, considered by Ndembu to be a remarkable phenomenon, with so many bird, animal, and insect scavengers about.

In divination, one meaning of *Mwaka* is a long illness. This often has the implication of a long process of bewitching or ensorcelling. The *Ilomba*, the human-faced snake familiar already mentioned is believed gradually to swallow its victim, beginning with the legs and proceeding upward. Only people who have drunk a potion called *nsompu* can see this happening. To others the patient appears to be suffering from a protracted illness.

Another meaning of *Mwaka* is "long delay before consulting a diviner." It can also stand for a protracted sorcery duel. I have heard the following described as a case of *Mwaka*: a man A had a younger brother B. Their mother lived virilocally with her husband (that is, in her husband's village). B went to stay with her and married in her husband's village. His wife had lovers there among her village kin. It is alleged that some of them bewitched B so that he died. A afterward came to the village and, it is said, killed two of its members in revenge by sorcery. He then fled from the village. After many years he returned there to visit his mother. Shortly afterward he died. One of my diviner informants told me that he inquired into this case when A's relatives consulted him. Clearly, he said, A had been bewitched by his mother's affines. But the enmity between the parties, the *chitela*, had a long history. This was first revealed to him by his *kaponya*, *Mwaka*, which came to the top four times in succession (*kawana muchilonda*). Then he searched out the details of the case.

The last *kaponya* I will mention here is a tiny carving in wood of a drum, known as *Ng'oma*, the Drum, or as *mufu wamwaka*, "a dead person from long ago." The appearance of *Ng'oma* means that a spirit and not a witch or sorcerer has caught or afflicted the patient. The term "drum" is frequently used for a performance of ritual, and there are few kinds of ritual which do not possess their own especial drum rhythm. Having ascertained that a curative and propitiatory ritual is required, the diviner finds out which particular curative cult should perform it. He does this by mentioning the names of the cults in order. The diviner says to his *tuponya*, "I am going to play the drum of the *Nkula* ritual, will you please let us know if this is correct?" If the Drum then appears two or three times in succession on top of the Elders, he knows that he is right. The different kinds of ritual are not individually represented in the diviner's basket, although sometimes the *Kayong'u* spirit and the propitiatory ritual named after it are represented by a seed of the *mudidi palm*, from which *ntombi*, palm wine, is made, drunk by adepts at *Kayong'u* rituals. *Kayong'u*, it will be remembered, is the ritual men must undergo if they wish to become great diviners.

On the face of it, divinatory symbols seem to be primarily fashioned under the influence of explicit human purposes. They are used to enable diviners to discover the causes of misfortune and as a result of their inquiries to suggest possible courses of remedial action. The diviner, as I have said, behaves in an astute and rational way, given his axiomatic beliefs in spirits, mystical forces, and witches. He is not above a certain low cunning at times, as we saw with regard to his manipulation of the figurine *Chamutang'a*. Nevertheless, the bases of his craft are rooted in mystical beliefs, and he is himself a believer. Without belief, I feel that he would not possess insight into Ndembu social life, which is governed by values with which he largely identifies himself. I say "identifies" advisedly, since the diviner himself believes that he harbors in his body the *Kayong'u* spirit, which more than any other spirit is believed to detect breach of norm and rebellion against and deviation from Ndembu moral prescriptions. The spirit is using the diviner's sharp wits on behalf of Ndembu society. That is why a diviner must be in a fit moral condition before he undertakes a consultation. For example, he must be sexually continent for some time before and during the period in which he is divining. He practices many food avoidances. He must not harbor malice in his heart against anyone, as this would bias his judgment. He must be a pure and empty vehicle for the *Kayong'u* spirit. For instance, he may not eat two species of burrowing rodents which fill up the entrances to their tunnels. It is believed that if he eats these they will "stop up" his chest and liver, the parts of the body which *Kayong'u* occupies during the act of divination.

The diviner feels that he is not primarily operating on his

own behalf, but on behalf of his society. At divinations, the physiological stimuli provided by drummings and singing, the use of archaic formulae in questions and responses, together with the concentration demanded by his divining technique, take him out of his everyday self and heighten his intuitive awareness. The opening sentence of the nineteenth-century French poet Baudelaire's *Journaux Intimes* might stand as an admirable epigraph for a paper on Ndembu divination: *"De la concentration et de la vaporization du moi, tout est là"* ("Everything is in the concentration and vaporization of the ego"). In concentrating on the special problems posed by his clients the diviner ceases to be his everyday self, swayed by self-interest and ephemeral desires and ambitions. He is a man with a vocation. He measures actual behavior against ideals. As we have seen, several of the symbols he manipulates owe something of their meaning to values attached to openness, honesty, and truthfulness. One of his avowed aims is to make known and intelligible in Ndembu terms what is unknown and unintelligible. Underlying his task is the presumption that unless people bring their grudges and rancors into the open, these will fester and poison the life of a group. Spirits afflict the living with misfortune to bring such hidden conflicts sharply to the attention of members of disturbed groups before it is too late. The diviner can then recommend that a cult association be called in to perform ritual which will not only cure an individual patient, but also heal disturbances in the group. But where animosities have become deep and cankered, they become associated with the lethal power of witchcraft. The malignant individual himself becomes a social canker. At this point it is little use trying to cure the selfish or envious sorcerer or witch. He must be extirpated, rooted out of the group, at whatever cost to those of his kin who love him or depend on him. The diviner may even risk his own life in giving a public decision, for I have been told of diviners who have been speared or shot by the kin of those they have accused of witchcraft. I am satisfied that some diviners are convinced that they are performing a public duty without fear or favor. It is a grave responsibility to be possessed by the *Kayong'u* spirit and become a diviner, for henceforth one is not entirely one's own man. One belongs to society as a whole, not to one or other of its structured subgroups.

The diviner is a ratiocinating individual, but the premises from which he deduces consequences may be nonrational. He does not try to "go behind" his beliefs in supernatural beings and forces. That is why divinatory objects are better classed with symbols than with signs, although they have some of the attributes of signs. He treats as self-evident truths what social anthropologists and depth psychologists would try to reduce to rational terms. These scholars, in their professional role, do not concede that spirits and witches have existence, most of them see these entities as symbols for endopsychic or social drives and forces, which they set themselves the task of discovering.

Although my main concern in the field of Ndembu religion has been with the symbolism of life-crisis ritual and curative ritual, I feel that certain distinctions can be made between divinatory symbolism and the symbolism of these classes of ritual.

In divinatory symbolism, the cognitive aspect is much more pronounced; in the symbolism of life-crisis rituals and rituals of affliction the orectic aspect, that concerned with feelings and desires, is clearly dominant. The diviner, granted his premises—which are shared by his consultants—

is trying to grasp consciously and bring into the open the secret, and even unconscious, motives and aims of human actors in some situation of social disturbance. In the public ritual of the Ndembu, symbols may be said to stimulate emotions. Both kinds of symbols have multiple meanings, but in ritual symbols proper those *significata* [6] which represent emotionally charged phenomena and processes, such as blood, milk, semen, and feces, are fused and condensed with *significata* which stand for aspects of social structure, such as matriliny, marriage, and chieftainship, or virtues such as generosity, piety toward the ancestors, respect for the elders, manly uprightness, and so on. The emotional, mainly physiological, referents may well lend their qualities to the ethical and normative referents, to make what is obligatory desirable. They seem, as Edward Sapir once wrote, to "send roots down into the unconscious," and, I would add, to bring sap up to the conscious. But when one examines the semantic structure of divinatory symbols one finds that the senses possessed by a symbol are not so much "fused" as sharply distinguished. Their semantic structure has "brittle segmentation." I mean by this that a divinatory symbol possesses a series of senses, only one of which is relevant at a time, that is, at an inspection of a configuration of symbols. An important symbol in a ritual of affliction or of life crisis is felt to represent many things at once; all its senses are simultaneously present. Divinatory symbols may therefore be called analytical and ritual symbols synthetical. The former are used to discriminate between items that have become confused and obscure; the latter represent fusions or unifications of many apparently diverse and disparate *significata*. The brittle seg-

[6] *Significatum:* that which is shown or made known as by a sign, words, or a sensorily perceptible vehicle of meaning.

mentation of divinatory symbols may be because the same symbols are used in a series of inquiries, each of which has its own specific aim, for example, to discover a relationship between witch and victim, to find a motive for ensorcelling, to seek out the precise mode of spirit-affliction, and so on. The meaning of each individual symbol is subordinated to the meaning of a configuration of symbols, and each configuration is a means to a clearly defined and conscious end. The system of meanings possessed by the ritual symbol proper derives both from some deep and universal human need or drive and from a universal human norm controlling that drive, which govern its idiom of association and pervade it with orectic quality. A divinatory symbol, on the other hand, is a device to help a conscious individual to arrive at decisions about rightdoing and wrongdoing, to establish innocence or allocate blame in situations of misfortune, and to prescribe well-known remedies. His role falls between that of a judge and that of a ritual expert, but whereas a judge inquires into conscious motives, a diviner often seeks to discover unconscious impulses behind antisocial behavior. To discover these he uses intuition as much as reason. He "feels after" the stresses and sore points in relationships, using his configurations of symbolic objects to help him to concentrate on detecting the difficulties in configurations or real persons and relationships. Both he and they are governed by the axiomatic norms and standards of Ndembu society. Thus the symbols he uses are not mere economical devices for purposes of reference, "signs," but have something of the subliminal quality of ritual symbols proper. With their aid he can say, for instance, that a spirit is "making her granddaughter ill because the people of such-and-such a village are not living well with one another," or that "a man

killed his brother by sorcery because he wanted to be headman." With their aid he can prescribe remedial ritual measures, but he cannot diagnose the empirical causes of social
conflict, any more than of sickness or death. The diviner's
sphere of conscious knowledge and control is limited by su-
praconscious social and moral forces and unconscious bio-
psychical forces. Yet divinatory symbols are as close to signs
as they are to Jung's symbols, pregnant with unknown meaning.

Divination as a Phase in a Social Process

Divination is a phase in a social process that begins with a
person's death, illness, reproductive trouble, or misfortune at
hunting and continues with informal or formal discussion in
the kinship or local group of the victim as to the immediate
steps to be taken, the most important of which is a journey to
consult a diviner. The fourth stage is the actual consultation
or séance, attended by the victim's kin and/or neighbors, followed by remedial action according to the diviner's verdict.
Such action may consist of the destruction or expulsion of a
sorcerer/witch, or of the performance of ritual by cult spe-
cialists to propitiate or exorcise particular manifestations of
ancestor spirits, or of the application of medicines according
to the diviner's prescription by a leech or medicine man.

The consultation is the central phase or episode in the total
process, and it both looks back to the antecedent phases and
forward to the remedial measures. Since death, disease, and
misfortune are usually ascribed to tensions in the local kin
group, expressed as personal grudges charged with the mystical power of sorcery/witchcraft, or as beliefs in the punitive
action of ancestor spirits that intervene in the lives of their
surviving kin, diviners try to elicit from their clients re-

sponses which give them clues to the pattern of current tensions in their groups of origin. Divination therefore becomes a form of social analysis, in the course of which hidden conflicts between persons and factions are brought to light, so that they may be dealt with by traditional and institutionalized procedures. It is in the light of this "cybernetic" function of divination, as a mechanism of social redress, that we must consider its symbolism, the social composition of its consultative sessions, and its procedures of interrogation.

Inevitably, the standards against which social harmony and disharmony are assessed are those of Ndembu culture and not of Western social science. They are those of a society which has only a rudimentary technology, limited empirical skills and knowledge, and consequently a low degree of control over its material environment. It is a society highly vulnerable to natural disasters, such as disease, infant mortality, and intermittent food shortages. Furthermore, its ethical yardsticks are those of a community composed of small residential groups of close kin. Since kinship controls coresidence and confers rights to succeed to office and inherit property, the major problems of Ndembu society bear on the maintenance of good relations between kin and on the reduction of competition and rivalry between them over office, wealth, and prestige. Furthermore, since persons of frequently incompatible temperaments and characters are forced into daily propinquity by kinship norms which enjoin respect and cooperation among them, interpersonal hostilites tend to develop which are forbidden direct expression. Hidden grudges (*yitela*) rankle and grow, as Ndembu are well aware. In the idiom of Ndembu culture these grudges are associated with the mystical power of sorcery/witchcraft.

It is hard to say to what extent, if at all, the specific struc-

ture of Ndembu society—matrilineal, virilocal, gerontocratic, and so on—is responsible for social conflict. From the
evidence of my own observations, from popular saws, folk
tales, and village gossip, from a study of ritual symbolism, I
would rather say that social conflict among the Ndembu has
its source in a human nature they share with us. Ndembu
themselves list jealousy, envy, greed, pride, anger, the desire
to steal, lust, as causes of discord in group life, and these
vices are by no means unfamiliar to us. Nevertheless, these
symptoms of a disordered human nature erupt from a social
body of a specific structure. In their attempts to diminish the
disastrous consequences of these "deadly sins" in social life,
Ndembu bring into operation institutionalized mechanisms
of redress which are ordered toward the maintenance of that
social structure. Divination, as we have seen, is one of those
mechanisms, and in its social form and cultural content we
can observe many idiosyndcratic features of that framework.

In the first place, the diviner clearly knows that he is in-
vestigating within a social context of a particular type. He
first establishes the senior chief's area, then the subchief's,
then the vicinage, and finally the village of the victim. Each
of these political units has its own social characteristics—its
factional divisions, its intervillage rivalries, its dominant personalities, its nucleated and dispersed groups of kindred, all
of them possessing a history of settlement or migration. An
experienced diviner is familiar with the contemporary state
of these political systems from previous consultations and
from the voluminous gossip of wayfarers. Next he ascertains
the relationship between the victim and those who have come
to consult him. He is assisted in this task by his knowledge
of the categories of persons who typically make up the per-
sonnel of a village: the victim's matrilineal kin, his patrilateral

kin, his affines, and unrelated persons. He finds out the victim's relationship to the headman, then focuses his attention on the headman's matrilineage, and discovers into how many sublineages it may be segmented.

By the time he has finished his interrogation, he has a complete picture of the contemporaneous structure of the village and of the position occupied in it by the victim and by those who came to consult him. Since it is common for representatives of each of its important segments, as well as affines of members of its matrilineal nucleus, to visit a diviner in the event of an important man's death, and since these representatives may not make the same responses to key questions, the diviner does not have to look far for indications of the structural cleavages in the village. Diviners are also aware that there is a general association between the kind of misfortune about which he is consulted, the sex of the victim, the composition of the group of clients, and the size and structure of the political or residential unit from which they come. Thus only a few close kin or affines will normally consult a diviner about a woman's barrenness or a hunter's bad luck. But a large party, representative of all segments of a subchiefdom, will come to him when a subchief dies. This association does not always hold true, however, for the death or even illness of a child may sometimes be taken as the occasion to make explicit the dominant cleavage in a large village which is ripe for fission. But diviners have learned by experience—their own and their society's incorporated in divinatory procedure and symbolism—to reduce their social system to a few basic principles and factors and to juggle with these until they arrive at a decision which accords with the views of the majority of their clients at any given consultation.

They are guided in arriving at such a decision, not by an objective analysis of the social structure, but rather by an intuition into what is just and fitting in terms of Ndembu moral values and of an ethical code which would be recognized as valid by all human groups. Just as Africans have been shown to operate in their judicial processes with the universally recognized concept of the "reasonable man," [7] or "man of sense," so do they operate in their divinatory processes with the universally recognized concept of the "good man" or "moral man," *muntu wamuwahi*. This is the man who bears no grudges, who is without jealousy, envy, pride, anger, covetousness, lust, greed, and who honors his kinship obligations. Such a man is open, he has "a white liver," he has nothing to conceal from anyone, he does not curse his fellows, he respects and remembers his ancestors. The diviner looks for sorcerers and witches among those who do not measure up to this standard of morality. Indeed, he looks for them among the positive transgressors, among those whom his clients admit to be wrongdoers or "slippery customers." In the cases of illness, infertility, and bad luck at hunting, he applies the same measure of the moral man to individuals, although he also applies the yardstick of the moral group, which lives in mutual amity and collectively reveres its ancestors and respects its political authorities. But here it would seem he is on the lookout not so much for "mortal sins" as for "venial sins," for grudges that have not grown murderous, for offences that may yet be forgiven, for quarrels that have not yet split up a group.

A sinner (*mukwanshidi*) is defined as "one who has ill feeling for other people [*mukwanshidi watiyang'a kutama nawak-*

---

[7] Gluckman (1955:126) argues that the Lozi concept of the "upright man" embraces both "sense" and "uprightness."

wawu antu]." *Ku-tama*, "to be bad, evil, unpleasant, ugly," is linked with the symbolism of blackness, darkness, death, sterility, and night in Ndembu ritual. It is the opposite of *ku-waha*, "to be good, morally upright, pleasant, beautiful." It is also linked with witchcraft/sorcery, theft, adulterous lust, and murder. *Ku-tama* is associated with "secret things" (*yis-wamu*), with the concealment of thoughts or possessions from others. What is good, for Ndembu, is the open, the public, the unconcealed, the sincere. A man is said to be good when he performs his duties from "the liver," not from calculated policy, concealing malice beneath outward politeness. A man is bad when there is a marked inconsistency or disparity between his public behavior and his private thoughts and feelings. The former is outwardly correct, but it conceals malice and envy. Thus the hypocrite is the real sinner, "the whited sepulchre." We find in the diviner's basket a representation of the weeping hypocrite (*Katwambimbi*) and several references to the duplicity of bad people, the witches and sorcerers.

Thus the diviner has to take into account both the specific structure of Ndembu society and a set of moral values and norms. Both these categories of referents are represented in the symbolism of divination. The symbols are mnemonics, shorthands, cyphers; and each one refers to a whole series of stereotyped ways of thinking about and evaluating Ndembu society and culture. They serve as reminders to the diviner of certain general rubrics of Ndembu culture, within which he can classify the specific instance of behavior that he is considering. Moreover, they have to be of such a nature as to lend themselves to configurational analysis.

The constellation of symbols rather than the individual symbol forms the typical unit of interpretation. A symbol may appear as a substantive, and in this role it may possess, say, half a dozen basic senses. Those symbols which are spatially juxtaposed with it will then become qualificatives or modifiers of one of those basic senses. The diviner arrives at this basic sense principally by means of his interrogation of clients and attenders at the divinatory séance. He notes the kind and intensity of their reactions, positive and negative, to his questions and statements, and from these clues makes a guess, or "formulates a hypothesis" about the circumstance he is considering: the name of the deceased, the relationship between the deceased and the clients, the kind of grudge cherished by a kinsman against the deceased, and so on. Once he has established the basic sense of the substantival symbol he can allocate senses to the modifiers. Here the vagueness and flexibility of the referent series of each symbol leave him free to make a detailed interpretation of the symbol configuration which corresponds to the diagnosis he is making of the state of relationships between his clients and the deceased and between the living kin concerned in the matter. Once he has established a *chidimbu*, a definite point of divination, and obtained agreement on its veracity or likelihood, he has a point of departure for further inquiry, something firm to go on. He may then deduce logical consequences from the *chidimbu*, regarded as a set of premises. Furthermore, he has established a certain psychological ascendency over his audience, "softened them up," so that they tend to become less guarded in their replies, for with growing credulity in his divinatory powers they become more eager to give him the hard data he requires. I believe that this is one of the reasons why a basket diviner tries to find the name of the deceased quite early in the séance. Diviners have learned that the vast majority of Ndembu names can be classified under relatively few main heads—water, hoofed animals, chieftainship, and so on, and after the manner of the English party game "Twenty Questions," they can quickly proceed from the general to the particular, from the category to the subcategory to the instance (see below, pages 276–282). In a society not specially remarkable for its interest in abstract thinking, the diviner's ability to do this must appear little short of miraculous or superhuman. When the diviner names the deceased, therefore, he has already reduced the skepticism and increased the credulity of his audience to such a pitch that he can elicit key information without much difficulty. In other words, the logician is felt to be a magician.

It may be said in conclusion that the diviner occupies a central position with reference to several fields of social and cultural relationships. He acts as a mechanism of redress and social adjustment in the field of local descent groups, since he locates areas and points of tension in their contemporary structures. Furthermore, he exonerates or accuses individuals in those groups in terms of a system of moral norms. Since he operates in emotionally charged situations such norms are restated in a striking and memorable fashion. Thus he may be said to play a vital role in upholding tribal morality. Moral law is most vividly made known through its breach. Finally, the diviner's role is pivotal to the system of rituals of affliction and antiwitchcraft/sorcery rituals, since he decides what kind of ritual should be performed in a given instance, when it should be performed, and sometimes who should perform it. From the Ndembu point of view, the diviner is a man who redresses breaches in the social structure, enunciates the moral law, detects those who secretly and malevolently transgress it, and prescribes remedial action both on the social-structural and cultural levels in the form of redressive ritual. Since diviners are consulted on many occasions, it is clear that their role as upholders of tribal morality [8] and rectifiers of disturbed social relationships—both structural and contingent—is vital in a society without centralized political institutions.

---

[8] Divination as a system of thought exhibits the "paranoid style" (see above, Introduction), but diviners regard themselves as acting in the public interest—compare politics and politicians in Western society!

CHAPTER 5

Some Kinds and Methods of Ndembu Divination

During my field work among the Ndembu of Mwinilunga District in Northern Rhodesia (now Zambia) from 1950 to 1954, I interrogated a number of diviners on their profession. Death, sudden or protracted illness, reproductive disorders, and persistent misfortune at hunting are all thought by Ndembu to be due to supernatural causes, such as witchcraft or the action of ancestor spirits. It is the task of the diviner to locate the precise supernatural cause and where possible to prescribe remedial action. There are many kinds of divination, and all involve the use of material apparatus. In the past divination into death was a public occasion, often taking place at the village of a subchief or important village headman. But the European administration introduced legislation against witchcraft and witch-finding (White, 1947:10). Divination into the cause of death was consequently, at the time of my field work, done either in secret or across the border of Portuguese Angola. I was never able to attend such a public séance, although I had a series of private interviews with an Angolan Ndembu diviner who visited Ikeleng'e Area in 1952. This man showed me how he used his apparatus. Since I have not actually observed divination into death in its natural setting I have presented full accounts of my interviews with diviners and other ritual experts. To compensate for the lack of direct observation, the Ndembu here tell in their own words how they think and feel about the subject matter of divination, the mystical consequences of transgressing the moral order.

I had five informants, of whom three had practiced or were practicing divination at the time of my inquiry. The other two were a subchief and my cook, who might be described as "an intelligent layman." In addition I picked up pieces of information from a variety of persons in the form of unsolicited comments and conversations overheard in the men's shelter in villages. My best informant was Muchona. I have published elsewhere a character sketch and short biography of this ritual specialist (Turner, 1967:131–150). His account of divination is my main source here, with my comments on it in the light of other informants' statements and of my own observations of Ndembu life and ritual. This account is the product of a series of interviews spread out over several weeks. I was most competently assisted in these sessions by Windson Kashinakaji, a teacher at the Nswanakudya Mission Out-School. He elucidated for me some of the technical terms and idiomatic phrases of divination that peppered Mushona's narrative.

Basket Divination

The kind of divination now regarded as most accurate and least liable to fraudulent misuse by Ndembu is called *ng'ombu yakusekula*. *Ng'ombu* is a generic term comprehending not only the art and practice of divination, but also the material apparatus employed. *Yakusekula* means literally "of shaking up" and refers to the characteristic practice of tossing up a heap of symbolic objects in a flat, round winnowing basket. The diviner ostensibly makes his diagnosis on the basis of examining the configuration of objects on top of the resulting pile.

This kind of divination, which I shall call basket divination, is no mere manipulative technique, and it requires more than a knowledge of the meaning of the symbolic objects. A basket diviner must have first undergone a ritual known as *Kayong'u*. Only after "passing through" (*ku-hitilamu*) *Kayong'u* may a man become an apprentice diviner (*mpumba*). *Kayong'u* belongs to that class of Ndembu rituals which I have called rituals of affliction (Turner, 1957:292–303).

These are performed to propitiate or exorcise ancestor spirits which are believed to bring illness or misfortune. The victims are their living kin. Reasons for afflicting vary, but it is commonly alleged that the victim has neglected to make offerings to the spirit or has forgotten the spirit in his heart. Affliction is a sharp rebuke for such negligence. In almost every case I have observed of illness treated by ritual of affliction there seems to have been an additional factor of social disturbance. The victim is afflicted as a representative of a disturbed social group (a village or a matrilineage), even if he or she is not held to be personally in the wrong. I have heard it suggested that such affliction is good because the ritual to remove it brings to light and so dispels the quarrels and grudges in the social group. If these go on for long, it is said, people may resort to sorcery or witchcraft and start killing one another. Thus a ritual of affliction is prophylactic against witchcraft.

There are several modes of affliction. Women, for example, are afflicted with a number of well-defined reproductive troubles, each kind corresponding to a mode of affliction. Thus an ancestress who has "come out in *Nkula*" (as Ndembu say) afflicts her living kinswoman (nearly always in the matrilineal line) with menstrual disorders. Another, coming "in *Isoma*" causes miscarriages. Hunters are afflicted with bad luck in the chase by ancestors manifesting in various modes. For example, *Mukala* is a mischievous manifestation that drives game away before the hunter can take proper aim.

To each mode of manifestation (*Nkula, Isoma, Mukala, Kayong'u*) there corresponds a curative cult bearing the same name. Its members are recruited from among its former patients. Cult members are "doctors" insofar as they are regarded as herbalists or medicine men, and "adepts" with regard to their role as repositories of a cult's secret knowledge (*mpang'u*). Similarly, those treated are "patients" or "candidates"—the same term *ayeji* is used in both senses. Cult associations cut across kinship and local groups. Their rituals are performed contingently, as occasion arises. The diviner specifies just what cult's ritual should be performed for a sick or unlucky person. He is the diagnostician; the cult association is the team of therapists. Theoretically the same man may be both diviner and doctor, but this is extremely rare, and I have never heard of an actual instance of it.

Kayong'u, then, is a ritual of affliction, performed to propitiate an ancestor spirit by a cult association of *Kayong'u* adepts. As in other rituals of this type the spirit's victim is suffering from illness of a particular kind—what kind we shall find out presently. I shall give Muchona's account of the *Kayong'u* rites that made him a diviner, just as he told it to me, but with interpolated comments to clarify or expand the argument.

Muchona's account

The *Kayong'u* ritual

"*Kayong'u* comes from the Chokwe or Lwena peoples. There are two kinds [*nyichidi*]: one for divination [*nakuhong'a*]; one for sickness [*yikatu*]. It is the diviner who decides which kind. The spirit-manifestation of *Kayong'u* [*ihamba da-Kayong'u*] can come from either the father's or the mother's side. My own *Kayong'u* comes from three spirits, from two mothers' brothers and from my father. A woman can have a *Kayong'u* spirit, but she cannot become a diviner herself. But she can give the spirit to her brother."

Comments. Ndembu seldom use the term "*ihamba*" generically to mean "spirit-manifestation." This is a Luvale usage and would agree with Muchona's remarks about the origin of this cult. Ndembu normally mean by *ihamba:* (1) an upper front incisor of a deceased hunter which is inherited by a hunter kinsman and kept in a special pouch as a sort of talisman; (2) a particular manifestation of a hunter spirit which in the form of such a tooth embeds itself under the skin of a living relative and causes sharp pains in his or her body; (3) a curative cult of hunters which propitiates (2).

Ndembu frequently employ the term *mukishi* (plural *akishi*) for any manifestation of the ancestor spirits.

Muchona's account. "When I became sick, some people said, 'Muchona is going to die,' some said, 'soon,' others 'tomorrow.' Some said, 'He has been shot by a *wuta wawufuku.*' "

Comments. A *wuta wawufuku* or night-gun is a miniature muzzle-loading gun, carved from a human tibia, which is believed to be used by (male) sorcerers or by the familiars (*tuyebela* and *tuhwehwu*) of (female) witches. It is loaded,

Ndembu say, with pellets of decomposing flesh, bits of human bone, and graveyard soil, and then it is discharged at the victim in the dead of night through a hole in the wall of his hut.

Muchona's account. "They said, 'You must find a goat and a fowl for the *Kaneng'a* drum' [*Kaneng'a* is a kind of ritual performed to cure a person of illness caused by sorcery/witchcraft]. Some people went to another [*sic*] diviner who said that 'Muchona has *Kayong'u.*' The first group were telling lies, because what I felt in my body was not like that [the sickness] of a night-gun. I agreed with those who said, '*Kayong'u,*' for I had first dreamed of my [deceased] mother's full brother [who had come] with his *ng'ombu yakatuwa* (see pp. 326–328) apparatus of moving-calabash divination. My dead uncle told me to 'tremble' [*ku-zakuka*—to undergo *Kayong'u*]. Before that he told me to move the *ng'ombu yamwishi*, the divinatory pounding pole (see pp. 322–324). I 'trembled' in my sleep. My uncle told me, 'That is your *ng'ombu*' [*Kayong'u* divination]. He then said, 'There is a *kakuyu* [a spring hare] for you.' Then I woke up. I began to reason with myself why I should have had such a dream, and not long after dawn I went to inspect my traps. In the first one I found a *kakuyu.* I went on to my other snares [*yidiya*] and discovered many rodents [*amfwa*] in them. I said: 'This accords with my dream.' So I took them home. That is how my *Kayong'u* began. When I went home, I spent a month in good health. Then began a pain in my back which went on for several weeks. Some people thought I would die, as I said. I have diviners on both my father's and mother's sides. I also dreamed of my dead father. My father had a pounding pole [*mwishi*]; he gave it to me and said, 'Divine with it yourself, I have given it to you.' Then I began to tremble. But this was before I dreamed of my mother's brother. At that time I was living in the village of my father's [matrilineal] kin.

"At that time, too, I dreamt of my mother. But she was so weak that the diviner did not recognize her later.

"*Kayong'u* begins with a heavy sickness in the body. A person nearly dies of it—I myself nearly died. My relatives went to a diviner [*mukwakuhong'a*] who divined for me. I had divided pennies among them to pay for the divination. They were told that I was suffering from the sickness of *Kayong'u* [Muchona here employed both the following phrases: *mukishi waKayong'u*, 'the ancestor spirit of *Kayong'u*,' and *yikatu yaKayong'u*, 'the physical illness of *Kayong'u*,' to describe his condition]. Those *Tuyong'u* [plural of *Kayong'u*] were three. My relatives brought me *mpeza* [powdered white clay], they asked me whether I wanted to have the *ku-lembeka* drum played or the *ku-tumbuka* drum. I said, 'No, let me have both drums on the same day, not separately.'"

Comments. Ndembu used the term "drum" (*ng'oma*) as a shorthand both for "a performance of ritual" and "a kind of ritual"—as in *ng'oma yaKayong'u*. Most rituals of affliction have three main phases: (1) *Ku-lembeka* or *ilembi*, said to be derived from *ku-lemba*, "to be sorry or penitent," a performance of ritual, followed by (2) a period of partial seclusion from secular life, often with interdictions on certain kinds of food, and concluded by (3) *ku-tumbuka*, a complex and elaborate performance with drumming, singing, and dancing as accompaniment.

Muchona's account. "Next I gave my relatives some money to buy a cock and a he-goat. They bought them and brought them to my place. Then I sent my relatives to bring my

'Mother of Huntsmanship' [*Mama daWuyang'a*], Sanyiwangu Chingangu [1] [to perform *Kayong'u*]. All this was in Senior Chief Kanongesha Sakayoli's Area in Angola. *Chingangu* is a Lwena word for a diviner, but this man was a Lunda. I was just over thirty years old at this time. It is the same *Kayong'u* treatment for the cure of sickness as to make a diviner. It depends on the patient whether he will go on and become a diviner."

Comments. It may seem a little odd to refer to a man as a "mother," but this term is commonly employed among the matrilineal southern Lunda with reference to a superior who is at the same time a benefactor—and often an instructor in some branch of tribal lore. Thus an apprentice circumciser refers to his master as *Mama danfunda*, "Mother of the lodge medicine" and will be called reciprocally *Mwana wanfunda*, "Child of the lodge medicine." A generous chief will sometimes be eulogistically described or addressed as *Mama yetu*, "our Mother."

Muchona establishes an interesting connection between *Kayong'u* and the set of hunters' cult rituals. [2] For *Mama da-Wuyang'a* is the title applied not only to a great hunter who instructs apprentice hunters in both the technical and ritual aspects of huntsmanship, but also to the senior adept or practitioner at any performance of hunting ritual or of the *Ihamba* ritual—which is included in the hunting-cult complex. An apprentice hunter is known as *Mwana waWuyang'a*, "Child of Huntsmanship."

I asked Muchona whether Sanyiwangu Chingangu was his

---

[1] Sanyiwangu was Muchona's father's wife's brother, a brother of Muchona's mother's cowife.

[2] White (1947:9) has compared the initiation of a diviner to the initiation of hunters.

personal instructor in hunting or whether *Mama daWuyang'a* was the title of the senior officiant in *Kayong'u*. He then told me that *Kayong'u* was a spirit of *Wuyang'a* or *Wubinda*. *Wuyang'a* is the cult of hunters who use firearms, *Wubinda* is the ancient cult of hunters who use bows and arrows, spears, or traps. "*Kayong'u*," he went on, "also prevents or hides [*waswekang'a*] huntsmanship [*Wubinda*]." In other words, the *Kayong'u* spirit, in addition to causing ill health, could cause bad luck at hunting. "*Kayong'u* is a very strong spirit; he knows everything. Because he is strong, he gives power to divine." Hence *Mama daWuyang'a* was the senior officiant's title, and *Kayong'u* was a ritual associated with the hunters' cult.

It is likely that Ndembu see an analogy between hunting, the tracking down of elusive animals, and divination, the tracking down of witches and spirits, but Muchona did not state the connection in those terms.[3]

Muchona's account. "Many calabashes of beer were brewed. When Sanyiwangu Chingangu arrived he told my relatives to bring firewood. They stacked it up near the doorway of my hut about an hour before sunset. Sanyiwangu went with his wife *Nyamuneng'a* [a title, not a personal name] and the other doctors to collect medicines, while I stayed in the village. Before they went they circled my hut singing: '*Chaliya ng'ombu chalumbulula.*' [What a person with divination eats explains itself], and also '*Kalumbweye mweza kutambula ndumba kuwulu.*' [Kalumbu (a woman's name) will be likely to take a witchcraft familiar to (her) place of marriage.] I hid myself in my hut while they were singing."

Comments. The first song, Muchona explained, refers to a

---

[3] See his comments on duiker-horn divination on page 336, below, where the divining apparatus is compared to a leopard following the scent.

diviner's food avoidances, which we will discuss below (pages 285 and 288). These are of so obvious a nature that they give him away when he eats with others.

The second song deals with what Ndembu believe to be a common cause of death, a wife's witchcraft. Some women are believed to have familiars, known as *andumba, tuyebela,* or *tushipa,* which take varying forms, such as undersized men with inverted feet, jackals, hyenas, owls, or rats. These are inherited matrilineally, in the sense that the familiars of a dead witch (*muloji wamumbanda*) are said to "run around the villages" until they find one of her matrilineal kinswomen, to whom they attach themselves. They compel their "owner" (*mweni*) to become a witch, to permit them to kill her kin, and not infrequently, it is thought, her husband, and to take part with them in necrophagous feasts on the bodies of their victims.

The song also has reference to the diviner's role as a witch-detector.

Muchona's account. "The doctors collected medicines in the bush. They returned to the village. They brought with them a sapling of the *muyombu* tree [*Kirkia acuminata*], which in *Kayong'u* is called *muneng'a.* They also had *nsompu* [pounded-leaf medicine] with them. The *muneng'a* sapling was decorated with lines [*nyifunda*] of white clay and of red clay [*mukundu*]. In *Kayong'u* red clay is called *nkung'u.* This took place at about sunset."

Comments. Muneng'a is said to be derived from *ku-neng'a,* "to be sad." Quick-set saplings of the *muyombu* tree, which has vigorous vegetative propagation, are planted in most Ndembu villages as shrines to the ancestor spirits. On the occasion of such a planting a village member will usually inherit the name of a deceased matrilineal village relative of the same sex. It is believed that this ancestor spirit has been visiting sickness or misfortune on his or her relative as a punishment for negligence or forgetfulness. Sociologically, the inheritance of a name often marks the social incorporation of an individual into the local descent group. Ndembu have high personal mobility, and a person is reckoned to have definitively affiliated himself to a local descent group after a year or two's continuous residence.

The *muyombu* tree has a dazzling white wood; whiteness represented also by white clay, white beads, white cloth, white beer (maize and bulrush-millet beer) stands, among a host of other things, for harmony and accord between the ancestors and the living. It also secretes a clear gum, described by Ndembu as tears (*madyilu*) and representing, they say, mourning for the dead.[4]

The use of this tree as a dominant or focal symbol in *Kayong'u* seems to emphasize the theme of ritual death. There is a close affinity with the use of the *muyombu* tree at the boys' circumcision ritual (*Mukanda*). Immediately after the novices have been circumcised they are passed over a *muyombu* branch. This represents their ritual death from childhood and dependence on their mothers.

Red clay is employed as decoration in many Ndembu rituals. It always has the generic sense of blood (*mashi*), but may be contextually specified to mean what Ndembu themselves describe as many kinds (*nyichidi*) of blood: blood of circumcision novices (*mashi awanyadi*); blood of animals (*mashi atunyama*—in hunters' cults); maternal blood (*mashi amama*) revealed when a woman gives birth; and the blood of slain men (*mashi awubanji*). *Kayong'u*, as we shall see, involves the bloody killing of animals. The juxtaposition of white and red

[4] See the derivation of *muneng'a* from *ku-neng'a*, see above.

markings on the *muneng'a* also has reference to the use of these colors in all forms of divination to indicate, respectively, innocence (*ku-ying'a*) and guilt (*ku-luwa*) of the sin (*nshidi*) of witchcraft/sorcery. Witchcraft is red, Ndembu say, because witches eat the red meat of their victims. They speak in this connection of the blood of witchcraft (*mashi awuloji*).

The employment of special terms for common things, such as *muneng'a* for *muyombu*, and *nkung'u* for *mukundu*, is fairly typical of African cult ritual and ritual of transition. The idea behind it perhaps is to impress upon the participants that these common things are not at all what they seem to be but possess a hidden meaning and hence a profound ritual efficacy when they are used in the context of the cult.

Muchona's account. "When the doctors returned they put the medicines by the firewood, then went round my hut, in which I was again hidden. This means that the spirit must hide in the hut with the patient. Then they said: '*Putu walwa, Mung'ong'i he-e,*' [To begin with, beer—*Mung'ong'i* ritual]."

Comments. "To go round" (*ku-nyeng'umuka* or *ku-jing'umuka*) means in Ndembu ritual "to make sacred" or "to taboo" (*ku-jilisha*). *Putu* is an ideophone, connected with *ku-putuka*, "to commence." *Mung'ong'i* is the name of a funerary association that possesses a system of cult ritual and initiates novices into its ranks at the funerals of its members. Here I take the reference to this funerary cult as a further exemplification of the theme that the patient is dying a ritual death.

Muchona's account. "At dark they brought in drums. The 'Mother of Huntsmanship' cut the vegetable medicines into pieces and put them in one big ritual pot [*izawu*]. They lit the fire. Then Sanyiwangu brought black alluvial soil [*malo-*

wa] [5] and plastered it around the base of the *muneng'a* sapling. *Malowa* in this case stands for peacefulness, on account of its coldness. *Muneng'a* stands for the [*Kayong'u*] spirit. This is to make the spirit peaceful [*ku-fomona mukishi*]. Then they covered *muneng'a* with a mat. At dark Sanyiwangu took medicine leaves [*nsompu*] in his hand and people brought him a meal mortar [*iyanda*] and its pounding pole, putting them near the fire. *Nyamuneng'a* [this title means the mother of the *muneng'a*] pounded the medicines. All the doctors stood around to witness it. To stand is to be a witness [*chinsahu*].

"Sanyiwangu told me to take off all my clothes in my hut except my waist-cloth [*mukotola*], drawn up between my legs [*ku-ta mukotola*]. I had a belt [*muya*] around my waist. Then he told me to sit on a stool near the fire. He began to wash my whole body with water and *nsompu* medicine. The *nsompu* was put on a plate and the plate was laid over the mouth of the meal mortar. For the *Kayong'u* spirit does not like dirty things, but likes a clean plate. The mortar would have been too dirty. Then Sanyiwangu took pounded medicines from the plate and put them in my mouth. I spat some medicine first to the right, then to the left. This was to keep away the *ayikodjikodji*, the spirits of troublemakers, witches, and barren people. Then I drank two or three times. Now some medicine was put on my head, on my chest, on my arms, and then on the rest of my body. Next the big doctor [Sanyiwangu] gave me his *musambu* [6] and lifted me as I held onto it.

[5] Usually collected from the bed of a stream.

[6] Described to me by Windson Kashinakaji as "a musical instrument made from *tubobu*, soft branches [gourds ?] which grow in the streamside forest [*itu*]. It is a sort of rattle with seeds of the *mundoyi* tree inside it."

"Now they played the drums and sang songs like those I mentioned before. I was taken from the stool and put on a mat on the ground. I found I was thrown on the mat by violent quivering [ku-zakuka]. I jerked about very much. I did not know how I was doing it. It was on account of the power [ng'ovu] of Kayong'u which attacked me suddenly there. I had one bout of trembling, then another, but the third time I was given a katema, which is another name [used in Kayong'u] for mpashi, a cowry shell. Katema is really two shells joined together on a string. The feathers of a red cock are tied to both cowries. The string was fastened round my neck."

Comments. Muchona told me how he felt during his trembling fits:

Neyi nidinakuzakuka natiyang'a mumuchima luku neyi anamweti namuhinyi.

(When I am trembling I feel in the liver lightning-struck as if beaten by a hoe handle.)

A person in this state "can only say 'hoyi' " (an ideophone for difficult or labored breathing). "His ears are completely blocked [mumatu majikang'a pati]. His eyes and his whole body are like those of a man who has drunk beer. He slips onto the ground in an epileptic fit [wadimbukang'a hamaseki nakukonya]."

I once observed a curative Kayong'u performed at Sandeji Village in Ikeleng'e Area. There the patient could not be induced to tremble, and his head was covered with a blanket, and he was made to inhale the vapor from a boiling pot of leaf medicine. I asked Muchona why this was done. He replied that it was "to introduce Kayong'u into the body of a person who did not have Kayong'u."

I inquired why a person should want "to have Kayong'u."

Muchona replied: "A person who has *Kayong'u* is safe from witchcraft. *Kayong'u* is a terrible [*wafwana*] spirit. If someone tried to bewitch me, *Kayong'u* would kill that witch. My three *Tuyong'u* remain in my body to help me. They want me to give them food and to remember them. All spirits want to be remembered." He then went on to discuss the spirits of evildoers, the *ayikodjikodji*: "A person who gives others food and a welcome will not become a *chikodjikodji*. Now if I became a *Kayong'u* after death I would give my relatives animals to eat. But a *chikodjikodji* could also become a *Kayong'u*, a very powerful one that could kill someone. Thus Mashata [a headman who had died with the reputation of sorcery] would become a terrible *chikodjikodji*. That is why I spat to the right and to the left—to keep away the *ayikodjikodji*. To spit straight forward is for the beloved spirit, for the one who helped others during his life. Sometimes I drink medicine in his memory. To spit to the right and left means that one does not love the dead but will nevertheless give them some medicine."

Muchona's account. "Then the doctors brought a calabash of beer and everyone drank from it. Sanyiwangu said, 'Now I am going to give him [Muchona] *masaku* medicine. *Masaku* are the skins of small animals, such as the bush baby [*katontu*], mongoose [*kambunji*], or genet cat [*nshimba*]. The skin of the giant rat [*chituba*] and the shell of the tortoise [*mbachi*] are also called *masaku* [singular *isaku*]. Sanyiwangu had a *kambunji* skin and a tortoise-shell *isaku* container. He took some powdered medicine [*yitumbu yakutwa* or *luseng'a*] and gave me some to eat. Then he put his fingers in the *kambunji* skin which contained powdered red clay and marked me on the outside of each eye with one hand. Then he put his fingers in the tortoise-shell and took some medicine mixed with oil [*imonu*] and marked my liver [*muchima*], just above the navel, with it. Also my forehead. At that time I did not know what medicines he used."

Comments. In speaking to Muchona in another connection—about hunting rituals—I learned that "to bring a doctor to perform *Kayong'u* they tie red beads round an arrow and take it to him." He then spoke of the red clay used in this ritual and why it was called *nkung'u* both in *Kayong'u* and in divination. "The name is changed because when a diviner was once divining he found that a witch was near him. He collected some powdered red clay in his hand and sang a song about giving *nkung'u* to a murderer [*mbanji*] or a witch, to deceive the listening witch. Later the same red clay is put on the witch's head by the diviner as a sign of guilt." He went on to discuss the relationship between the *Kayong'u* manifestation of an ancestor spirit and the red blood symbolism. "The *Kayong'u* spirit [*ihamba daKayong'u*] is regarded as a murderer. He is 'an elder of murder' [*mukulumpi wawubanji*]. A *Kayong'u* may cause a person to live in bad ways, to be noisy and quarrelsome. The spirit of a murderer comes through [*wedikila*] in [the manifestation of] *Kayong'u*. I received one of my *Tuyong'u* from my father; I am not yet free from it." He said that a *Kayong'u* could "help a diviner strongly and kill his enemies," but that if it was not propitiated it could do much harm to those it "caught."

Muchona's account. "Now the drums were played again. I began to tremble again; so did Sanyiwangu, the big doctor. We trembled very much. Then Sanyiwangu fetched the *musambu* rattle and rapped it on my head and over his liver [*muchima*] to prevent my falling into the fire in an extremity of shaking.

"When it was nearly dawn Sanyiwangu fetched a red cock

and held it out extended from head to feet. Then I myself came quickly and bit its neck through to sever the head from the body. I was still trembling. Its blood spouted out and I beat the blood-stained head on my heart to quieten [*ku-wundisha*] it. Then Sanyiwangu said: 'Cut off the goat's head too.' Then the assistant doctors severed the goat's neck. Blood poured on the ground. I came and supped some of the blood. The cock's head was now drawn over the head of the *muneng'a* sapling. It was now just after dawn. My wife was given the cock to cook for me. The cock was cut up and put into a clay pot specially chosen for the performance, then my wife cooked it. Sanyiwangu came with a cup to collect some blood from the goat."

Comments. I asked Muchona why a cock and a goat were used in this ritual. He replied: "The cock represents the awakening of people; when it is nearly dawn the cock begins to crow and people are awakened by its crowing. The goat represents awakening also. At dawn the billy-goat begins to bleat when it is running after she-goats, and people are awakened by its sound."

He then went on to compare these kinds of awakening with the *Kayong'u* spirit. "*Kayong'u* awakens any person it has caught by a hoarse breathing sound [*ku-tomena*, which also means to belch] which is made by people who have it." The Angolan diviner I met in Ikeleng'e Area used to punctuate his conversation with this deep, wheezing, asthmatic sound.

Muchona went on to say, "It is the power of *Kayong'u* which is responsible for the patient's killing a cock with his teeth. *Kayong'u* makes a person a little mad [*ku-zaluka chanti*]. He feels as though he were drunk or epileptic. *Kayong'u* makes you sick in your whole body, but especially in your chest. It makes it hard to breathe. In the lungs you feel a pricking of needles. In the chest you feel as if you have been pumped up with a bicycle pump. But after the performance I felt much better. I could breathe easily."

Muchona's account. "Sanyiwangu now carried a hoe and the goat's blood in a cup and went with the other doctors along a path from the village. The hearts of the goat and the cock were carried in that cup. Then they went to 'the tree of greeting' [*ishikenu*] for *Kayong'u,* which was a *kapwipu* tree [*Swartzia madagascariensis*]. They found the *kapwipu* like this: when they came to the place where two paths separated, the *makenu,* the doctors went straight on, following neither path, to look for a *kapwipu* tree. Near the *kapwipu* tree Sanyiwangu told them to make a mound of earth in the shape of a crocodile [*ng'andu*] with legs and a tail. Soon he stood ready with a bangle [*ikayi*], a knife [*mpoku*], and a string of beads [*wusang'a*]. He then buried one of these objects at the head and another at the tail of the 'cocodile.' Next he pricked the cock's heart with the sharp end of a needle and the goat's heart with the point of a razor [*ntewula*]. He then hid these hearts somewhere. He also hid his [stock of] red clay [*nkung'u*].

"Now they brought drums along. Only doctors were allowed to attend. They began to play the drums. I was called to sit on the 'crocodile's' neck facing the head. Sanyiwangu asked me, 'What have you come here for?' I replied, 'I am sick.' 'How are you sick?' 'It is *Kayong'u* who has already killed me.' 'How did *Kayong'u* kill you?' 'I do not sleep well. I have three *Tuyong'u* just now.' 'You must let *Kayong'u* help you now.' 'Yes, *Kayong'u* can help me.'

"Sanyiwangu said, 'Will you play the *kutamba* drum [rhythm] for him?' This is the special drum of *Mung'ong'i* [the funerary association mentioned above]. Sanyiwangu asked me, 'Will you let me know your *ankung'u* of witchcraft?' [The plural of *nkung'u* is used here, seemingly to mean not only red clay but also abilities to divine guilt.] I then began to dance and went on dancing until I found the place where the red clay was hidden. My *ihamba* told me where it was, my *ihamba* of *Kayong'u*. I took the red clay and brought it where the people were. Sanyiwangu and all the people were surprised and said, 'Your *ihamba* is a powerful one. It showed you where a concealed thing [*chuma chakusweka*] was.'

"Then they sang the *ng'ombu* song [which is sung when a basket diviner is about to expose a witch]. When they had finished they asked me, 'Where have we hidden the other things?' I then began to clap my hands, by throwing both hands forward, palms facing the people, then clapping. The people responded by clapping. I told them, 'One thing is kept here near the head of the crocodile, and one is kept near the end of the tail, and the other is hidden where the women are.' Sanyiwangu asked me, 'Will you tell me the names of the things, one by one?' They played the *ng'ombu* drum once more. I began to tremble and to divine [*ku-taha*]. I said, '*Kayong'u* is near the neck [of the crocodile].' The doctors said, 'If you know it, please will you hold it now.' In the neck of the crocodile they had hidden *nyibulu* ankle-rings. I removed some earth and found them. Then they asked me again, 'What is hidden near the tail? Of a dead person?' 'It is now near the tail,' I said. 'Exactly where is it?' they asked. I said, 'Let me see it' and took off earth and found a bangle. Then I said to the women, 'You have hidden an ax.' They said, 'Which woman has it?' I said, 'An ax is with this child who is standing near my wife.' They praised me with joy.

Sanyiwangu said, 'Let us now return home,' but secretly he said to the doctors, 'There is one thing Muchona must announce to all—that is the name of someone who has died.' He sent two doctors swiftly to my village, to the place of *muneng'a*. There they hid something else. They returned to bring Sanyiwangu and me back to the village.

"Everybody gathered round the *muneng'a* and the *ng'ombu* drum was played. All the people danced round and round and round. I gave them 'a hand of clapping' [*kuyinka chikasa chakusakwila*]. Then I began searching round the *muneng'a* tree for what was concealed. I said aloud, 'Something is hidden near that *muneng'a* of mine. I see that you have hidden something here for the name of a dead person. The horns of a duiker [a small woodland antelope] are kept here.' Sanyiwangu and his friends agreed: 'You are right.' Then they praised me very much indeed. I said, 'That is the dead person's name, *Nkayi* which means Duiker. Just as an animal, like a duiker, lives in the bush, do does a human being [*muntu*] live in a village.' All this was just a test to see whether I would divine correctly or not. The *Mama daWuyang'a* and the other doctors try to deceive the candidate [*muyeji*] by mentioning the wrong things. They want to be sure that he will not divine someone as a witch who is not really a witch.

"Sanyiwangu then said, 'This is a man who will make a real diviner. Everyone who has been here must now go home. There is nothing left here for you all.' All returned, but I stayed with Sanyiwangu. We slept at the village, but in different huts because Sanyiwangu was my mother's brother [*mandumi*]. I slept with my wife Masondi. Masondi cooked the meat of the cock and goat killed at the *muneng'a*. The hearts of the goat and cock were given to me when I was sitting on the 'crocodile' to swallow uncooked. I did not swallow the needle and razor stuck in them. These were put on an *isaku* skin.

"Sanyiwangu divided the meat among the other doctors, then said to me, 'Let us now see what you are going to do for me.' I gave him four yards of cloth as payment for the *muneng'a*; then a further two yards of cloth for 'mentioning the dead man's name'; then two yards for 'sitting on the crocodile' made by Sanyiwangu. I gave some more little ritual gifts [*nyishing'a*] for other services. That is the end of *Kayong'u*."

Comments. Muchona explained some of the symbols and procedures of the last episodes of *Kayong'u* as follows:

"*Makenu* is a fork in a path. When people come to a fork they must choose just where to go, which means that even a *Kayong'u* diviner must choose the exact way to go. If he goes along a path he must know beforehand the proper way to go. *Makenu* means the place where a choice must be made, either one thing or another. That is ordinary knowledge. But the diviner goes between the paths. He knows what everyone else does not know. He has secret knowledge.

"The pricking of hearts with razor and needle represents the pain [*ku-yeng'a*] of the *Kayong'u* patient. Because it has already been done in the hearts of the animals he should not feel it again. But he feels the pain again when he is divining. This is what tells him to look closely at the symbolic objects in his divining basket when he is divining. The pricking is caused by the spirit-manifestation [*ihamba*] of *Kayong'u*.

"If a patient guessed wrongly where the things are hidden, he would be laughed at by the doctors. *Kayong'u* is certainly not like teaching somebody something first, then asking him questions about it later. A person who is believed to have *Kayong'u* is also trusted to know all the things of *Kayong'u*, because his own *Kayong'u* tells him about them or gives him the power. He has the *ihamba* of *Kayong'u* in his liver [or heart—*muchima* can mean both in Lunda]."

The phrase *ihamba kumuchima* is roughly equivalent to having the gift of clairvoyance or "second sight."

Muchona continued his explanation: "The crocodile is a symbol [*chinjikijilu*] of divination or of the *Kayong'u* spirit. Its many teeth represent needles.

"The diviner must be sharp like a needle, cutting like a knife. His teeth should be sharp to bite off the cock's head. He must know the points of divination [*yidimbu*]."

Ndembu make an interesting association between sharp pain and sharp wits. It would be tempting to speculate about the psychological requirements and conflicts of diviners, who have the dangerous and unpleasant task of bringing to light and announcing in public the secret undercurrents of hostility and envy between close kin. Such a task must cause the diviners almost as much pain as they know they will bring upon others. But an inquiry of this sort lies outside the scope of this mainly ethnographic account.

Muchona then told me how Sanyiwangu instructed him in the knowledge of *Kayong'u* medicines.

Muchona's account. "From that time Sanyiwangu wanted me to divine for huntsmanship [*naWubinda*]. He was my 'Mama yang'ombu' or 'Mother of divination.' He taught me the medicines [*yitumbu*] of *Kayong'u*. If I am very sick I use them. My *Kayong'u* comes to help me.

"Sanyiwangu told me to go first to a *muhuma* tree to collect medicine from it. We made *mpandula* first [they took leaves from the tree, put them underside up on the back of their left hands and smacked their right hands down on the leaves, uttering a brief invocation to the appropriate ancestor spirit].

Then we took a piece of [a parasitic plant called] *chinang'amu* from a branch of the *muhuma* tree. We took leaves from both for *nsompu* medicine. Then we went to a *mutete* tree and gave *mpandula* to it. We took some leaves. Then we brought this medicine and pounded it in a meal mortar. We put *nsompu* in a plate in front of the *muneng'a* [tree-shrine]. Muchona prayed [*ku-kombela*] with white clay: '*Eyi mandumi mpemba oyu, eyi tata mpemba oyu nkwashenu*' [Thou uncle, this white clay, thou father, this white clay, help me], '*ifuku dalelu ami nakata hama*' [this very day I am sick exceedingly]. '*Kayong'u kami ching'a wuhiti hohana wahitang'a wunkwashi, mpemba oyu*' [My *Kayong'u* you must pass as you always pass that you may help me, this (is your) white clay].

"I put *nsompu* medicine in my mouth and spat to the right and to the left [as described on page 257]. Then I took some with my right hand and drank, then with my left hand. I took some more and washed my arms, chest, forehead, back of head, and legs. Then my whole body. I did this at the performance itself and after it had ended. And whenever I am sick."

Comments. Muchona explained that *muhuma*, the name of a species of tree, was derived from *ku-huma*, meaning "to butt with horns," like a goat or an antelope, "to strike with the elbows," and "to strike" generally. "A *muhuma*," said Muchona, "is a man or a spirit that goes to attack [*ku-huma*] animals. *Muhuma Matang'a* is a hunter-name which means one who attacks the herds [of animals]. It's just a name [*ijina hohu*], there is nothing in the tree that explains why it should have that name." [In other words it has no natural property or habit.]

"The *Kayong'u* spirit is one which attacks animals. If it finds them it 'butts' them toward the hunter.

"*Chinang'amu* represents the spirit of *Kayong'u*. It comes from *ku-nang'ama*, 'to alight upon,' as a bird from flight."

Muchona did not explain the meaning of *chinang'amu* further, but it is possible to get at this meaning by analogy with another interpretation of his. This concerned the ritual use in the hunters' cult *Ntambu* of another parasitical plant *mutuntamu*, which grows on the *mukula* tree (*Pterocarpus angolensis*). *Mutuntamu* has a similar primary sense to *chinang'amu*, for it is derived from *ku-tuntamia*, "to sit upon." In *Ntambu* this plant means that "the hunter's spirit must come and sit upon an animal so that it is blinded and the hunter can kill it easily." It might also have the meaning that the spirit has seized (*wunakwati*) the patient. In ritual, antithetical senses are often possessed by the same symbol.

I asked Muchona the meaning of the *kapwipu* tree which marks the site where the patient's divinatory skill is tested. He replied: "In *Kayong'u* the *kapwipu* tree is called *mutete*. This is short for a Luvale saying, which is also a special hunter-name—*Mutete manyangi wuta wachashi*, 'the one who cuts up huntsmanship [huntsmanship here stands for meat—this is an instance of the central African tendency to substitute an abstract noun for a concrete one], the unloaded gun.' The unloaded gun refers to one who misses animals when he is shooting at them. It is a praising name for the following reason: a hunter usually kills animals, but once or twice he fails to do so. They tell him that he must hold his gun properly, for the shaking [*ku-zakuka*] of his mind causes him to miss his aim. When he was first instructed he never missed. After being told this he kills animals again. So now he praises himself: 'At first I used to kill animals, later I missed, then after missing I kill animals once more.' "

In this explanation we get some impression of the complex

semantic involutions of an Ndembu dominant symbol. In the first place, the ordinary name of the tree is replaced by a ritual term borrowed from Luvale. This term itself is highly allusive, since it is the first word of a sentence. The sentence—which is also a name given only to ritually initiated hunters—requires a further interpretation. This interpretation can only be understood against a wider background of Ndembu religious values, for it refers to the Ndembu belief that one can only obtain the highest ritual—and also material—benefits by suffering misfortune first. This is not all, for misfortune is believed to be frequently caused by ancestor spirits. These beings are punishing one for a breach in the social or ethical order, committed either by oneself or by a member of one's kin group. But these spirits are not merely punitive; they wish to become one's guardians and to bring help in one's worldly affairs. First, however, one must perform a ritual to honor and propitiate them. All this is implied in the single word "*mutete.*" Truly symbols condense and economize!

There seem to be further allusions in this symbolism, borrowed from hunting, to the diviner's role as a hunter of witches and sorcerers and a discoverer of ancestor spirits.

Further training

After the performance Muchona's *Mama daWuyang'a* taught him "how to *ku-sekula*"—the art of shaking up symbolic objects in a winnowing basket and of interpreting their meaning. He was taught both in his own hut and in Sanyiwangu's. The latter gave him some *tuponya* to start him off as a diviner. He also commissioned a woodcarver to make some for him. In pre-European times, Muchona said, a candidate diviner would give his instructor in the art of using *tuponya* a present of forty yards of cloth and a muzzle-loading gun, or even of a slave. Today, he went on, only forty yards of cloth or (in Angola) a cow is required.

The diviner's tally

According to Muchona, a diviner collects faggots [*tushinji*] of firewood from the funeral fires of persons into whose deaths he has divined. He keeps them in a little *Kayong'u* hut [*katala kaKayong'u*], not far from his own hut. He does not keep his medicines there, but only bits of charred firewood. He keeps his *tuponya* in an *ibang'u* basket with a lid.

The process of basket divination (*ng'ombu yakusekula*)

I give here Muchona's account of the divinatory process, just as he gave it to me, with my comments interpolated, as above, where further elucidation is needed.

"When a person dies his relatives go to a diviner with a fowl or a two-yard or four-yard piece of cloth. Nowadays they may take two or three shillings. When they reach the diviner's village [Northern Rhodesian Ndembu usually cross the border of Angola to find a basket diviner], they go either to the village shelter [*chota*] or stand near the diviner's hut. When the diviner sees them coming he begins to breathe heavily [*ku-tomena*, which also means to belch], then he goes to meet them. He tells them to keep still, then informs them that they have come for divination; he knows it by means of his '*ihamba* of divination.' 'Come and sit down, please,' he says. But the people put him to the test [*kweseka*] by replying, 'No, we did not come here for that purpose. We are going somewhere else.' He says, 'No, I know you have come to me.' Satisfied, they sit down. The diviner says, 'Let me go to the path you have come here by.' He looks closely on either side of the path. He sees an arrow on one side of the path and returns with it, showing it to the relatives of the dead person.

"About this arrow. During the mourning camp [*chibimbi*] for the deceased, one of his relatives brought an arrow and some red beads on a string. He said, 'These are for the birth-name [*ijina dakusemuka*] of the dead person.' This is the name which is divined for by a baby's father shortly after birth and comes from an ancestor spirit. Arrow and beads are taken to the diviner, to be discovered by him. Sometimes several arrows are taken in a quiver and the diviner has to select from these 'the arrow of the name' [*nsewu yejina*].

"Then they go to a special place to divine, usually in the bush. Long ago when a diviner wanted to divine for sickness he used to divine in his own village. For a dead person, he divined outside his village. Often the diviner was invited to the village of the sick or dead person. The first thing was to divine at his own village to get some ideas. The second was to go to the patient's village, to repeat the divination in the presence of many relatives of the patient. The third thing was to go all around the area to divine for sick people.

"To go back to the first case. The diviner tells the people who came to consult him not to go back alone to their village. They must go with him. When they are about half a mile away he says, 'We must leave the path and go and wait in the bush.' He then sends one of his own villagers to announce to the dead man's people that they are ready in that place. When they hear of this they bring to the diviner a goat, some fowls, some baskets of cassava, and some calabashes of beer for the diviner and his people. They stay there all day and all night. The diviner himself is not allowed to drink beer, for otherwise he would give drunken answers.

"At dawn they clear a special site [*ibulu*] [7] in the bush. They make a framework of three poles [like a soccer goalpost] just like the one at the boys' circumcision ceremony [*Mukanda*], under which the novices [*anyadi*] must pass on their way to being circumcised.

"The diviner is now ready to divine. All the relatives of the dead are there. The headmen and people of neighboring villages also come to see it well. For the people have thought, 'Why should this person have died young? Why did he not grow old? It must be because of witchcraft.' Three headpads of the kind used by women when they carry calabashes or baskets on their heads are placed on the crossbar of the *mukoleku* frame. Everyone who attends must pass under the *mukoleku* and give a present as he passes through. These presents may consist of beads, bracelets, or *isumba* neck ornaments. Money is now given too.

"The headpad is a sign [*chinjikijilu*] to the diviner not to forget anything, nor must he be ignorant of anything, for a witch [*muloji*] may use medicine to deceive the diviner or conceal things from him. The headpad is medicine to prevent this because the grass from which it is made is twisted like a witch's attempts to deceive. It is made of *kaswamang'wadyi* grass. This name is from *ku-swama*, 'to hide,' and *ng'wadyi*, 'the bare-throated francolin.' Such birds love to hide in this grass. Witches and sorcerers also hide from view.

"The people sit around the *ibulu* clearing, facing the place where the diviner sits. When they passed under the *mukoleku* frame the diviner was not present: he was inspecting the paths leading to the clearing to learn about people who had come there with their witchcraft.

[7] This term is now applied to an airfield.

"When the diviner arrives they begin to drum, sing, and dance in the fashion of *Mung'ong'i*, the funerary association. The diviner is decorated with strips of white and red clay. When he dances the lines of red and white seem to undulate about [expressed by the ideophone *wayiwayi*]. This is the song—which is [partly] in the Lwena language:

Hele tala ngongu mweza eye hele eyeye, olo tala muyinda mweza, eye-leya muyindi wamutambika netiya e-e yele eheleche chimbungu mwakeza he-e.
(Look, a terrifying thing [like a lion or a witch] is coming, look, a giant is coming, a giant, when you call it answers, the hyena will come.)
[*Ngongu*, *muyinda*, and *chimbungu* are terms denoting witches, sorcerers, and their familiars.]

"After that song, the diviner comes and sits on a stool. When he sits, he begins to look at the people one by one. He asks them, 'Why have you come here?' All the people answer, 'We have come for your divination.' The diviner asks, 'Have you come well [*chachiwahi*] or ill [*chatama*]? If you have come well, you will see well. If you have not come well, you will see badness here. Sit down properly all of you, men, women, and children and listen to me.' He speaks strongly with authority [*wanta*].

"Then he drinks pounded-leaf medicine mixed with cold water from one cup and then from another. [Its composition, Muchona told me, is a professional secret.] He brings a basket with a lid, called *chisuku*, which contains his *tuponya* divining objects. He begins to shake them up and examine them. He looks again at each person, one after another. He does not at this point disclose what he has seen. He shakes the *tuponya* again twice and drinks again from each calabash cup [*lupanda*]. Now he takes medicine from two or three *malembu* containers he carries. These *malembu* are small calabashes cut across the center, filled with medicine, then joined together again. They contain magical ingredients [*mpelu*]. These include:

"1. Some skin or bone from the forehead [*ihama*] of a dead chief. This represents renown or fame [*mpuhu*];

"2. A piece of nerve from inside an elephant's tusk.

"This is called *nsomu*. If someone eats *nsomu* by chance, he finds that it has made him impotent. It was a thing well-known by experience to the ancestors that *nsomu*-eaters became impotent. For the elephant is a big animal. When hunters killed it, many gathered to collect meat. They removed the tusks [*mbing'a*]. Exactly where the tusks met the mouth, the people found something very soft, like meat, they put it in their pots and tried to eat it, young people among them. Later they found that those who ate *nsomu* had become impotent. *Nsomu* is long and soft, like a limp penis. A man who ate *nsomu* entered a hut where young women [*tunkang'a*] were and found he was unable to have intercourse with them. So the women laughed at him, and said, 'Two weeks ago you were strong in this thing, but now you can't do it. Why have you now no power?' The young man complained to the elders, who went into the bush to collect medicines to restore him. Sometimes these medicines cure people, sometimes they fail.

"Diviners use *nsomu* to see secret things that happen to occur just on that occasion, just as a hunter when he goes hunting expects to meet animals by chance, they just turn up, suddenly they are seen. *Nsomu* is like a torch at night, by its aid the diviners can see witches openly and clearly. This is because *nsomu* is a secret thing that has been brought into the open."

Comments. Nsomu would seem to be a symbol for the rapid, unexpected action of witchcraft which can cause death or impotence in the twinkling of an eye. In that it represents witchcraft it is of service ("like a torch") to the diviner: it is "a secret thing that has been brought into the open" like the nerve concealed in the elephant's tusk. There is in *nsomu*, too, an element of treachery or deceit, for who would expect an animal that provides many people with meat to produce impotence along with plenty?

Muchona's account. "Other ingredients [*jipelu*] [of contagious magic] include:

"3. The hair of an albino [*mwabi*]. This to see everything clearly, for an albino is white or clear. It also can mean good luck.

"4. The wing case of a Goliath beetle [*mpumpi*]. This *mpelu* stands for meeting together [*chipompelu*] because such beetles assemble in groups to feed on the leaves of *mwala* trees. It also stands for a meeting of witches, who gather together to eat human meat. It means too that the diviner should meet with a witch now, just at this time.

"5. The feather of a gray parrot [*kalong'u*]. This means good luck, fame, or reputation, for all must know that a great diviner is present.

"6. Charcoal [*makala*] from the site where a witch was burnt. This stands for seeing witches. When witches are seen [by the diviner's art] they should be burnt.

"7. Part of the burnt heart (or liver) of a witch [*muchima wawuloji*, literally 'liver of witchcraft.' This has the same meaning as 6.]

"8. Charcoal from the fire on which the novices' food is

cooked at the boy's circumcision ceremony. This fire is called *ijiku daMukanda*, 'the fire of circumcision.' It represents a *chipompelu cheneni*, a big gathering of people.

"9. A root from beneath the cooking fire of a circumcision novice's mother [*Nyamwadyi*]. This fire is the *ijiku daMukanda*, just mentioned" [and the root has the same sense as 8].

The divination séance

Muchona's account. "Although the diviner looks everywhere he does not suspect small children [*atwansi*] of witchcraft, for they do not possess familiars. Children just come to watch.

"The diviner rubs his *malembu* medicines [just described] between his hands and smells them. Then he extends his arms before him, claps his hands together, while the people facing him do likewise, crying, '*Wo-o!*' Whenever he asks a question he does this and the people respond accordingly.

"He begins by an address or invocation [*ku-kombelela*] to the ancestors of old chiefs:

Nyakabamba Musompa hadi Luweji Ankondu kukung'ulula nyanta ye-jima, amavulu enjili nankanu, chitwenjili hamu nankanu jetu twenjili ntahi dinu? Twenjili A-Cheza [8] *chisemi namwana, nshinta nakuyanda. Twenjili nanka? Twenjili nachiyang'a mukwa kuloza wubinda wanyonji, wukwawu wanyivuwa kumeji, nimuloji hamu, ni mukwanshidi wa-tiyang'a kutama nawakwawu antu, ni chivumbi wendang'a nakukama ang'odi jawakwawu. Twenjili namonu tahindi? Twenjili nakufwa. Tu-hani monu.*

(Nyakabamba Musompa who is Luweji Ankondu to gather together all the chiefs, many came with *lukanu* bracelets, when we came together with our *lukanu* bracelets, in what way did we come? We came [from] Cheza [of Mwantiyanvwa], a barren woman

---

[8] The plural prefix A—before personal names—is a sign of respect.

with suffering. What did we come with? We came with a gun-hunter, one who shoots [firearms], [with] hunting by string traps, [with] another [kind of hunting] by fish traps in the water, and also with a sorcerer [or witch], with a sinner who has ill feeling toward other people, with an adulterer who comes to sleep [with] the wives of others. Did we come with life? We came with death. [Please] give us life.)

Comments. Nyakambamba Musompa is a legendary figure sometimes identified by Ndembu with Luweji Ankonde or (as here) Ankondu [9] who married the founder of the Mwantiyanvwa dynasty among the northern Lunda, called the Luunda of whom the Mwinilunga Ndembu were an offshoot. Sometimes Nyakabamba or Nyakapamba is regarded as a separate person from Luweji. Cheza is another term for Luweji. The reference here to Luweji's barrenness is connected with a tradition that she suffered from menorrhagia and could not conceive children. Once during a long seclusion in the menstruation hut her husband, Chibinda Ilung'a, claimed that her *lukanu* bracelet (made from human sinews and genitalia), the royal emblem par excellence of the northern Lunda, was rightfully his. She had left the *lukanu* in his care, that it might not be polluted. Previously she had held it by inheritance from her father Yala Maku. After Chibinda usurped his wife's chiefly office, many Lunda royals of Yala Maku's blood fled the country with their followers, and, according to many central African traditions, founded chieftaincies in distant lands. An Ndembu myth tells of how

[9] See my article (1955) for a translation of the Portuguese ethnographer Carvalho's account of the northern Lunda (or Luunda) version of Luweji Ankonde's marriage to the Luban hunter Chibinda Ilunga, who founded the great Mwantiyanvwa dynasty.

Luweji was cured of menorrhagia by a newly devised cult of ancestor propitiation—her condition was reputedly caused by an ancestor spirit who disapproved of her Luban husband's succeeding to a Lunda chieftainship. This cult, Nkula, flourishes today in Mwinilunga District, where it is performed to rid women of menstrual disorders and sterility reputedly brought upon them by ancestor spirits. Luweji was said to have borne a child after passing through *Nkula*.

In this highly allusive text, a relationship is established between Luweji's affliction and the departure of the chiefs from Luunda with their *lukanu* insignia. The diviner does not seek to explain the origin of witchcraft and sin (*nshidi*), but claims that witches and sinners, with hunters, fishermen, and adulterers, came with the migrants from the Lunda homeland. Sin's origins are not pushed back to mankind's beginning. They have come 'from Luunda."

Muchona's account. "The diviner finishes by saying, '*Diyaya*, *diyaya* [Luvale *liyaya*], *Momo*, *mono*."

Muchona then described how a diviner questions his audience and supplied characteristic queries made by the diviner to his clients:

Ilang'a chimunapompeli munapompeli yika? Munapompeli wusungu indi? Indi munapompeli mukamba namovwa? Chalema mukamba. Mukamba wawantu akuhanda indi wawantu afwa?

Munapompeli mukamba wawantu afwa? Hadi kufwa? Kufwa hiyala indi mumbanda? Wafwa mumbanda yaku hamumbanda. Ochu wafwa eyi muntu wafwa nyisong'u tahindi? Wafwa wupong'u? Tahindi wafwi wudidi? Ochu wafwili musong'u wakuweni hadihi? Wakuweni nawufuku tahindi? Wakuweni namwana? Tali-i. Wakuweni namwana hela nawufuku. Hamwana nyisong'u yakuweni itang'wa hadihi?

(Now that you've assembled, what have you assembled for? Have you gathered [for] fish poison? Have you come [for] a special cassava root? [10] It is a heavy matter, a cassava root. [Do you mean] the cassava root of living persons or of dead persons? [11] [The diviner establishes successive "points" of divination. It is supposed in this account that the people are giving him the replies he wants.]

(You have come [about] the fate of dead people? Is there death? Is it the death of a man or a woman? If a woman died [may divination reveal] a woman. When you died, you person, did you die [of] diseases? Did you die [in an] accident? Or did you die [of illness after lying long] in bed? If you died of illness what part of you was affected? Did illness catch you at night? Did you become sick in the day? Let me see. You became ill either by day or at night. If illnesses caught you by day when [precisely] did they catch you?)

Muchona continued:

Jakuweni namwana antu akwiteja nawu namwana. Musong'u wakuk-watilili kumutu tahindi? Kumakasa tahindi? Mumujimba tahindi kun-yendu? Nyisong'u neyi yamukwatili mufu kunyendu nawu kunyendu, hela mumujimba nawu mwomu mumujimba, hela kumutu nawu kwoku ku-mutu, hela kukabavu nawu kukabavu—antu akwiteja. Wakamini mafuku ang'ahi akukata? Neyi muntu wakatili ifuku dimu akwiteja nawu dimu, neyi wakatili mafuku ayedi akwiteja nawu dimu, neyi wakatili mulungu wumu akwiteja nawu dimu, neyi wakatili kakweji hela chaka akwiteja nawu dimu. Hikukwata kunyikambu yamusendeleluwu neyi amusuwili nyonji amukasili nachu hayisalu akwiteja nawu dimu. Ngonji yambuka neyi asuwili nyonji yakansula akwiteja nawu dimu hela yamupuchi hela yamusamba hela yamwanda hela yamukung'u yoyu yamusuwiluwu akwi-teja nawu dimu. Neyi mufu amupopeleli muchikasha akumutena nawu amupopelelumu. Chitawija nawu letenu mushing'a, wakwiteja nachu. Ahanang'a chilala chakwiteja nachu.

(If it was by day the people agree, saying, "By day." [Or if by night, they likewise agree.] "Did the disease catch you in the head?

---

[10] *Mukamba* (cassava root) is a euphemism for the human body, hence a person's fate or luck.

[11] Do the clients wish him to divine into death or illness?

Or in the arms? In the body or in the legs?" If the diseases caught the dead person in the legs, they [the clients] say "in the legs," or in the body, they say "just there in the body," or in the head, they say "just in the head," or in the side, they say "in the side"—the people agree. "How many days did he sleep when he was ill?" If the person was ill for one day they agree that it was so, if he was ill for two days they agree that it was so, if he was ill for one week they likewise agree, and similarly for a month or a year. If they held the poles of the litter with which they carried the dead person, and if they stripped off bark string to tie him on the mats, they agree that this was so. Bark strings are of different kinds (and) if they stripped off bark strings from the *kansula* tree, they agree (with the diviner) that it was the case or of the *mupuchi* or *musamba* or *mwanda* or *mukung'u* trees, they agree that they were stripped from those trees. If they nailed (the body) into a box they mention that they have done so. When agreement has been reached they say "Bring a ritual payment." He [the diviner] agrees to this. They give a four-yard piece of cloth for the [process of reaching] agreement.)

Comments. Ndembu attach great importance to the species of tree from which the bark strings of their funeral litters are taken. I have recorded several cases in which persons were said to have been afflicted with illness or misfortune by the spirits of angry deceased relatives whose deathbed instructions about the kind of bark string to be used for their litters were ignored. Perhaps the point at issue is not the species of tree used, but the fact that respect for the dying person has been publicly attested.[12]

[12] From my notebook I summarize the following case, which perhaps explains some of the burial preparations: "A man named Kanyombu, of Mukanza Village, in November 1951, on his deathbed told his relatives to prepare his corpse for burial in a specific fashion to annul the effects of a medicine called *mwiyanawu* which he had taken. This medicine is said to avenge its owner's death on the sorcerer or witch who killed him—or on the witch's kin. Kanyombu told his elder brother, the village headman, to

In this preliminary interrogation the diviner shows his skill by establishing in detail those incidents in the illness and death of his clients' kinsman which Ndembu regard as significant.

Muchona's account.

Kusekula mung'ombu kuyinka nkoshi, aneteji; ijina dakundama kumaseki tahindi, kunyitondu tahindi, kumenji tahindi, kutububu tahindi kutunyama tahindi kunshi tahindi, kudihi?

(There is shaking up in the *ng'ombu* [apparatus], he [the diviner] gives them a clap, they respond. (He asks: "Does the name belong to the earth, to the trees, to the water, to insects, to animals, to fishes, where is it?")

Comments. Muchona explained that there were different classes of names (*nyichidi yamajina akusemuka*—literally "classes of birth names," names given to infants by their fathers as a result of *mwishi* pounding-pole divination and usually selected from those of paternal deceased kin). Each

---

go to the Lunga River to collect leaves from a water lily, named *ntambayamenji*, 'sweet potato of the water' and also some *malowa*, black alluvial soil from the river bottom. The headman was to put these substances in his mouth, spit them on his hands, and then rub Kanyombu's body, with them. *Malowa*, in ritual, often has the sense of 'to cool' or 'quieten' (*kufomona*) 'hot' persons, things, and activities, such as sorcery medicines, angered spirits, or sexual desires. Here it would seem that the dying man was urging his brother to express in ritual terms his intention to revoke or annul his revenge medicine. Kanyombu also requested that his body should be tied onto the bier with *mukung'u* bark string. Moreover, he asked that the bier be dragged along the ground for a time before it was lifted. These actions were all directed against the *mwiyanawu* medicines. According to my informants, Kanyombu's kin neglected to fulfill his dying wishes. When many people fell ill in the village, a diviner was consulted, who told the headman that Kanyombu's spirit, angry at their negligence, had afflicted them in punishment. Later, a *muyombu* shrine-tree was planted in his memory, and the epidemic ceased."

class or category contains many items, all of which possess
some outstanding common attribute. Thus there is the category *Tunyama*, "wild animals." This category is further sub-
divided into *Tunyama twamafumbu*, "animals with padmarks"
and *Tunyama twayikwa*, "animals with hoofmarks." The diviner, in this cross-examination, establishes that the name of
the dead person fell in the class of animals with padmarks.

Muchona's account.

*Neyi ijina damufu dakundama kutunyama twamafumbu hikuyitena
hejina hejina. Ijina dakundama kumutupa tahindi? Chisumpa hela mumbu
hela chizozu hela kang'widi kela kabonzu?*

(If the name of the deceased belongs to the animals with padmarks, he mentions them name by name. "Does the name belong
to the lion? [or to] the leopard, hyena, wild dog, or wild cat and so
on?")

Comments. Further classes of names include: (1) *Woma*,
"fear." This contains such names as Muzala and Kazadi from
ku-zala, "to shiver" (with cold or fright). (2) *Chilung'a*, the
pumpkin vine, including Sailung'a (the title of the Kosa-
Lunda senior chieftainship), Katamba or Katambi, literally, a
trap for small arboreal animals. (3) *Menji* or *Kenji*, "water,"
including Malowa, "black alluvial soil," Mulumbi, "a torrent," Chifuwu, "a bush overhanging the river," Ndembi, "a
fish with small teeth." These last three are the personal
names of three Ndembu senior chiefs, incumbents of the
Kanongeshaship. The *ka-* prefix is employed in ritual contexts to designate aquatic phenomena such as *kenji* and *kachinana*, "the red river," a trench filled with reddened water used
to teach boys tribal mysteries during the circumcision ceremony. (4) *Wanta*, "chieftainship," for example, Chinyaweji,
part of the salutation to an important chief, a term formerly

applied to the Supreme Being. The diviner is sometimes called *Sakamulami*, "the one who selects" with reference to this mode of proceeding from the general to the particular.

Synopsis of Muchona's account

When he finds the dead person's name he puts away his *tuponya*, divining symbols. He is given another present for finding out the correct birth name. Next, according to Muchona, he establishes the relationship between the dead man and his clients, "by means of his *ihamba*, by asking questions and by mentioning things one after the other." If, as sometimes happens, the clients deliberately give him incorrect replies, he says sharply in Luvale, *"Munangongi,"* "You have deceived me" (the correct Luvale is *munangwongo*), and asks further questions.

First he asks whether the dead man came from the area of a particular senior chief, Kanongesha, Musokantanda, Kazembe, and so on. Having established the senior chief's area, he then finds out by question and answer the subchief's area—Ntambu, Chibwika, Mwininyilamba, Ikeleng'e, Nyakaseya, Mukang'ala, and so on. He then ascertains the name of the *Mwenimbu* or headman of the oldest established village in the vicinage or cluster of neighboring villages in which the deceased resided. Finally, he fixes on a single village.

Then he finds out whether the dead person is related to the client on the father's or on the mother's side (*kukatata tahindi kukamama?*). Unrelated persons (*ayilolu*) have come to consult him, persons who "have a relationship of the face [*asemuka kumesu hohu*], not of the matrilineage [*ivumu*, literally, 'womb']"; these are persons who "just sit in the *chota*" (the men's shelter in the middle of the village). If there are, say, "three wombs" (sublineages), in the village it is the diviner's task to count how many sublineages there are, and to find out from which of them the dead person came. On the other hand, the deceased may have been a woman married into the village, "He catches [considers] the married women" (*hikukwata amasumbu iyasumbolawu niwena*). Uxorilocally married men are also taken into consideration. So too are slaves (*andung'u*), and chiefs (or headmen) (*anyanta*). Eventually the diviner establishes the social relationship between clients and deceased and locates the deceased in his appropriate category of village relationship to the headman. Now he goes on to identify the witch or sorcerer.

Muloji neyi iyala wukwiluka neyi hiyala, neyi himumbanda nawa wukwiluka neyi himumbanda. Neyi mumbanda diyi muloji wukwiluka neyi ndumba jindi diju jajahayi nachu muntu. Neyi hiyala hikutena yuma yajahayi nachu muntu, hela nkala hela kalulu, hela ilomba, hela ikishi, hela katotola, hela nzoji, hela nanzaji, neyi hadi chimbu chijahayi nachu muntu. Chamwekanang'a nawa munkishi ni nakayong'u kehamba; antu ejima akwiteja nawu eng'a dimu.

(If the sorcerer is a man he will know if it is a man, if [the witch] is a woman he will know if it is a woman. If it is a woman who is a witch he will know if her familiars are the ones by whom the person was killed. If it was a man he will mention the things by which the person was killed, whether [it was] the Crab-monster, or the Half-Hare, or the Man-Snake, or the Masked Demon, or *Katotola*, or *Nzoji* [an animated figurine], or by Lightning-medicine, [or] if there was a Hyena-being by which the person was killed. It goes on appearing thus in the divining objects and with [the help of] the *Kayong'u* spirit; all the people will agree and say, "Yes, thus it is.")

Comments. These familiars or "things" of sorcery are described in greater detail in Turner 1968:passim. A good account appears in C. M. N. White's article (1947:12–14), and

Melland (1923) mentions some of these beliefs and practices (notably the employment of the *ilomba* or Man-Snake).

Muchona's account. Muchona then described how the diviner finds "the grudge" (*chitela*) which induced the accused to employ sorcery or witchcraft:

Neyi muntu wamujaha nachitela hela chambiji hela chakuheta hela cha-winyi hela chakuzuwa hela chawuvumbi hela chawukombi chikumwekana nawa ankishi kumwinka Kayong'u nindi dima.

(If the person was killed by a grudge [arising from] meat or wealth or pride or anger or adultery or theft this will appear [from] the divining symbols and *Kayong'u* tells [the diviner] likewise.)

Comments. The above is a succinct list of the kinds of motives which Ndembu believe impel persons to have recourse to sorcery or witchcraft. I have elsewhere (1957:passim) in a series of case histories, shown how these alleged motives are caught up into the intrigues of local politics and manipulated by village factions to discredit their rivals. Detailed studies of such political contexts are necessary if one wishes to make an adequate study of the sociology of witchcraft. Muchona's texts throw light principally on the cultural structure of sorcery/witchcraft and on Ndembu stereotypes of the psychology of its practitioners.

Windson Kashinakaji's summary of Muchona's account. Windson Kashinakaji, my assistant in eliciting information from Muchona, pithily summarized his account so far in the following terms:

"If people came from a far country, such as Chief Muso-kantanda's Area in the Belgian Congo, to divine here—where there is a diviner—the first thing he would do would be to find the reason why they came here. He would find the arrow they leave by the path, as described. Then he would divine in a private place for those strangers [ang'eji]. In the end he would find out what their village is, then separate them into each [village] lineage. For example, he might say: 'You, the first man here, you are the dead person's older brother. This one is your younger brother, but this one here is your brother-in-law [ishaku], and that one is your father-in-law [muku].' He would ask them if they were in agreement with what he said. If they agreed, he would ask them whether they lived in the same village or in different villages. He would find just where they lived and whether they had resided with the dead person or not. The father-in-law, for instance, might live separately. Then he would begin to divine to find the name of the dead person. Then he would ascertain who had killed him. Then he would find out the kind of grudge which had provoked witchcraft."

Muchona's account. "If a person is sick, the diviner prescribes the exact treatment, whether the rituals of *Nkula, Chihamba, Isoma,* or *Kaneng'a* should be performed. It is the *ihamba* [spirit-manifestation] which is in the diviner's liver which begins to shake. Then the *tuponya* will act in the same way.

"One *kaponya* represents one kind of *Chihamba*—that for the water—and another represents the *Chihamba* for the bush [these are variant forms of the ritual; in the former, medicines collected from the streamside forest and in the latter from the dry bush have the major therapeutic role]. If a small rattle [*nzenzi*] appears [at the top of the *tuponya*] in a *chisekula* [the shaken-up heap of *tuponya*], this represents either kind of *Chihamba* [in which rattles play a prominent part]. If the *nzenzi* rattle appears again on top with a piece of looking-glass, called *Chibanjilu,* after the diviner has asked if this is a

Chihamba for the water, then he is sure it is for the water, since *Chibanjilu* stands for water. Once the diviner has begun shaking up the objects he does not add any new ones to the basket later."

Before Muchona discussed the *tuponya* in detail he listed a diviner's principal ritual interdictions.

Food avoidances and other ritual interdictions

"A diviner must avoid eating bushbuck [*mbala*] because it has a spotted hide. When he divines [after eating bushbuck] he will find that he is getting astray from the main points of the divination. Just as the spots are divided so he will stray from the point. The zebra [*chingalika*] is avoided for the same reason, for it has many stripes. The blue duiker [*kasenda*] is avoided because it is darkish in color; there is darkness in divining [*mwidima kutaha*], the main points will be obscure. The yellow-backed duiker [*ikuma*] is avoided for the same reason. Diviners do not eat the *mukung'a* fish because it has sharp bones [*nying'a*]. These sharp bones might prick [*ku-lemeka*] the diviner's liver, and then he cannot divine well. A needle and a razor were inserted in the cock's and goat's hearts at the *Kayong'u* ritual to prevent this from happening [an example of the prophylactic use of symbolism].

"When a diviner finds that his *ng'ombu* [divination] has been successful, he can eat the giant rat [*chituba*], also blue duiker, yellow-backed duiker, and *mukung'a* fish. But he may not then eat bushbuck or zebra.

"He is not allowed to eat spinach leaves of the *wusi* and *kalembwila* varieties [commonly used as relish by Ndembu] because these are slippery, and his divination might slip away from him.

"He may not sleep with his wife until divination is over."

The Angolan diviner's account

Earlier I mentioned an Ndembu diviner (of the Ayiseng'a branch of the tribe) who visited Mwinilunga District from Angola early in 1952. The circumstances of his visit are worth mentioning. He had been called in from his village near the Kazombo Posta by a man in Chief Ikeleng'e's Area whose younger brother had been suffering from a wasting illness, probably tuberculosis. The diviner arrived, consulted his *ng'ombu yakusekula*, and proclaimed that the older brother himself was the sorcerer who was trying to kill the sick man. Indignantly, the older brother went to the chief's court and told Chief Ikeleng'e that he had consulted a diviner in Angola (since this mode of divination was, he said, illegal in Northern Rhodesia), who had declared him a sorcerer. In the past a person divined as a sorcerer had the right to appeal to a chief's poison oracle (see page 319). The older brother wanted Ikeleng'e to put the diviner's decision to the poison oracle test (*Mwaji*). Chief Ikeleng'e told him that unless he kept silent about the whole matter he would be compelled to send him under escort to the district commissioner's court. He was "wanting in sense" to make such a request since he knew that divination into sorcery and witchcraft was illegal.

By using personal influence and by the inducement of gifts I managed to persuade the Angolan diviner to visit me and talk with me about his profession. The account I was given was much sketchier than Muchona's and at the time I had much less knowledge and experience of Ndembu ritual. But I present it here in summary, since it represents the narrative of a diviner who was actively plying his trade at the time of interrogation.

15. An Angolan diviner and the tools of his trade.

Summary of the Angolan diviner's account

The way to become a diviner (as to acquire all ritual eminence among Ndembu) is "to begin [by being] sick," *watachika wakata*. "You are sick and at the same time dream of a dead relative." The diviner seemed to have had some kind of bronchial or asthmatic complaint; his breathing became heavy and labored. He dreamed constantly of his older uterine brother. Another close relative of his consulted a

16. Disfigurement of the Angolan diviner's hand.

diviner who told him that the spirit wanted to make my informant a diviner too. This meant that he would have to undergo the *Kayong'u* ritual.

Ritual interdictions

Before the performance and after, once he had become a diviner, he had to avoid the following foods:

Three species of fish: *mukung'a*, a fish with sharp teeth, "resembling the filed teeth of Luvale tribesmen"; *chinkola*; *musonji*, the "bubble fish."

Three species of animals: *mbala*, bushbuck; *mpumba*, mole rat; *chituba*, giant rat (*Cricetomys sp.*).

Leaf relishes (*mafu*), including cassava leaves and sweet potato leaves.

During the period he is divining and preparing to divine he must keep away from river and streams.

His wife is the only person then allowed to pass before his doorway or enter his hut to bring him food.

Comments. The diviner told me that relish leaves are avoided on account of their slipperiness (*ku-senena*), both in the sense of their glossy appearance (in the case of *wusi* leaves—a kind of spinach, and *ntamba* leaves—sweet potato leaves) and in that they slip down easily into the stomach. The principle underlying the avoidance is that the *tuponya* symbolic objects will not remain in position after being shaken but will slip down from the heap. The same principle governs fish avoidances. The mole rat and the giant rat are rodents that fill up the holes they dig behind them. In the same way, if they are eaten they will stop up the chest and liver of the diviner, so that he will be unable to make a correct diagnosis. I could get no interpretation from this diviner of the avoidance of bushbuck except that "it had spots." [13]

Angolan diviner's account. He must "pass through *Kayong'u*" to become a full diviner (*chitaha*). Toward the end of the performance he must kill a cock by biting through its neck—no knife must be used.

Training

After *Kayong'u* an established diviner will teach the novice his skill on payment of one cow (cattle are kept in the Angolan districts bordering on Mwinilunga). After a while he will examine the novice thoroughly on his knowledge of divination. When the apprentice has assisted his teacher at a number of séances, he will make a *ng'ombu* of his own and set

[13] But see Muchona's interpretation of this avoidance on page 285.

up in private practice. There is no such thing as a guild or association of diviners; they compete against one another. A successful diviner is one who finds the arrow brought by a dead man's relatives and one whose verdicts are consistently upheld by a chief's poison oracle or ordeal—in Angola the Senior Chief Kanongesha Sakayoli performs this *Mwaji* test himself.

A diviner begins his apprenticeship when he is between about thirty-five and forty years old. My informant told me that he began when he was about my cook's age, thirty-eight. Muchona was in his early thirties when he went through *Kayong'u*. My informant's right hand was peculiarly disfigured. All the phalanges of the second and fourth fingers were missing, and two phalanges of the first and third fingers were missing. I wondered whether this was a ritual amputation of the type practiced by Damara shamans, but he insisted that his disfigurement was the result of an accident before he became a diviner. At intervals he breathed heavily and exhaled a groaning breath. He said that this was due to "his spirit," that of his older brother. He could not see spirits when awake, but he saw them in his dreams. The arrangement of symbolic objects in his basket and the way his hand correctly selected the arrow of the dead was controlled by his spirit, which was in communication with the spirit of the dead person.

He said that if a *Kayong'u* or diviner-making spirit "catches" a woman, she cannot become a diviner, but may "give the spirit" to a close male relative, such as a brother. He then told me that when his son was old enough he would teach him how to divine, a statement that contradicted his remark that it was necessary to "start sick," that is, to be caught or chosen by a spirit first. His own mother's brother had been a diviner. He was accompanied by his sister's son who repeatedly spoke up about technical points, indicating that he was learning how to divine.

In Angola, he said, diviners are paid more often in cloths, sheep, goats, guns, and gunpowder than in money. If Northern Rhodesian Ndembu pay in money, they pay 30s. for a successful divination into death. For divination into illness or bad luck at hunting a woman must pay 3s. and a man 2s. 6d. This discrimination between the sexes is due to the fact that women do not offer hospitality to visiting diviners—though they may be asked by their husbands to cook for them—while men are offered a discount because they do so.

Nowadays, a diviner wears no special clothing during the performance. My informant wore an old jacket and trousers and a battered felt hat. In the past, according to White (1947:9), the diviner was daubed with red and white clay, wore a grass kilt and necklet, with a feathered headdress.

What happens after a divination séance

After he has identified the witch or sorcerer, the diviner and his assistants depart in haste to avoid any subsequent dispute with the kin of the accused.[14] If the chief's poison oracle (ordeal) establishes the innocence of an accused person, the chief insists that the diviner pay the accused half of his fee; he is allowed to retain half for his "hard work." He also suffers through the loss of his reputation. If the poison oracle confirms the accused's guilt, the latter must nowadays pay a

[14] A diviner called Ihembi once told me that divining was a dangerous profession. He mentioned that a diviner, Kaseleng'i, from Chief Ishinde's Area in Balovale District was killed by the sorcery of relatives of a man he had divined as a sorcerer. Another diviner was shot in the arm by the son of a man he had found to be a sorcerer and had to have it amputated.

large fine to the chief and to his victim's relatives and leave
the area immediately and for good. In the past a sorcerer or
witch would have been beaten to death or burned. My informant denied what others had told me, that a person cleared
of guilt by the poison oracle had to pay the chief a slave or
his equivalent in kind.

When the relatives of a dead person go to consult a diviner, he said, they bring with them a brand of firewood
from the funeral campfire, which he retains if they are satisfied with his diagnosis. This forms a sort of tally of the
number of successful divinations into death a diviner has
made. My informant said that he had amassed twenty-five
brands in 1951. He reckoned that in the same year he had
made three or four times as many divinations as that into the
causes of illness or misfortune. He claimed that he had made
three divinations into illness on his current visit to Rhodesia
in the course of a week. It is clear that in Angola a successful
diviner is a man of considerable wealth and influence.

The *tuponya*—symbolic objects used in divination

I carefully examined the contents of the diviner's flat,
round winnowing basket, while my wife took photographs of
the basket and the twenty-four divining objects it contained.
My wife and I made sketches of most of the *tuponya*.

The basket also contained a pouch made of the skin of a
species of mongoose (*kambunji*), filled with powdered red
clay, which the diviner applies to his temples and midbrow
during séances. There is also a solid piece of white clay or
chalk in the basket. After he has finished scrutinizing his
tuponya, he dances while quivering in every limb. While he
dances he carries a gnu-tail switch in one hand and a bell,
called *ng'eji*, in the other. During the actual process of basket

divination, he places the winnowing basket on several genet (*nshimba*) skins, which dangle tail first.

Some of the *tuponya* appeared to be coated with dried blood. According to the Angolan diviner, his *tuponya*, with the exception of the horns and hoofs of antelope, were given to him by the diviner who had instructed him in their use. But new *tuponya* may be made by professional woodcarvers and sold to diviners. They are periodically washed in the blood of a goat or a cock, some say before each consultation.

I present here interpretations of the different *tuponya*, first by the Angolan diviner and then by Muchona.

Fig. 1, no. 1. Chamutang'a (the slippery customer or the prevaricator). A wooden figurine with arms bent over chest, and legs crooked.

Angolan diviner: "*Chamutang'a* is a person who does not want to go to a diviner or to pay compensation to the relatives of the deceased. He is one who says, 'I don't like to do this or that.' "

Muchona: "*Chamutang'a* is the sort of person who when one tries to know what he is like escapes one. One fails to know him. If one tries to think of him in one respect, one fails; similarly in another respect. The figurine also stands for a matter which is not at all clear [*yalumbuluka chanti hohu*, or *chamutang'a hinsang'u*—literally 'a story']. He is 'a failure of beeswax' [*mukang'anya wandunda*], for when beeswax is taken to the fire it melts and when it is taken away from the fire it becomes hard. Such a person may give many presents to others and at other times he may give nothing to others. He is the same man who laughs very much with people and laughs very little with people. He is often very angry and often not at all angry. You do not know how to take him.

"How is *Chamutang'a* used in divination? Some people go

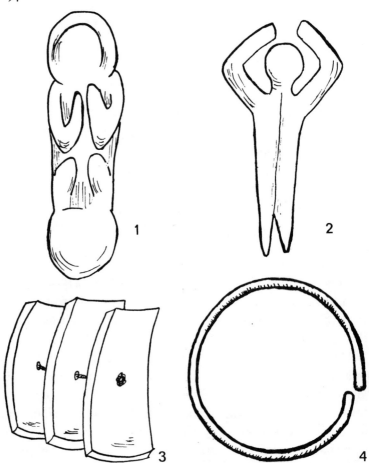

Figure 1. The divining objects. 1. *Chamutang'a* (the Prevaricator)—carved wood. 2. *Katwambimbi* (the Tale Bearer)—carved wood. 3. *Yipwepu* (Possessions)—pieces of calabash. 4. *Lukanu* (Chief's Bracelet)—iron.

to a diviner about the matter of a dead relative. The diviner points out a relative of the dead person as the killer of that man. The relative denies this and says, 'I am not the one who killed him; I never killed anyone in my life.' Another relative supports him. Yet another relative says, 'I am not quite certain whether our relative killed him; he might have been killed by somebody else.' A third relative says, 'This diviner is mistaken. Don't let us agree with him, for our relative never killed anyone.' Then the diviner resumes his divining. Suddenly they see *Chamutang'a* come to the top of the *tuponya*. The diviner asks *Chamutang'a*: 'Why have you come here? Does this mean that my divination is incorrect?' He goes on shaking his basket. If *Chamutang'a* appears again [on top] twice or thrice, the diviner tells the people: 'My divining is now at an end. I can't continue with this death matter. Please give me two four-yard pieces of cloth as the price of my work for you. You haven't agreed with me. I must close up my divining apparatus on this occasion.' Thus *Chamutang'a* appears when there is a big disagreement between the diviner and his clients.

Fig. 1, no. 2. Katwambimbi (the Weeping Hypocrite or the Tale Bearer). A wooden figurine representing a person holding his head, elbows bent, in the traditional Ndembu posture of mourning.

A.D.: "This stands for the person who is forever going from one man to another, causing enmity between them by telling each that the other had threatened to ensorcel him [*kumubawuka*]. If one of them should die—perhaps by the other's sorcery—the *Katwambimbi* is the one who weeps loudest at the funeral camp."

M.: *Katwambimbi akishamu mulong'a kena diku kaletang'a, yayivulu. Antu chakwinzawu nakutaha neyi owu muntu wudi chachiwahi hakufwaku kena diku kakubatama nakuswama. Neyi kena kakumwekana hanti nahanti hanyitu yawankishi, antu akwiluka nawu muntu wutunenzi nakuhong'ela wukufwa. Neyi kadinakwinza hanti nahanti tukwila netu iwu muntu wukukeng'a kufwa, wukufwa tahindi wukuhanda? Neyi wuku-*

*handa eyi Katwambimbi fumakuhu, hankishi jawakulumpi. Neyi wu-
kufwa chalala twaya nawa cheng'i hankishi jawakulumpi. Neyi akusha
ankishi jawakulumpi kwishina dayuma yejima, nakuselula kumona hihak-
winza ankishi inka wawu, Katwambimbi hikakuswamaswama nakufu-
mahu hankishi jawakulumpi. Netu komana muntu tukumukabakena wukuhanda. Neyi kushahu Katwambimbi hiyakwinza nakujika hankishi hohu
kushahu chochu nawa kamu hela kayedi hela katanu akwiluka nawu iwu
muntu hakuhandaku wukufwa. Mukwakuhong'a wayilejang'a anenzi nakuhong'a nindi iwu muntu hinamumoni chachiwahuku ching'a mwaka-
shuhu ng'ovu jamukukeng'ela chimbanda weneni weluka kuuka chacheni
kulonda akamuuki muyeji akahandi. Bayi mutwala muntadi muntu wakafwa.*

(*Katwambimbi* is put in [the basket] because it is the one which
brings many things. When people come to divination, if the person
is well, is not [going] to die, this [*Katwambimbi*] is the one which
will keep on hiding itself. If this one appears from time to time on
the heads of the Elders, people will know that the person whom we
have divined for will die. If it comes [up] continually we will say:
"That person is likely to die, will he die or live? If he is to live,
you, Tale Bearer, just go away, [do not come] on the Elders. If he
will really die then come again on the Elders. If they place the
Elders under the other things, suddenly they see the Elders coming
alone, the Tale Bearer goes on hiding itself and keeping away from
the top of the Elders. We say, 'Indeed we will take trouble over the
person, he will live.' When they put the Tale Bearer in and it
comes merely to cover up the Elders, if this is done once or twice
or five times they will know that this man will not live, he will die.
The diviner tells those who have come for divination: 'This person
I have not seen properly in [my *tuponya*], you must exercise your
powers to seek out for him a great curative specialist who knows
best how to heal so that he may cure the patient that he may live.
Do not go on arguing [or] the person will die.')

Muchona then explained to me the etymology of the term
"*Katwambimbi.*" *Ku-twa* means "to pound," he said, and

mbimbi here means "weeping." The noun *Katwambimbi* really means "He-who-starts-the-weeping" (or mourning—for *chibimbi* means a mourning camp lasting for several months between the burial and final mortuary ceremonies). A *Katwambimbi*, properly speaking, is a tale-spreader (*kakobukobu*), who carries tales from A to B and B to A, claiming that each is trying to bewitch or ensorcel the other. When A or B dies, *Katwambimbi* weeps the loudest although he has the greatest responsibility for the death. He is "the first messenger of death, the one who starts the weeping." From the diviner's point of view, not only the actual sorcerer (who did the killing) but also the tale-spreader would "receive a case" (*tambula mulong'a*), that is, he would be publicly denounced as responsible for the death.

Fig. 1, no. 3. Yipwepu (Possessions). Pieces of calabash.

A.D.: "When a woman changes her place of residence at divorce, on her husband's death, when her village builds on a new site, she takes her possessions [*yipwepu*] with her. It also stands for bad medicines a person sends on before him to kill someone."

M.: "*Yipwepu* represents 'water,' because water is carried in a calabash, and *chipwepu* means any part cut from a calabash, like a calabash cup. But it also means 'a matrilineage' [*ivumu*], for before a calabash is used for drawing water it has many seeds inside it; such seeds are the members of a matrilineage. When those little seeds are planted anywhere, they produce more and more calabashes. It is just the same with the men and women who come to a single lineage. Without a womb [*ivumu*] people would not become so many. There are many people in one lineage.

"When a woman marries a man she comes with her possessions, she has her cooking pot [*inung'u*], her calabash [*nswa-ha*], her big round basket [*ibang'u*], her plate, her cup, she pours all her seeds [for sowing] into her cabalashes, she brings to her husband's place her long open basket for carrying cassava, these are the *yipwepu* she brings into her marriage.

"*Yipwepu* represents water because when someone requires water a woman puts it into her calabash, and that water is then drunk by many people at the village; it also represents beer which is brewed in a calabash. It can also represent 'cassava mush' [*nshima*] with [bad] medicine in it. The diviner considers that in this case the grudge might have come from a calabash.

"Here is another example: a woman wanted to go to Chief Ikeleng'e's Area, and before she went she collected all her *yipwepu*. She put in her long *mutong'a* basket a calabash containing cassava meal [*wung'a*], and in another she put some uncooked beans, and in yet another she put some salt [*mung'wa*]. Afterward she died quite suddenly in the place where she had been visiting. The diviner would then shake his *tuponya*. *Yipwepu* he found on top of the pile. Then he would ask: 'Is the meaning of this *Chipwepu*, the Way, or does it mean "beer," or "water"?' He then asks, 'Is it the Way?' and shakes the *tuponya* again. If *Yipwepu* comes uppermost again, he is satisfied that the Way (meaning a journey or visit in this case) is correct. Next, he asks his *tuponya:* 'Did this woman put her possessions in a bundle [meaning a long visit], or not?' He keeps on asking until he comes to a real point of divination [*chidimbu*]. For every *kaponya* has many senses [a sense or *significatum* is *mwakulumbilila*, 'how it is explained,' or *muchaya*, 'wherein it goes'—the question 'what does it mean?' is in Chindembu *chaya mudihi?*, literally, 'wherein does it go?].

"*Yipwepu* also means 'a collection of goods' [*ku-long'eja*]. This is, properly speaking, a woman's possessions which she takes away with her when she has quarreled with her husband. Or it can mean a man's possessions too. Thus it means that a person has left a place on account of a quarrel [*ndombu*], gone off in a huff.

"It can also mean a collection of horns in which medicines [usually sorcery medicines] are kept. It can also mean an assemblage [*yikuyung'ulu*] of *yipwepu*, a set of kits. A man who has many sorcery familiars is said 'to have *yikuyung'ulu*.' "

Fig. 1, no. 4. Lukanu (the Chief's Bracelet). An iron open-ended band, called after the bracelet worn by senior chiefs (such as Mwantiyanvwa, Kanongesha, Musokantanda, Ishinde, Nyakatolo, the Luvale chieftainess), which is made of dried human sinews and portions of genitalia, and washed periodically with secret medicines.

A.D.: "It stands for chieftainship."

M.: "*Lukanu* represents chieftainship [*wanta*]. If a chief dies, his people want to know the cause and go to a diviner. The Chief's Bracelet comes up and he says: 'You have come to divine for a chief, or for a chief's brother, or for his son, or for a member of his lineage.' Then he finds out the particular person in question."

Fig. 2, no. 3. Majiku (the Funeral Fires). A piece of wood with three notches burned out of it at approximately equal intervals.

A.D.: "*Majiku* [literally, 'fires'] represents the fires kindled inside a *chota* [the unwalled shelter in the middle of each village where the men gossip, eat, and discuss village matters] when the headman decides a domestic case, or when a council of village elders are deciding whether or not to go to a diviner in the case of illness or death."

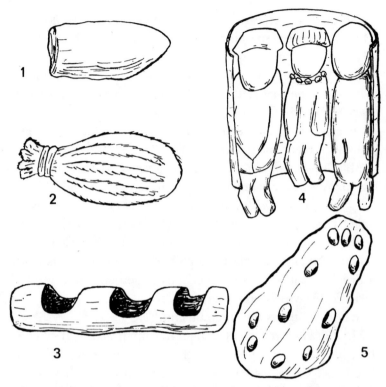

Figure 2. The divining objects. 1. *Mpemba* or *Mpeza*—white clay, see pages 168–169. 2. *Mukundu*—powdered red clay in mongoose pouch. 3. *Majiku* (the Funeral Fires)—a piece of wood. 4. *Akalumpi* (the Elders: woman, child, man)—carved wood and horn (note the white beans around child's neck). 5. *Chimbu* (the Hyena)—wood studded with red beans.

M.: "This *kaponya* stands for death [*ku-fwa*]. This is how it is used:

Neyi muntu nayi nakutaha wukumona mung'ombu mudinakwinza majiku. Majiku diyu ntanda. Mukwakuhong'a wayilejang'a antu anenzi nakuhong'a nindi mung'ombu yami chimudinakwinza majiku antanda chinalumbululi nawu muntu wakafwa ching'a chimwakafunta kumukala

wenu mwakenkuku ng'ovu jakuuka muntu kulonda akahandi; neyi kwin-
kaku ng'ovu nehi ona muyeji wakafwa.

(If a person goes to divine he will see in the diviner's basket the
Funeral Fires coming [up]. *Majiku* is a group [of fires].[15] The diviner tells the people who have come for divination: "In my basket
has come up a group of Funeral Fires, which means that someone
will die unless you return to your village with the strong intention
of curing the person that he may live; if you do not apply power [to
this aim] that person will die.")

"This means," Muchona went on, "that the people must
find a better doctor than they have hitherto employed; he
must be a doctor who will give the correct [*alala*] medicines
to the patient.

"The Funeral Fires may also come up if a patient has already died. After his death the headman and his people gathered in the village shelter to discuss the matter. The headman chose a group of his villagers 'to go to a different place'
[*nakuya kwekwawu*—a euphemism meaning to consult a divin-
er]. When they have arrived, the diviner shakes up the Funeral Fires to the top; he asks them [the Funeral Fires] why
they have come—they must represent death. Then he asks
his clients, 'Have you come about a living or a dead person?'
They answer [to test him], 'He is alive.' The diviner shakes
his *tuponya* again, and finds the Funeral Fires on top. He insists that the patient has died. Then the clients agree that he
has.

"*Majiku* can also stand for a funeral camp [*chipenji* or *chibimbi*]."

Fig. 2, no. 4. Ankishi (the Figurines, or Akulumpi, the Elders).

[15] At a Ndembu funeral camp people attend from near and far, and each
village group has its own fires, one for seniors, one for juniors.

Three rude stylized figurines carved in wood and united by a band of horn.

A.D.: "These represent a man, a woman, and their child, or a husband, his wife, and their child."

M.: "The *Ankishi* represent the Elders (*akulumpi*). They are the most important of the *tuponya*. The man is like Mwantiyanvwa, the paramount chief of the Lunda, the woman is his wife, the child is their offspring. Diviners shake them in the name of chiefs, saying that the grudge came from chiefs. Or it might be from a headman or his family.

"They also stand for husband, wife, and child. If the piece of white chalk came to the top with them, this would show that these people were free from suspicion.

"*Ankishi* are also used to divide between sublineages [*mavumu*]. For example, suppose there are five sublineages in Mukanza Village, and the diviner wanted to find out from which of them a sorcerer came, he would ask his *tuponya*, 'If the dead man was killed here [in the sublineage under consideration] will you please let us know? Show us by bringing *mpeza*. But if he found that the *Ankishi* came with red clay, he would say that the grudge 'is in this sublineage I have just mentioned.' For red clay means guilt of witchcraft.

"If, in this way, a chief is found to be a sorcerer, the diviner does not mention his name, but mentions a stone [*ilola*], the sky [*iwulu*], or a rock.

"This group also represents sorcerers. Thus it happened that one day a sorcerer killed someone. He was not a well-known sorcerer so the matter was taken to a diviner. The diviner used his *tuponya*. He shook them up. He saw the *Ankishi* come to the top along with the Hyena [*Chimbu*, see next object], red clay, white clay, and the Dead [*Mufu*]. He then began to ask questions [*nyikunyi*] of his *tuponya*. First he asked the white clay: 'Why have you, *mpemba*, appeared here, does it mean that there is no sorcerer here at all?' Then he put the *Ankishi* right under the heap and shook again. If the white clay then disappeared, he said, 'That *mpeza* appeared here for no reason.' Then he put the *Ankishi* underneath again and shook the pile up. But before he did this he said: 'I saw the Hyena. Does this mean that the Hyena killed someone?' If the *Ankishi* then came up next to the Hyena this showed him that there was a grudge present. Then he took the set of three figurines and put them under again, saying, 'I have seen the Hyena twice. Did you, Hyena, come from the mother's side, from the father's side, from the group of unrelated persons in the village, or from the women married into the village?' [*Eyi Chimbu wunafumi kukamama tahindi kukatata? Tahindi mudi ayilolu tahindi kudi ambanda amasumbu?*]

"After that he finds a sublineage or group from which the sorcerer came, by using the *Ankishi*.

"The *Ankishi* can also represent ancestor spirits [*akishi*]."

Interpretation by studying configurations of objects

Muchona at this point interpolated that a configuration of *tuponya* was called *kudiwung'a hamu* or *kupompa hamu* and that such configurations were made up of four, five, or six objects, and never more than six. They were to be interpreted in conjunction with one another as described under *Ankishi*.

Fig. 2, no. 5. Chimbu (the Hyena). This is an irregularly shaped piece of wood studded with hard red seeds (*jikeng'enyi*) from a thorn bush called *chiputa mazala* ("dirt [in] the fingernails": this tree is thought to be used in sorcery medicine and in love magic).

A.D.: "This *kaponya* means a sorcerer or witch [*muloji*]; the red seeds stand for a hyena's spots."

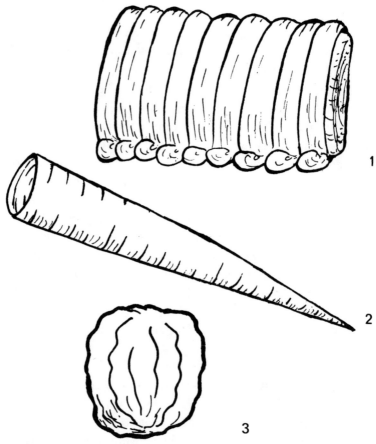

Figure 3. The divining objects. 1. *Mufu* (the Dead)—wood and bark string. 2. *Izu* (the Word)—duiker horn. 3. *Mwaka* (Longevity)—*mucha* fruit stone.

M.: "*Chimbu* means a sorcerer or witch. You should know that there are two kinds of hyena. There is a small striped one called 'little hyena' [*chimbu chanyanya*] or *kawubi;* there is a big one called *chimbu cheneni* ['big hyena'], with a spotted body. The *kaponya* stands for the big hyena. The people near Kalene Hill also call the lion '*chimbu.*' "

Fig. 3, no. 1. Mufu (a dead person). A piece of wood wound round with bark string.

A.D.: "This *kaponya* represents a recently dead person."

M.: "*Mufu* stands for a dead person tied onto his bed [*baka-didi*] or on grass mats [*bayisalu*] to be carried to the grave.

"When a diviner finds *Mufu*, his task is to explain the cause of death and then to find out who the sorcerer was.

"Or *Mufu* can represent an ancestor spirit. For example: a hunter found that his hunting power had vanished, he could kill no animals. So he went to a diviner, who found *Mufu* in his divining basket after shaking. The diviner then explained in detail just how the hunter-ancestor kept his client's hunts-manship away and how he must deal with the spirit, whether he must wash himself with pounded-leaf medicine or whether to pray at a hunter's shrine [*chishing'a*], or whether to have a drum played [perform a ritual of the hunter's cult] for him."

In different divinatory contexts *Mufu* may represent a corpse, a recently dead person, or an ancestor spirit which is afflicting its living relative with bad luck at hunting, repro-ductive disorder, or illness.

Fig. 3, no. 2. Izu (the Word). A small duiker horn with a small piece of *mpemba* inserted in the opening.

A.D.: "This stands for cursing [*ku-shing'ana*]; by such curs-ing a sorcerer can raise up a *musalu*, the body of a dead per-son with long hair and fingernails, and send it to kill someone he has a grudge against."

M.: "It is a word either of a dead or of a living person. Or it is a curse which caused something bad to happen. They divine to find out why someone spoke such 'a word.' The white clay stands for someone who spoke properly or justly. If that person spoke well, the *kaponya* called *Izu* would stand upright with the white clay uppermost. But if it lay on one side, that person spoke badly or evilly."

Fig. 3, no. 3. Mwaka (longevity). The durable stone of the *incha* fruit of the *mucha* tree (*Parinari mobola*).

A.D.: "It stands for a case [*mulong'a*] that took place a long time ago [*mwaka*]."

M.: "A *mucha* tree takes four or five months to produce ripe fruits, but the stones of those fruits take two or three years to decay. Thus it can mean in divination that someone has been ill for a long time. For a sorcerer, in order to escape detection, sometimes puts a small amount of medicine on one part of his victim's body, then a little more, then more, until he has killed him in gradual stages. A diviner, inquiring into this case, sees *Mwaka* and knows that the victim has been killed in this way, by gradual, secret applications of medicine. Or a sorcerer's snake familiar [*ilomba*] may catch the victim by his leg, without medicine being used, and swallow him slowly from the leg upward. Only a sorcerer, a diviner, or a doctor who has drunk *nosompu*, pounded-leaf medicine, can see this happening.

"*Mwaka* also indicates when people have long delayed consulting a diviner. For example: once upon a time a man called Chifwetafweta had a younger brother, whose wife had many lovers [*andowa*]. Some of them ensorcelled the younger brother and he died. Chifwetafweta brought medicine with him and killed two of the lovers, who were living in the same village. They were not related to him. Fearing revenge he fled from his own village, where he lived with his mother, to a distant place. Three years later he returned to his mother's village. But the relatives of those he killed ensorcelled him and he died. This is a case of *Mwaka*, for although Chifwe-

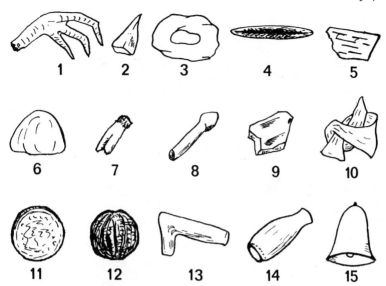

Figure 4. The divining objects. 1. *Kaneng'a* or *Kasumbi* (the Fowl)—cock's claw. 2. *Chipaji* (Situtunga Hoof)—piece of hoof. 3. *Ng'oji* (Carrying Cloth)—hide. 4. *Njila* (the Path)—grooved wood. 5. *Wutali* (Smelted Iron)—iron. 6. *Itung'a* (the Country)—piece of red gum. 7. *Chikwa Chankayi* (Duiker Hoof)—hoof. 8. *Ilomu* (the Penis)—carved wood. 9. *Madilu* (Tears)—green glass. 10. *Matang'isha* (the Twister)—twisted leather. 11. *Mali aPotugeshi*—50 centavos of Angolan money. 12. *Mpuhu* (Fame)—black withered fruit. 13. *Muhinyi* (Ax Handle)—piece of wood. 14. *Ng'oma* or *Mufu* (the Drum)—carved wood. 15. Bell (Hunting)—iron.

tafweta ran away for a long time, the sorcerers did not forget to take revenge."

Fig. 4, no. 1. Kaneng'a or Kasumbi (the Fowl). A claw of the cock killed by the diviner's bite [see page 259] during his initiation in the *Kayong'u* ritual.

A.D.: "This means that a cock should be sacrificed, instead of a black goat, in the *Kaneng'a* ritual performed to cure a person of illness sent by a witch or sorcerer."

M.: "If this *kaponya* comes up, it means that people have

come on behalf of someone who is very ill. The diviner diagnoses that a cock should be killed at the *Kaneng'a* ritual, or at the *ku-kupula* rite of sweeping a person with medicine brooms to drive away familiars. But it can stand for any ritual in which a cock is killed, such as *Kalemba, Chihamba, Nkula,* or *Kaluwi.*"

Fig. 4, no. 2. Chipaji (the Situtunga's Hoof). A split-off portion of the hoof of a situtunga antelope (*nvudi*).

A.D.: "This represents a person who goes to consult a diviner but is really himself the sorcerer who killed his relative."

M.: "The word *nvudi* [situtunga] comes from *kavulachima,* 'negligence.' Here is a story to explain it: Someone died in a certain village. The headman and his kin said: 'Oh we are sorry to see that our relative is dead. Perhaps tomorrow or the day after we shall go to a different village to consult a diviner about his death.' Everybody went on weeping for the dead man, and they wept and wept for many days. But they never went to the diviner. Such men were negligent about the matter of the death. Others might delay about consulting a diviner on behalf of a sick person. In both cases, the diviner would be led to think that the negligent people were themselves guilty of sorcery. He would think this if he saw the Situtunga's Hoof come to the top of the *tuponya* several times.

"But *Chipaji* can also stand for huntsmanship [*Wubinda*], particularly for the [hunter's] mode of praying [*ku-kombelela*] to their hunter spirits."

Fig. 4, no. 3. Ng'oji (the Carrying Cloth). A piece of hide with a hole in the middle.

A.D.: "This stands for the cloth in which women carry their children."

M.: "*Ng'oji* means 'in tribes' [*munyichidi*] or 'in matrilineages' [*mumavumu*]; it means that a person [represented] in *ng'ombu* belongs to such and such a group."

Fig. 4, no. 4. Njila (the Path or the Way). A piece of grooved wood with a deep line incised along the middle of it.

A.D.: "*Njila* means that one of the persons in *ng'ombu* went away.' "

M.: "This is something that is found on the path along which a person is traveling. That person may have met death, or perhaps been bitten by a dog or a snake. For example, if I were to go to another place and leave my home, I might find a grudge [*chitela*—here referring to sorcery medicines concealed in the path by someone with a grudge against Muchona] on the path. It also means 'something that happened between two places.' It is a symbol [*chinjikijilu*] of something happening."

Fig. 4, no. 5. Wutali (Smelted Iron; also called Chikung'u, Iron). A small irregularly shaped piece of flattened iron.

A.D.: "This means that the happening described by the diviner has been seen by a person's own eyes—he was an eye-witness [*chinsahu*]."

M.: "It stands for 'food.' For example, a person was given 'bad' beer (beer doctored with sorcery medicine), then he became ill and died. All grain crops from which beer can be made are cut with a sickle of iron, or the trees which are cut down, and burned to ashes, in which millet is broadcast, are cut down by an ax of iron. Or it can represent a hoe, hence 'food.'

"But it can also mean 'what a person has seen [*ku-tala*] [16]

---

[16] This is an example of fictitious etymology. *Wutali* cannot be derived from *ku-tala*, since the former has a long radical *a*, and the latter a short one. But fictitious etymology, like homonymy, is a device whereby the semantic wealth of a word or symbol is augmented.

with his own eyes.' It is also a thing that belongs to another thing—thus: a person died from drinking beer; this, then, belongs to 'beer.' A diviner can see this in *Wutali*. It means 'to one side' also. Or a man was bitten by a snake because he was cursed in a particular way—the way of *kumbila*, when something in snake form was thrown at a person to kill him, by a sorcerer."

Fig. 4, no. 6. Itung'a (the Country or Realm). A smooth piece of dusky red gum.

A.D.: "Its meaning depends on its position after shaking. It stands for any place, like a chief's area or a cluster of villages."

M.: "It means 'a country.' For example, it may mean that a person goes far away, perhaps to the Belgian Congo, which is another territory. When he goes there he dies. So the grudge which caused his death must be there. Or someone went to Angola and there died or was attacked by a terrible disease. The grudge must be there where he went, not here in his village. Or even in Bembaland or Nyasaland, where something terrible [*chafwana*] happened to him, the grudge belonging to that place. *Itung'a*, then, is the country to which a person went."

Fig. 4, no. 7. Chikwa chankayi (the Duiker's Hoof). A small duiker's hoof.

A.D.: "It means 'a hunter' [*chibinda*]."

M.: "This represents huntsmanship [*wubinda*]. If the *kapon-ya* called Hyena comes in contact with this hoof, it means that the witch, the owner of the hyena familiar, came to take away a man's huntsmanship, his power to kill animals."

Fig. 4, no. 8. Ilomu (the Penis). A carved piece of wood representing a circumcised penis.

A.D.: "This stands for 'a man' or 'anything male.' "

M.: "A woman must come into contact with a penis in order to conceive a child. Thus *Ilomu* stands for 'everybody' [*antu ejima*], for everyone must be conceived and born again [*acheng'i*—this may refer to the Ndembu belief in a modified form of reincarnation—to the inheritance of certain personal character traits of a deceased relative, usually on the father's side]. Without the penis no one would be seen.

"Another meaning is a woman who is always committing adultery—she was caught by her husband and cursed by him. Then the husband went to the lover to claim compensation, say a goat or a gun or, as it is today, £5. While the case [*mulong'a*] is going on, people are cursing one another because of this adultery. It may then happen that a sorcerer [*muloji*]· who lives far away comes quickly and kills the woman with his medicines. The sorcerer thinks: 'Although I am the one who killed the woman, no one here knows me. Everyone will think she died because of the case she brought [from the sorcery of one of the protagonists]. They will think that perhaps the husband or the adulterer killed the woman.' When a diviner is divining about this matter he goes into all the details and he concludes that the woman is dead because it was her own choice to commit adultery with the penis. If she hadn't done so, she would not have died. There is a Luvale proverb: '*Kunyi janjamba jakudi chayila*' [the wood-fire of the elephant is collected by himself], that is, it is the victim's own will that caused his death. The sorcerer killed for food only [this refers to the necrophagous purpose of Ndembu sorcery and witchcraft]. He had no personal grudge against the woman.

"*Ilomu* also stands for anything masculine. Here it could mean that the *muloji* was a man.

"Or it can represent a man who is in the habit of committing adultery."

Fig. 4, no. 9. Madilu (Tears, or Masoji; tears in Chi-Luvale). A piece of broken glass rubbed smooth.

A.D.: "This stands for the weeping and lamentation of women after they hear the news of a death."

M.: "It has two senses: (1) It shows that someone has died, that people were weeping, tears were running down from their eyes. (2) It is usually black in color, which means darkness [*mwidima*], which means that someone was having a dream in the night. His trouble came from the darkness while he slept. Someone came to bewitch him at night, or he dreamed of a dead relative who was making him ill or causing bad luck."

Fig. 4, no. 10. Matang'isha (the Twister). A small piece of twisted leather.

A.D.: "This means a person who goes hither and thither, or one who gives evasive answers. Such a person is likely to be a sorcerer or a witch, for sorcerers go to one place one day and to another the next."

M.: "The Twister stands for 'deceiving a diviner' [*kumudimba mukwakuhong'a*]. For example: a diviner may say to his clients, 'You have come to consult me about the death of a chief,' but they disagree with him. Or he may say, 'I have seen the drum of *Kaneng'a*, I have seen the cock crow that you have killed. Is this not so?' But they deny it. But a diviner can convince people that he is a real diviner. When people come to consult him they hide an arrow near the path by which they came. The diviner says, 'All right, if I am incorrect, let me go to that path.' There he finds the arrow and says, 'Isn't this your arrow, the sign that you wanted to consult me?' Then the people say, 'You are a true diviner. All

you said was correct. We have just been testing you out.'
How did he know all this? He saw the Twister coming up
three or four times in his basket."

Comments by Muchona on diviners and divination

One goes to a distant diviner. Muchona here interpolated that
it is wise to go to a distant diviner rather than one who lives
in the neighborhood, since the latter may be in some way
connected with the subject of divination, or with his kin or
affines or with the witch's relatives. He illustrated this point
with a proverb: *"Kajila kadi kunsa yawuta kakukwasila muk-
wenu, bayi eyi awenuku,"* [Your friend should shoot the bird
on the end of your bow, you should not shoot it yourself.]
Matters that are too close to one are best left to an outsider's
judgment. Muchona said that even a diviner would consult a
distant diviner, if one of his own relatives died.

Professional etiquette among diviners. This led Muchona by a
natural transition to talk about the need for good manners between diviners. For example, they must not quarrel during a
consultation. It sometimes happens that two diviners are
brought together to inquire into the same case. If one is older
or more experienced than the other, he holds his peace while
the latter is divining. If he sees that mistakes are being made,
he quietly asks his junior if he may assist for a while and
takes over for a few shakes of the basket. Then he will say,
"Now, I'm tired, please carry on for a while, my younger
brother." This procedure is repeated until divination is complete.

The assistant known as *mpumba* is not a true diviner, initiated at the *Kayon'gu* ritual. He is the man who sits beside
the candidate at *Kayong'u* and who later may assist him at
séances by handing equipment to him and by placing white

clay on the heads of the innocent and red clay on the guilty. He is usually taught the meaning of the *tuponya*, though he may not undertake basket divination.

Fig. 4, no. 11. Mali aPotugeshi (*Portuguese Money, or Ikuta, a small coin*). A fifty-centavo piece of Angolan money.

A.D.: "This may indicate that a man has been killed [by witchcraft] for money."

M.: "It represents the loss of money. If a man loses, say, 5s. or 10s., he consults a diviner. If the diviner sees *Ikuta* coming up, he says, 'You have come because you have lost money.'

"It may also stand for the loss of other kinds of property, such as sheep, goats, or fowls. The diviner must find out who the thief was and where the money is. If the money has been mislaid by the owner he will tell him where it is.

"*Ikuta* also appears several times if people grew envious of a rich man and killed him for his money. Perhaps his relatives wanted to inherit his wealth. Or he may have grown proud and taken many women, causing jealousy and starting a grudge."

Fig. 4, no. 12. Mpuhu (*Fame*). A black *mpuhu* fruit, withered around its stone, from a tree which grows in the evergreen streamside forest. *Mpuhu* means fame or reputation.

A.D.: "It represents a chief or an important person."

M.: "It stands for one who has a reputation for generosity, for a rich man, a great hunter, or a famous diviner. It can also mean a notorious evildoer, a noted sorcerer or witch. It represents a chief, for chiefs use *mpuhu* medicine during their installation rites.

"I myself use the shell [*nkesi*] of a water snail to represent good or ill fame. I use it because water is the first of things. For example, at a woman's first pregnancy the first thing to do is to spit water on her body; when a baby is born the women spit water on it, then give it water to drink.[17] All men drink water, even chiefs drink it, animals and birds must drink it, and thus water is the most important thing. Water is life [*wumi*]. Thus the snail shell, which comes from the water, means real fame [*mpuhu*], it is the most important or senior [*yamukulumpi*] thing. For water is the elder [*menji di mukulumpi*]."

Fig. 4, no. 13. Muhinyi (the Ax Handle or Hoe Handle). A small piece of wood shaped like an ax or hoe handle.

A.D.: "It represents a witch's familiar or zombie, called *kahwehwu*, the animated corpse of her bewitched husband, which kills at her will with an ax handle."

M.: "*Muhinyi* has three meanings: (1) it may stand for the grave [*kalung'a*], for when a man has died, the first thing to do is to bring a hoe with its handle [*muhinyi*] and dig a grave with it; (2) it may also mean 'raising the dead,' for diviners believe that after burial witches go privately to the grave and there raise up a hoe handle. Then they strike the grave with it and the dead person comes out quickly; they take him secretly to be cut up into portions of meat; (3) it may also stand for the ax handle or hoe handle used by a *kahwehwu* familiar. Here it would mean that a witch had been the cause of death."

Fig. 4, no. 14. Ng'oma (the Drum, or Mufu wamwaka, the Dead of Long Ago). A wooden carving of a drum.

A.D.: "This stands for someone who has been dead for a long time or for an ancestor spirit."

M.: "If a diviner sees the Drum coming to the top, he

---

[17] This is done before the infant is given the breast. Ndembu say that cold water is spat on a newborn child "to awaken its voice and life."

says, 'A spirit is coming here which likes a drum to be played' [mukishi wudinakeng'a kumwimbila ng'oma]. If his clients came on behalf of a woman [one suffering from reproductive disorders or from illness] they would then inquire, 'Are we to play the drum of Kayong'u or Nkula or Chihamba [three rituals of affliction] for her?' If the diviner told them Chihamba they would go home and play the Chihamba drum for her. There are ways of representing every kind of ritual [chidyika]. But there are not tuponya for all kinds of ritual. For example, to find out whether Nkula should be performed the diviner has to ask the right questions. Thus he speaks to all the tuponya and says, 'If the Nkula drums should be played, please let us know it.' If the Drum then appears just above the Elders, this is a sign of Nkula. But sometimes a diviner will add things that stand for various kinds of ritual. For example, the seed of the mudidi [18] tree [a palm tree from which palm wine, ntombi, is made] represents the Kayong'u spirit, for this spirit likes drinking palm wine. Kayong'u comes from the Belgian Congo where people drink palm wine. This is where the Lunda found Chibinda Chakatili [the Luban founder of the Mwantiyanvwa dynasty, who married Luweji Ankonde]. Red beads, standing for maternal blood [mashi amama], the blood that is seen at parturition, may stand for woman's rituals like Nkula or Isoma. But these are not necessary for the diviner has the red beads in his breast. He need only ask questions two or three times in succession [muchilonda], to test the truth of a question."

[18] The Angolan diviner told me that he had left a seed of the mudidi tree, representing Kayong'u, behind in Sewulu Village.

Some other *tuponya*

Muchona told me about some *tuponya* not found in the Angolan diviner's set. These included:

Nyikana yawandumba (*the groups of Witches' Familiars*). A piece of wood with notches cut into it.

M.: "It stands for groups [*nyikana*] of familiars used by witches.[19] If this *kaponya* appears two or three times, the diviner stops to reason about [*ku-tong'ojoka*] it, saying, 'Does this mean that a witch [female] was responsible for the death?' Then he would mention a name to the *kaponya*, say, the victim's mother or his sister."

Chanzang'ombi (*the Snake Familiar*). A piece of wood carved to look like a snake with a man's face.

M.: "It stands for the *ilomba*, the human-faced snake, made and sent by medicine. It is used by a sorcerer [male]. *Chanzang'ombi* is an old Lunda word, perhaps it is connected with *kwanzanza*, 'to talk aloud while dreaming,' or 'to moan when sick,' but I don't know that properly."

Kaswaha kawalwa (*the Little Calabash of Beer*). The neck of the calabash just where it joins the vine.

M.: "It means a person who died because he drank beer containing bad medicine, for the beer was in a calabash. The diviner will go from that point into details about the kind of medicine used, about the sort of grudge cherished by the sorcerer, and so on.

"The Little Calabash may also represent water and may stand for those manifestations of *Chihamba*, *Kayong'u*, or *Nkula* that catch people near rivers or streams.

[19] These are said to gather together with their owners under a *mwang'ala* tree and to share with them a ghoulish feast on the corpse of a slain victim.

"It may also stand for the water that is poured over a very sick person from a calabash to revive him.

"Again it may stand for ancestor spirits, for the beer that is poured out at their tree shrines.

"It may mean, too, the calabash of water that is poured over the mound of earth heaped up on a grave. This water softens the earth so that it can be moulded [ku-pembesh'ejamu]. They make its surface smooth and neat, so that if a woman comes to eat the corpse, her presence can be detected by the disturbance of the mound."

Nkumbilu (the Waterfall Stone). One of the stones found at the top or foot of a waterfall.

M.: "The *kaponya* stands for 'misunderstanding of the matter' [*museneni*, derived from *ku-senena*, 'to be slippery']. If *Nkumbilu* comes to the top with a series of different *tuponya*, he says there is misunderstanding or confusion here— '*museneni* has come from a sorcerer or witch.' The sorcerer may have given some of the consultants *museneni* medicine to make it hard for the diviner to find things out correctly. He now tells his *tuponya* to come up properly. He speaks publicly to his clients, saying, 'You have come with *museneni*, please stop it.' Now the power of the *museneni* goes away because it has been detected. It is just the same with legal cases [*nyilong'a*]. If a person can hide his evildoing, he will get away. But if there have been witnesses, he is known and then punished."

Comments by Muchona on innocence from witchcraft. Muchona said that when a person is cleared of a witchcraft charge by divination Ndembu speak about "making someone go forward as an innocent one" (*ku-twamijaku mwelu*). The term *mwelu*, here used for "someone who is not a witch," Muchona derived from *ku-welela*, "to wash (with medicines) on someone's behalf." Medicine has been washed on the *mwelu*, cleansing him. This is another fictitious derivation. *Mwelu* is actually composed of the prefix *mu* + radical *elu* and has the basic sense of light-skinned. The connotation seems to be the contrast between dark-skinned and sorcery or witchcraft, as against the light-skinned and free of such qualities.

Muchona on fees paid to diviners. "Long ago the fee for a divination into death was twenty-four yards of cloth and a slave; or twenty-four yards of cloth and two guns; or twenty-four yards of cloth and one gun. If the diviner failed to mention the name of the dead person [correctly], he would be paid twenty yards of cloth, or nowadays twelve yards of cloth. If a diviner was paid a conus-mollusk shell [*imba*], this meant that the case was left unfinished. If someone paid an elephant's tusk, a few things were added to that payment. Today £4 10s. 0d. or £5 0s. 0d. in Northern Rhodesian money may be paid. Witches and sorcerers were forced to pay some cloths to the relatives of their victims. The sorcerer's or witch's belongings were taken by the dead person's relatives. But some of the belongings of those relatives were then paid to the diviner."

Muchona on the chief's poison ordeal or poison oracle

"If a person divined as a sorcerer then appealed to the chief's poison-ordeal [*mwaji*] and was found innocent by it, the diviner did not have to return any payment made to him. Both kinds of divination were said to have been true. The relatives of the deceased person were adjudged to have no case against the alleged sorcerer, who had gone personally to the chief to report on the accusation. The chief had then told some of his own relatives to use *mwaji* privately somewhere to find out if he was innocent [*naying'i*]. If he was found innocent by *mwaji*, they returned and reported it to the chief. The chief upheld this verdict. But the alleged sorcerer must, in these circumstances, make a payment to the chief. When the man's relatives heard the news they came to praise the chief and helped their kinsman to pay two goats or twenty cloths or a gun or two slaves, according to the chief's wish. An official known as *Chivwikankanu*, 'The Invester with *lukanu*,' whose main ritual role is to place the chiefly *lukanu* bracelet on a new chief's arm and to wash it periodically with purifying medicines, may be entrusted with the task of administering the *mwaji* ordeal. A person cleared by this ordeal is known as *Nsanza mwaji* from *ku-sanza*, 'to vomit.' The subchiefs of the present Ndembu Native Authority were once called *ayilolu* (singular *chilolu*); only Kanongesha among the Ndembu was called a true chief (*mwanta walala*). But these *ayilolu* could administer *mwaji*. There are four ways in which *mwaji* may be given: to chickens; to human beings—sometimes it is given to a slave of an important man [20] divined as a sorcerer; to termites—a form called *chiswa* (see page 333); finally, the term *mwaji* may refer to the boiling water ordeal whereby a suspected sorcerer or witch must plunge his or her arm into a pot of boiling water and medicines. If the arm is not scalded the person is innocent.

"My father Kenji was once given *mwaji* to drink but he vomited it up. The *mwaji* tree [*Erythrophloeum guineense*] grows only in special localities, such as Mwininyilamba Area. It is a tall, thick tree, growing in the streamside forest [*itu*] or in thick [*Cryptosepalum*] forest [*ivunda*]. The *mwaji*

[20] White (1947:8) cites the case of Chief Ishinde Kawumbu who was accused of witchcraft; the poison ordeal was administered to one of his servants.

poison consists of scrapings from the bark. The collector makes a ritual address [*mpandula*] to the tree itself and to one or two of his ancestor spirits. It is sometimes given in adultery cases. If a man denied sleeping with another's wife, they might say, 'let us give you a taste of *mwaji.*' But it is usually administered to chickens, not to the man himself. If he is found guilty, he has to pay. If innocent, the husband must pay him."

A government subchief told me in 1951 that a person divined as a sorcerer would go to a chief's capital village (*ng'anda*) and tell him that he was prepared to pay him one of his junior relatives, usually a sister's child, if the latter would perform the *mwaji* test on his behalf. The chief would summon his *Chivwikankanu* or some other important headman to act as officiant. The officiant and the accused would both bring chickens. The officiant would first put *mwaji* in the mouth of the accused's chicken. If he was indeed guilty the bird would die instantly. If it vomited up the poison, another dose of *mwaji* would be given to the officiant's chicken— called "the chief's chicken." If this survived, a third chicken would be brought. If this one lived, the man would be regarded as innocent. The chief was then entitled to choose one of the man's relatives as his slave (*ndung'u*). Next he ordered the diviner to return the cloths he had received in payment to the relatives of the deceased man.

Fees for divination into illness. "For divination into illness a diviner receives 1s. 6d., 2s., 3s., 4s., or 5s., according to his liver [*muchima*]. In Angola today a man pays less than a woman, for a man is more hospitable to strangers than a woman. Long ago no difference was made between them."

Other Kinds of Divination

Muchona's account

Mwishi (divination by pounding pole)

"*Mwishi*, the pounding pole used by women to pound [*ku-twa*] grain and cassava roots into meal, is the senior [*muku-lumpi*] of Lunda methods of divination. It is the first one, we knew it before the basket method was brought in from the Luvale. When a person wishes to begin *mwishi*, he must get power [*ng'ovu*] in the back of his wrist [*nkuku*]. He need not dream first—this would mean that he has the *ng'ombu* of *Kayong'u*. Here only the medicine is important. He asks a senior *mwishi* diviner to help him and they collect medicines together. First they collect *mpelu* medicines [small portions of inorganic or organic objects and human personal leavings—these ingredients, by the principles of the part for the whole and of contagious magic, impart the powers and properties of those objects and persons to the set of medicines]. These consist of some *ibanda* salt, made from the ashes of burned river grass, and a piece of dried leech [*izambu*].

"Next, they go to a *kapwipu* [*Swartzia madagascariensis*] tree and collect some of its leaves, then to a *lweng'i* plant [*Draecena reflexa var. nitens*] for leaves. They chew these leaves up and place them in a potsherd [*chizanda*]. Then they mix these up with the *mpelu* medicines. Next the novice [*muntu wa-tachikang'a*] says, 'You, my relative X, who are dead, you are the one I am going to use in this *ng'ombu*. Come on to the back of my wrist. [*Twaya munkuku yami.*] I will make cuts on it so that you may catch points of divination with it. [*Nuku-sali kulonda wukwatang'a nachu hayidimbu*].' He then cuts marks with a razor [*ku-sala*] on his wrist and rubs the medicines into them. *Chidimbu* [*plural yidimbu*] means the point at which the pestle, as it is rubbed along the ground by the diviner, suddenly stops during an interrogation. The diviner's hand at this point presses down so that the underside of his wrist touches the ground."

The meaning of the mwishi medicine. "(1) *Ibanda* salt is used because it is tasty [*ku-towala*—this term is applied equally to salty substances, like blood and salt, and to sweet things, like honey and sugar]; this means that everyone should know that here is a man who knows how to divine properly—a diviner who has eminence [*kutiyakana*, literally, 'who should be listened to'], for salt is important [*dalema*];

"(2) A *leech* sticks to one; so should this *ng'ombu* stick to the point, stick firmly to the ground. For example, women call a man who does not divorce his wife an *izambu*, a 'leech,' or a *kanzeng'u*, 'a tick.' A woman who sticks to her husband is also an *izambu;*

"(3) *Kapwipu* is a hard tree, termites cannot eat it. Wild animals come to eat its fruit in large numbers—in the same way many people must come to the diviner and hear many things;

"(4) *Lweng'i* is used on account of its strong smell, this makes a person well understood—the diviner will be smelled by many people and will be well understood."

How mwishi is used. "A pounding pole or an ax handle or a hoe handle is rubbed along the ground. Since the diviner's power inheres in his wrist he can perform this kind of divination anywhere. He asks the *mwishi*, and not the people, questions. When his wrist presses down and the *mwishi* stops rubbing, he has his answer. He tells the people his findings when he has completely finished. Long ago all kinds of matters were divined into by *mwishi*, but mostly illness [*yikatu*]. Today it is used for illnesses and for finding a spirit-name [*ijina damukishi*] for infants. There are many *mwishi* diviners, but few *ku-sekula* [basket-shaking] diviners. Only a small payment is made for *mwishi* divination, about 3*d*. to a shilling. In the past, the kind of divination called *dawulang'ang'a* was used for catching sorcerers and witches. To rub the pounding pole is called *kukoka mwishi*, sometimes *ku-hong'a*."

Dawulang'ang'a or *ng'ombu yanzenzi* (rattle divination)

"*Ku-dawula* means to eat food early, at sunrise, before going anywhere. It is like the cock at *Kayong'u* (see page 259). The diviner [*ng'ang'a*] is the first awake, before others. In this kind of divination many *tuponya* are used as in *ng'ombu yakuse-kula*. Strong-smelling *lweng'i* is put in among the *tuponya*. The diviner touches the *tuponya* while he is divining and smells his finger. As in *ku-sekula*, the diviner must first have passed through the *Kayong'u* ritual before he can divine. The diviner holds a rattle [*nzenzi*] and all the attenders have two rattles apiece. When the diviner asks questions he shakes his rattle [*nzenzi*], and when the people answer they shake theirs. When the diviner sings, the people sing in reply. Here is a story to illustrate *dawulang'ang'a*:

"A person died at a certain village. His relatives went to a diviner's village and sat in its *chota*. When the diviner saw them, he began to breathe wheezily [*ku-tomena*], to show that he knew why they came. Then they tried to deceive him, saying, 'Farewell, we are going somewhere else on a visit.' The diviner said, 'Oh no, you have come to consult me. Why must you go elsewhere?' But they insisted that they must go. After a while, however, the diviner made them stay and went into his hut to fetch his big basket [*chisuku*] with a lid, containing the *tuponya*. He put it just outside his hut and began to take some medicines from his *malembu* [calabash containers], and rub them on his brow, biceps, and just above his navel. He moved the *tuponya* two or three times in his *chisuku* basket. Then he divined mentally [without using his apparatus] whether he was right in preventing the people from going away, but his *Kayong'u* told him that he was right. Then he gave each person present two rattles and began to sing:

Dawulang'ang'a dawula, nukushindi mukwetu, dawulang'ang'a dawula, chafuma hanka eyi? Dawulang'ang'a dawula, Nimukamba nimovi nimujimba namuntu? [21] *Dawulang'ang'a dawula, Tahindi kuwusungu kuwuzambi? Dawulang'ang'a dawula. Tuyenu kumukambi namovu, dawulang'ang'a dawula.*

(Eat early, doctor, eat early, let me see truly the matter you bring, [Refrain], what has your problem come from? [Refrain] Cassava root? or *movwa* tree root? or body? or a person? Is it for fish-poison or huntsmanship? [Refrain]. Let us go to the cassava root and *movwa* tree root. [Refrain].

Muchona's comment. "If it is to the cassava root [the clients] say:

Eng'a etu twendela mukamba muntu wakata, iyala namumbanda tahindi?
(Yes, we traveled for a cassava root, for a sick person. Is it a man or a woman?)

"If it is one man only, he says:

Wumu hohu, dawulang'ang'a dawula, nakwati hachidimbu, dawulang'ang'a dawula.
(One only. Eat early, doctor, eat early. I have seized on a point of divination. Eat early, doctor, eat early.)

"They agree that it is a man. If a woman, [they say]:

---

[21] All these terms refer to bodily illness. *Movwa* has a thick root similar to that of cassava.

Mumbanda nimuntu, dawulang'ang'a dawula. Ambanda ekali ayedi. Kansi indi mukulumpi?

It is a female person. Eat early, doctor, eat early. There are two women. Is it a child or an adult?)

"[If it is] an adult he says:

Mukulumpi.
(An adult.)

"If a child, he says:

Kansi.
(A child.)

"He puts down [the divining basket] after giving his decision."

"[Then he sings]:

Chikoli ye chikole-e wo-o, ng'ombu yalili matemwa nawandung'u.
(Strength, o strength indeed, [my] *ng'ombu* ate up hoes and slaves.)

"This means," said Muchona, "that he is praising his divining apparatus and divining power, which has acquired for him much wealth in hoes and slaves in payment for successful divination. He acquires hoes as follows: when a clearing [*ibulu*] is made in the bush for the séance, the hoes and axes used for the purpose are given to the diviner."

In most respects, *dawulang'ang'a* resembles the *ng'ombu ya-kusekula*, but *lweng'i* medicine is no longer used in *ku-sekula;* nor do the attenders carry rattles.

Katuwa kang'ombu (calabash divination)

"*Katuwa,*" said Muchona, "is a small round calabash with the neck removed. The same medicines used for *mwishi* divination [see above] are put inside it. Some powdered white clay and powdered red clay are placed on the ground in front of it, white clay to the right, red clay to the left. The diviner then grasps the calabash. If a man wants to find his huntsmanship, it moves by itself to the red clay. If he desires the *lukupu* ritual [to 'sweep away' (*ku-kupula*) witchcraft or sorcery], it also goes to the red clay. For sickness it goes to the white clay—also called cassava root,[22] as in other kinds of divination, such a root is the human body, but people mean that it is a sick body.

"*Katuwa* can also distinguish between different ancestor spirits. You can use it to divine for members of other tribes. For example, I was once employed at Broken Hill [Kawe] by a European to bring heaps of little stones to make a motor road. A Lamba fellow employee asked me to divine for a sick relative of his. I divined with *katuwa* and it led me to a hut where the patient was sleeping. Then I held *katuwa* at the far end of the hut from the patient. It then climbed up his legs until it reached his temples. After that it went into the fire and came out again. I told his relative, 'There is no need to give him medicine now,' for the man would die soon. At midnight the man died. For a fire means a 'mourning camp' [*chipenji*] and thus it means death. [See also pages 299–301.]

"When points of divination [*yidimbu*] are reached, if spirits of the water are indicated, or if a spirit wants *nsompu* pounded-leaf medicine, the *katuwa* often moves itself to calabashes in huts or kitchens, for this means that the spirit is needing water or, perhaps, beer. Or again, it might lead the diviner to a species of tree from which *nsompu* can be collected.

[22] Cassava meal (*wung'a*) is often used as a substitute for *mpeza* in ritual. It is pure white in color.

"It may go to both white and red clay for a spirit that likes to be decorated with lines or spots. But if the spirit only likes white clay it goes repeatedly to the white clay.

"The word *chidimbu* only applies to matters of divination. A point of law is *hansang'u* [literally 'on the story or history') or *hamulong'a* [literally 'on the case')."

Ng'ombu yamuseng'u wambala (bushbuck horn divination)

"Medicines are 'pressed in' [*ku-panda*] the horn of a bushbuck. The first of the *jipelu* magical ingredients collected is a portion of *mulukuta* or *kalulu*, taken from the Half-Hare familiar used by sorcerers—this stands for *yikatu*, 'illnesses.' "

"The next is a portion of vulture [*ikubi*], which eats dead people. This stands for huntsmanship. Then the *mwishi* medicines [see above] are collected in a potsherd and all the ingredients rubbed into small cuts of the wrist, and between the thumb and index finger of the left hand. Two cuts are made in the brow, others beside the eyes, and another in the middle of the chest over the heart, to make him remember things, and the medicines are rubbed in these. Then the same medicines are pressed into the bushbuck horn itself. After this the diviner takes the horn in his left hand at its base and speaks as follows:

" 'You, my *ng'ombu*, I wish to test you out to find out whether you are correct [literally, "good"] or mistaken [*china-wahi hela chinaluwi*]. Now, look, this is the sun which is just going to set. If this sun will not be seen tomorrow, or if this is the last time we shall see it, you, my horn, go straight away to the red clay [*mukundu* or *ikula*—this is from *ku-kula*, to mature, and here refers to the blood of menstruation]. If the sun will be seen, go to the white clay.' Then the horn leads the diviner's hand either to the red or the white clay.

He stops it moving by tapping it with a rattle [*nzenzi*], as in *katuwa* divination. If it goes in this case to the white clay his *ng'ombu* is all right [*chinawahi*].

"To designate something masculine, the horn will turn around and reach the diviner's penis; to represent something feminine it will point toward a woman's private parts—for example, to show that women's rituals [*yidika yawambanda*] should be performed.

"An elder is represented by white clay, a junior or child [*kansi*] by red clay.

"This *ng'ombu* likes to move about, it can go to people or trees. You distinguish the father's from the mother's side of a person by the movement or absence of movement of the horn. If you ask, 'Is it from the father's side?' and the horn moves, then you know that the answer is 'yes.' If it does not move, then 'the mother's side' is correct.

"As in *mwishi* divination white and red lines are drawn on the wrist of the diviner. Red and white stripes are drawn on the pounding pole and on the bushbuck horn.

"The movement of the horn in going about seeking for something is *ku-keng'akeng'a*.

"The horn can explain whether a patient has been caught or attacked by an *ilomba* snake familiar or not. If it begins to dig into the ground, the diviner will ask, 'Will this person, caught by an *ilomba*, die or not? Please show me if he will die.' If he is to die, the horn will go on digging more deeply into the ground, to show that a grave will be dug in the ground. If he is not going to die, the horn will lead to the white clay. In the latter case, the diviner will continue with his questions: 'What spirit can we now know, to have a drum played for it? If the illness comes from the spirits of the water, you must lead me to the red clay; if it comes from spirits not of water, to the white clay.' If the horn goes to the white clay, he says, 'You have gone to *mpeza* now, but this can mean many spirits. Which spirit can we recognize now?' The diviner begins by mentioning the spirits of huntsmanship, such as *Malanda kanzoji*, which dwells on large termite hills (*tuwumbu*); *Kaluwi*, which can enter a village and is the same as *Mukala*; *Lukatanyama*, a kind of *Kaluwi* that is a hunter's dead wife or sister—the ritual to propitiate her is performed on the threshold of a hut; *Monganyama*, another kind of *Kaluwi* with ritual on the threshold—*Lukatanyama* and *Monganyama* are children of *Kaluwi*; *Kayong'u*; *Ntambu*; *Malala wanyanta*—the revenge medicine of chiefs killed by sorcery; *Chihamba*; *Kalombu*; *Muyombu* for the name-inheriting ritual [*Ku-swanika ijina*] for a dead hunter; *Wuyang'a* for gun-hunters; *Chishing'a*—planting a forked-stick shrine to hunter spirits. Then he asks about rituals of illness or fertility: *Wubwang'u*; *Isoma*; *Nkula*—all these may be for the village or for the bush.

"It is the liver of the spirit which thinks that it is not well remembered by its relatives that makes its living relative ill. It is often because the whole group of relatives have forgotten the spirit that it attacks one as representative of them all. The spirit wishes to make that one its friend who will remember it well. Or if a group of relatives were quarreling or not living peacefully together, the spirit would come to a village and make one person ill. Often this is the headman's fault, and he is the one who is caught. Again if a person has committed individual wrongs or forgotten the spirit himself, he may be caught.

"If the horn goes to the white clay, then ritual to cure illness is the correct answer. If it goes to the red clay, that would be incorrect. In divination *Nkula* and *Wubwang'u* may be classed as rituals to cure illness, as well as for reproduction [*nakusema*]. So may *Chihamba*. But *Isoma* [also called *Tubwiza*] is for reproduction only.

"Once it has found the class [*muchidi*] of rituals, the horn then divines for the particular kind of ritual. If it goes to the red clay first, *Nkula* should be performed, if to the white clay, *Chihamba*. If it goes first to the white, then to the red clay, without stopping, then *Kayong'u* should be held, or *Kaneng'a*. White clay stands for (1) 'blessing' [*kiswila nkisu*]; (2) 'health' [*wukolu*]; (3) 'reproduction' [*lusemu*].

"Here is another example: if the ritual ought to be performed near water, the diviner asks: 'Are you going to have the drum played near the water or in the bush [*mwisang'a*]? If near the water, lead me to the red clay? Then he asks: 'Do we collect leaves from such-and-such a tree? If so, please lead me to its leaves.' Next he asks: 'Shall we mix pounded-leaf medicine with water or not? If you add water, show me?' Then the horn goes straight to the calabashes. He may divine for each medicine individually. But if some well-known ritual, such as *Nkula* or *Chihamba*, is divined, he does not specify the medicines, for they are known by the adepts. But he may in such cases tell them whether *nsompu* should be used or not.

"He will also tell them whether the afflicting spirit is that of the patient's father, mother's brother, older brother, mother, sister, and so on. The medicines of certain kinds of ritual are not fixed but are explained [*ku-lumbulula*] by the diviner to his clients who will tell the senior adept [*chimbuki wamukulumpi*] of the ritual. *Lukupu* medicines are so explained. A diviner may also divine for the medicines to cure sickness when no spirit is involved, but only a disease [*musong'u*].

"The diviner may divine for the time of day when the ritual should be performed. This is done by pointing. He asks his horn: 'Will it start at sunrise? If this is so, go to the white clay. If not, you must not move.' Alternatively, if it moves and stops, making a little hole in the ground, this marks a point of divination and means that the ritual should be held at sunrise. Or he may ask: 'If the drum is not to be played at that time, then you must move about without stopping and come back.'

"The diviner may point to different positions of the sun in the sky. If the horn stops after one of these has been pointed out, then that time is confirmed.

"Many rituals are performed in bright moonlight. If you see them being performed on dark nights, this means there is not time to wait, for the patient is very ill and will soon grow worse. The moon is white, like white clay and good health. The moon and the sun are signs of *mpeza*, darkness is the sign of blackness, bad luck, or death. The sun and moon are also signs of God [Nzambi]. A sign [*chimwekeshu*] is from *ku-mwekesha*, 'to cause to appear, to reveal.'

"There is no divination for new kinds of ritual, like *Tukuka* or *Masandu*. These are performed as the result of *ku-sakija*, 'fancying, imagining, thinking matters over.'

"Sometimes we divine for future things [*yuma yakumbidyi*], but not often. Usually we divine for things which have already happened. We reveal these. In the past people used *mwaji* poison, given to fowls, to find out future things. To bring luck in the future, people wear amulets [*nyitookela*]."

Chiswa

This is a collective term for several methods of divination, most of which involve the use of *mwaji* poison from the *Erythropholeum guineense* tree.

Mafwamfwa (small termite hills). Muchona explains: "*Mwaji* poison is pounded up. A small termite hill is cut in two. Then the diviner begins to address [*ku-sansa*] the poison and the ants to test them, as follows: 'You termite hill [*eyi ifwamfwa*], you my poison [*eyi mwaji yami*], if I shall see the sun and moon tomorrow, I must find the termites still alive. If I shall not see them tomorrow, then I must find that the termites are all dead.' After the address, he sprinkles some water on top of the exposed part, adds some powdered *mwaji* poison, replaces the top of the termite hill, covers the join with wet mud, and lays a branch of a tree on the termite hill.

"On the same day he goes to another termite hill, cuts it and says: 'If the sun and moon will not be seen tomorrow, I must find you all alive: if they will be seen, you must all be dead.' Then he replaces the top as mentioned before.

"The next day he goes at dawn to the first termite hill. If the termites are still alive, the poison is good. Then if he goes to the second termite hill. If the termites are dead, the power of the poison is confirmed.

"If one termite hill is right and the other wrong, they discard the *mwaji* poison; if both are wrong they discard it.

"Sometimes they go to five termite hills to test the *mwaji*.

"Another way of testing it is when someone has died. Then they go to the termite hill and address the dead: 'You, the dead person, we have buried you, you lie in the grave; if we shall see you again tomorrow, walking with us, then these termites must be found alive. But if we shall not see you forever [*haya nyaka*], tomorrow we must find all the termites dead.' Then they apply *mwaji* to the termite hill as described. If the termites are dead next day, then the poison is good.

"After testing *mwaji* in this way, the diviner can ask it questions, just as in other kinds of divination.

"Perhaps the word *chiswa* comes from *tuswa*, 'winged white ants'; or perhaps from *chiswamu*, 'a secret thing,' sometimes used for a sorcerer's *ilomba* or figurine."

Izawu (clay pot divination)

Muchona described this method of divination as a form of *chiswa*, though it has nothing to do with *mwaji*. I (V. T.) once saw, under tragic circumstances—which I suppose are the sort of circumstances under which much divination takes place—a performance of *izawu* divination. A small boy was dying of lockjaw, and a village headman called Makayi was divining into the cause of his condition. Makayi planted a straight, sturdy twig into the ground, then with great care placed a small, black clay pot [*izawu*] on top of it so as to balance there perfectly without wobbling. He had previously smeared some sticky chewed leaves on the bottom of the pot. He then made all the old people present collect a leaf apiece from trees growing in a circle around the village. Next he pounded these into *nsompu* in a meal mortar, poured water carefully into the *izawu* pot, added the *nsompu* to the water, and finally sprinkled powdered red clay and powdered white clay on the surface of the water. He then addressed the *nsompu* directly, bidding it to reveal quickly what the child was suffering from. Immediately afterward he walked in a circle widdershins [from right to left] around the village. He told me later that if the pot fell off the twig while he was doing this the patient would die very soon. The pot remained in position, but by the time he returned the red powder had agglutinated in a clump in the middle of the pot above the white powder. This meant three things, Makayi explained: since red was uppermost the child would die, for the white powder meant health and life; since the red powder was in the middle of the pot, someone closely related by blood to the child was bewitching him; since all the particles of red clay had collected together, there would be a gathering [*chipompelu*] of witches to eat the victim's body, together with their familiars. Thus the killer was a woman (since only female witches gather in covens) and a close relative of the dying child. Makayi vouchsafed some further information about witches' familiars or *tuyebela*. They have the power to produce in people what seem at first appearance to be the symptoms of ordinary illness or injury. They carry hoes and axes with which they beat their victims, producing swelling on their limbs, or cuts and slashes like those made accidentally during tree-felling or gardening. The little sick boy had been trembling and bubbling at the mouth, "just like a hyrax or coney [*chibatata*]." These symptoms had suggested to the people that the boy had eaten the flesh of this animal, tabooed to uncircumcised youngsters. But Makayi told me that his divination had shown him that the child's symptoms were caused by the beatings administered to him by witches' familiars.

Ng'ombu yamuseng'u yankayi (duiker horn divination)

Muchona told me that "the horn of a duiker killed by a wild animal, usually a lion or a leopard, is found. Then a hole is bored near the broad base of the horn with a strong needle. A string is drawn through the hole and tied to a stick of *kapwipu* wood. Next a number of *jipelu* [contagious magical] ingredients [23] are prepared, including: some bark-scrapings [*nyemba*] of *kapwipu* wood; a single hair from an albino [*mwabi*]; a leech; *mpelu* from a vulture; *ibanda* salt.

"*Kapwipu* [24] leaves are then chewed by the diviner, mixed with the *jipelu*, and pressed [*ku-panda*] right up to the end of the horn. Then powdered white clay is pressed in, until the whole horn is filled.

"Now they begin to divine. A duiker skin is spread out and the sharp tip of the horn is lowered by the diviner until it rests on the skin. The diviner holds the *kapwipu* stick, and the horn begins to turn around in a circle [*ku-nyeng'umuka*]. At a point of divination the horn spins around rapidly. Otherwise it just swings gently about.

"The spirit of one of the diviner's relatives is put into this *ng'ombu;* the spirit and the medicines act together to make the horn go around.

"We speak of such a *ng'ombu* as 'following the scent' [*ku-pepa*]. It is like a leopard that follows the scent of a duiker, kills it, eats its meat, then leaves its bones and horns. The *ng'ombu* must be like a beast of prey that follows the scent of wicked people who cause illness.

"Like bushbuck horn divination, and *chiswa*, duiker horn divination is an old Lunda method."

[23] See the medicines used in *mwishi* divination (page 322) and bushbuck horn divination.

[24] See the use of the *kapwipu* tree in *Kayong'u* (pages 260, 266) and in *mwishi* divination (page 320).

Museng'u yanteng'u (roan antelope horn divination)

This is similar to bushbuck horn divination, it its use of white and red clay. I could get no information about its medicines.

Ng'ombu yanzenzi (rattle divination)

Muchona told me that this is "a rattle with a hole in the butt and at the other end. A string is passed through both holes. One end of the string is held in the diviner's left hand, while the other is tied around his left great toe. Or it might be tied to a branch. The rattle is then thrown up by the right hand along the string; if it sticks midway and does not slide back again, this marks a point of divination, at which a definite answer is given to a question. If there is no point of divination, the rattle descends. Or it may come back when the diviner mentions the next point. I do not know the medicine for this *ng'ombu*. It is a Lunda method."

Ng'ombu yanzeli (stick bundle divination)

"Ten or twenty sticks," said Muchona, "are pierced at one end and threaded by a string. The diviner extends the string between his hands. When he pulls the string tight, if the sticks remain bunched in the middle this marks a point of divination. If they spread out along the length of the string, no point has been reached. This method was once used by the Lunda but not today."

Ng'ombu yambachi (tortoise-shell divination)

Muchona explained that in this method "medicines are put into the carapace of a tortoise, then a guinea fowl's wing feather is inserted, quill first, into the rear aperture of the carapace and twisted in firmly. White and red clay are placed to the right and left of it. The diviner holds the feather in his hand when divining and addresses the *ng'ombu*, just as in the case of the bushbuck horn method. A tortoise is used because it has a hard shell and hunts many little animals for its food, following them patiently—the *ng'ombu* must find hidden things [*yiswamu*] in the same way. A guinea fowl is sometimes called *nkang'a*, from *ku-kang'anya*, 'to fail.' This means that the *ng'ombu* must not fail, but find the wicked people."

Small black ants. Small black "sugar" ants, called *nzenkeneni*, are frequently used as *mpelu*, contagious magical ingredients, in all methods of divination, "because they are always looking for things," said Muchona.

Appendix

The following is an extract from an article *"Ankishi atiyake-sha ayimbanda mpuhu"* by J. K. Mulusa in the December issue of the quarterly journal *Talenu*, edited by R. J. Short, District Commissioner, Mwinilunga, and J. N. Chindefu, Native Authority Councillor of that District. *Talenu*, which was founded by R. S. Thompson, Information Officer at Kasama, and District Commissioner, Mwinilunga, from 1955 to 1957, consists of articles by Africans and Europeans living in Mwinilunga District on topics of local and general interest. Each article is both in English and Lunda. The editors are to be congratulated in bringing to light so much hitherto hidden local talent and such large quantities of useful ethnographic and historical information. Mr. Mulusa writes:

Nading'i nakutala chiwahi ng'ombu yaleteluwu kumesu a Mwanta Boma kudi Mashinja Kalani Funda. Diyu ng'ombu yaKatepa Mulomba wakumpata yaMwanta Ntambu. Lwalw'ilu lwenzala mbe natuyisosontu tweng'i natweng'i; nyiseng'u, yikunku yamakowa awanyama, mafwaha, yizanda yamanung'u nansaba makalashi, mabotolu malola ninkumbilu, yikwa yawanyama, tunchayila, ng'anji, tupamba, niyakwawu yasweja kuvula nankashi. Kachuma hikachuma kashimunang'a chuma chatama hela chachiwahi.

Tutalenu chichadi kumwekana kudi Kaji Muteba neyi waya kwaMulomba. Mulomba hakwinza nang'ombu yindi nakushakama muchitwamu china chazandama, nawayi dehi mukundu (ng'ula) nampemba kumesu hi-

kumwekana wubanji hohu, izu dindi wabalamuna dehi mwaka naleki dehi kuhosha Chilunda hakutomena mwidimi dacheng'i hohu.

Katataka hakutachika kusekula ng'ombu yindi; neyi munodiki nkishi yamumbanda yidi nzekesi, cheng'i himukulonda kanchayila. Kanchayila chidi neyi: nchawa janjamba jakudichayila [1] *—watema eyi aweni nchawa jakudikung'ila hamujimba weyi kulonda neyi kesi kanashiki dehi. Nkishi yamumbanda yidi nzekesi yashimunang'a wuvumbi; neyi wakama dehi namumbanda wakayawu dehi yitimbu kulonda kufwa.*

Indi ankishi amakwawu ashimunadi? Nkishi jasweja kuvula dichu tukuyilejaku chalumbululayi janti hohu.

1. *Nkishi namumbanda—yatena wuloji wakudi ambanda.*
2. *Nkishi yachiyala—wuloji hela chitela chakudi amayala.*
3. *Nkishi hela chivuvu—mufu hela afu.*
4. *Kesi hela Majiku—hikufwa—muntu waya mumbaka nafwi.*
5. *Museng'u wamfuma—muntu walema niyilwilu yindi.*
6. *Mboma hela Kapela—Ilomba hela mukishi wakukang'esha lusemu.*
7. *Izewu dachiheng'i—yuma yinaheng'i (chinatami oku kumukwinza).*
8. *Chibanjilu—meji hela mpola yikukumpula.*

Indi katepa Mulomba wamweni ng'ahi mwaka eli nindi ntung'i yamukala Chikundula wading'i nelomba? Hakutena nawa nindi ilomba dindi anadasi, nindi neyi Chikundula nakeng'i kuhanda watela kujaha muntu wakulamika nachu muchitu.

'I have been examining well the divining apparatus which was brought before the District Commissioner by District Messenger Kalani Funda. It belongs to Diviner Mulomba of the Area of Chief Ntambu. This basket contains dolls (figurines) of many kinds and shapes; horns, pieces of animal-skins, bones, pieces of broken pots and gourds, glasses and bottles, stones, hoofs, cocoons, certain hard stones of fruits, pieces of Lunda tools and very many other things indeed. Each of these items signifies something bad or good.

Let us see what happens to Kaji Muteba if he visits Mulomba. Mulomba comes along with his *ng'ombu* and sits in a high chair, he has rubbed powdered red clay and white clay on his face which

---

[1] See page 311 for Muchona's interpretation of this Luvale proverb.

looks just like murder, his voice he has changed, he has left off speaking Chilunda and speaks hoarsely in quite another tongue.

Immediately he begins to shake his basket up and down; if there appears a female figurine which is naked, then a cocoon follows it. The cocoon tells you: "the elephant's firewood was collected by himself," i.e. you cut (by yourself) the firewood and put it around your body so that for you fire has already arrived.[2] The naked female figurine signifies adultery; if you slept with a woman doctored with medicines (intended) to kill.

What do the other figurines represent? The figurines are too many to describe here; a few only may be explained.

1. A figurine of a woman—signifies female witchcraft.

2. A figurine of a man—sorcery or a grudge (associated with) men.

3. A figurine of rotten, decayed wood—a ghost or ghosts.

4. A fire or The Funeral Fires [3]—death—a person who went to the Copperbelt has died.

5. A horn with a drawing-pin—an important person and his deeds.

6. A python or snake—a Snake Familiar or an ancestor spirit which hinders female reproduction.

7. A warthog's tooth (tusk)—things are crooked (matters have gone wrong).

8. A bit of glass—water or a torrent which sweeps you away.

How did diviner Mulomba come to the conclusion that village headman Chikundula had an *Ilomba* familiar? He mentioned that his *Ilomba* was shot, and that if Chikundula wanted to live he must kill a person (to obtain from him) a patch to stick on (his body).

Comments. Mulusa is here referring to a Lunda belief, mentioned in my book *Schism and Continuity in an African Society*,

---

[2] Or as we might say, "If you play with fire you will get your fingers burned."

[3] See Muchona's account of *Majiku* on pages 299–301.

that a sorcerer may be killed by coaxing his *ilomba* from the stream in which it is concealed with a proffered chicken and then shooting it with a nightgun (*wuta wawufuku*), see above, pages 247–248). If the *ilomba* is killed, its owner too will die. But if it is only wounded, the wound will be reproduced on the owner's body. The sorcerer will recover only if he kills a child, euphemistically described as a black goat (*mpembi yeyila*), and covers the wound with a patch of the victim's skin.

Mulusa's account

Nikishi jindi jamulejeli, Kapela, chibinda wasenda wuta, nkishi yanyanya, ijiku dakesi, chibanjilu, nijikwawu nawa, dichu hakuchilumbulula nindi Chikundula anamwasi mwilomba nawuta wakesi, neyi nakeng'i kuhanda sampu kuhana muntu wakujika nachu muchitu.

His figurines told him: a Snake, a Hunter carrying a gun, a Child Figurine, a Funeral Fire, Glass, and others, that he simply interpreted as follows: "Chikundula has been shot in [his] *Ilomba* by a flint-lock, if he wants to live he must get a person [to obtain from him] a patch to cover [his wound]."

Bibliographical References

Butterfield, H. 1959. *Christianity and History*. London: Collins, Fontana Books.

Dante Alighieri. (1319) 1950. *The Divine Comedy*. Tr. J. A. Carlyle and P. H. Wickstead. New York: Vintage Books.

Douglas, Mary. 1968. "The Social Control of Cognition: Some Factors in Joke Perception." *Man*, 3 (September), 361–376.

Gilson, E. H. 1956. *The Christian Philosophy of St. Thomas Aquinas*. New York: Random House. First published in 1919 as *Le Thomisme, Introduction au système de saint Thomas d'Aquin*.

Gluckman, M. 1955. *The Judicial Process among the Barotse of Northern Rhodesia*. Manchester: Manchester University Press for the Rhodes-Livingstone Institute.

Horton, Robin. 1964. *"Ritual Man in Africa." Africa*, 34: 85–104.

Jung, C. S. 1949. *Psychological Types*. London: Routledge & Kegan Paul.

Junod, H. A. 1927. *Life of a South African Tribe*. London: Macmillan.

Langer, S. 1958. *Philosophy in a New Key*. New York: Mentor Book, New American Library of World Literature.

Melland, Frank. 1923. *In Witchbound Africa*. London: Seeley, Service.

Melville, H. 1952. *Moby Dick*. London: Macdonald.

Munday, J. T. 1961. *Central Bantu Historical Texts*, I, Part I, Kankomba. Livingstone Institute Communications, No. 22.

Paul, Sherman, ed. 1950. *Moby Dick*. New York.

Turner, V. W. 1953. *Lunda Rites and Ceremonies*. Rhodes-Livingstone Museum Occasional Paper, No. 10. Livingstone, Northern Rhodesia.

——. 1955. "A Lunda Love Story and Its Consequences." *Rhodes-Livingstone Journal*, No. 19.

——. 1957. *Schism and Continuity in an African Society*. Manchester: Manchester University Press for the Rhodes-Livingstone Institute.

——. 1967. *The Forest of Symbols*. Ithaca: Cornell University Press.

White, C. M. N. 1947. *Witchcraft, Divination and Magic*. Lusaka Government Printer, Northern Rhodesia.

White, C. M. N. 1961. Elements in Luvale Beliefs and Rituals. Rhodes-Livingstone Paper, No. 32. Manchester: Manchester University Press.

Whitehead, A. N. 1928. *Symbolism*. Cambridge: Cambridge University Press.

Index

Acquittal of *Chihamba* candidates, 112, 157-158
Act-of-being, 18, 179-180, 182, 183, 184, 185; and whiteness, 194-196, 202-203
Adepts, 78-79, 83-84, 113, 246
Afflicting spirit, 39, 45-46, 51
Affliction with sickness, 39, 118, 142
Akishi (plu.), ancestor spirits, *see Mukishi*
Albino, 273
Ambiguity: of *Kavula*, 21, 74, 179; in *Moby Dick*, 189
Andumba, witchcraft familiars, 117
Angolan diviner, 268-288
Ankishi; human figurines, 216-217; figurines of "Elders," 219-221
Antondu, uninitiated persons, 38, 44
Ants, small black, 338
Anus, 134n.
Aquinas, Thomas, 18, 19
Arrow: in *Chihamba*, 44, 47, 77, 84; in divination, 269
Artifactual source of meaning, 166
Asthma and divination, 214, 259
Ax, 84, 85, 146
Ayikodjikodji (plu.), malevolent dead, 62-63, 64, 136, 255, 257

Backwards approach, 80, 81, 90
Barthes, Roland, 31
Basket divination, 213-242, 244-321
Baudelaire, C., 230
Beads, 45, 260
Beans, 70
Beating, in ritual, 90, 91, 97
Beer, ritual, 44, 54
Black, Max, 31

Black mud, *malowa*, 125, 134-135, 141, 151, 152, 225
Blake, William, 21
Blood symbolism, 64, 109, 110, 127, 135, 143, 258-259
Bow, 46, 84
Boys' circumcision, *Mukanda*, 47, 56, 61, 79-80, 82, 97, 140, 143
Brittle segmentation of divinatory symbols, 232-233
Bruce-Miller, W., 167
Burning bush, 180-181
Bush ritual of *Chihamba*, 153-154
Butterfield, H., 195-196

Candidates in *Chihamba*, 38, 45, 89-93, 97-98, 113, 114
Carvalho, 61
Cassava, 70; cutting, 124; root, 138-139
Castor oil, 257-258; leaf, 78
Catching of candidates, 90-93
Chains of connotata, 165-166
Chasing: in *Chihamba*, 89-97, 101-102; in *Moby Dick*, 193-194
Chesterton, G. K., 203
Chidimbu, point in course of divination, 219, 240
Chiefs: Kanongesha, 47; Ikeleng'e, 286
Chief, symbolic: *Kavula*, 103, 173; Jesus, 188; in *Moby Dick*, 190
Chihamba, 17; social effects of, 19; and communitas, 23; expression of theory of goodness, 27; ritual of affliction, 27-28, 37, 39-40; symptoms of affliction by, 39, 151; two phases of, 39, 150; fieldwork, and observation of, 40; variations in per-

Chihamba (*cont.*)
  formances, 41; names, 45, 67, 69, 71; and excretion, 52n, 108, 134n.; originated by women, 56, 113; forms of, 73; taboos, 100; *ku-lembeka* phase, 150-157; and white symbolism, 167-171; cross-cultural comparisons with, 180-181, 186, 187-203; therapy, 185-186; ecstasy after killing *Kavula*, 185-186
Chihamba episodes: list of, 42-44; sending of the arrow, 44; ceremonial beer drink, 44-45; prayer before village ancestor shrine, 47; taking ember from chief's fire, 47; blowing white clay on rattles, 47, 48-49; collecting *isaku* medicines, 51-59; preparation of *isaku* medicines, 59-61; preparation of washing medicine, 61-64; entry of patients into hut and interrogation by *Kavula*, 65-72; public dance, 75-76; rousing candidates with cock's feathers, 76-77; inserting arrow into thatch, 77-78; marking out sacred barrier, 78-80; sacralizing *musoli* tree, 80-81; dragging meal mortar to *isoli* site, 81-82, 83-84; preparation of *isoli*, 83-88; fitting arrowhead to shaft, 88-89; the chasing, 89-97, 101-102; *mpanda* slave yokes, 97-98; interrogation of candidates, 99-101, 107-111; greeting *Kavula*, 102-105, 112-113; the killing of *Kavula*, 105, 108-114; concluding oration at village, 114; cutting of *ikamba daChihamba* root and collection of *kantong'a* medicines, 119-121; *yibi*, 121-123, 134; making of *kantong'a* shrine, 124-130, 134-136; cutting medicines for pots, 130-132, 137-145; planting beans and maize around *kantong'a*, 132; "stopping up" *Chihamba*, 133; ceremonial payment of adepts, 145; taboos, 147-148; lifting of taboos, 148
Chikinta dance, 75, 76
Chileng'a, *see* Rattles
Chimbuki, doctor, 38

Chinang'amu, parasitic plant, 265, 266
Chindefu, J. N., 339
Chinguli, 61
Chinjikijilu, symbol, blaze, landmark, 55, 195, 212
Chisolu, fence, 84, 87, 107
Chituba, giant rat (*Cricetomys*), 52
Chivwikankanu, Investor with *lukanu*, 320
Chokwe slave raiding, 89, 93, 167
Classification of symbols, 159-162
Cock, 84; *see also* Red cock
Cognitive symbolism in divination, 231-232
Communitas, 21-22, 28; as Godhead, 23; interchanging with social structure, 29
Complex symbols, 160, 161-162; *see also* Medicines *and* Shrines
Composite symbols, 160
Compound symbols, 160, 161
Conflict: symbolic, 90, 133; social, 235-236
Connotation, 162, 163
Conversion, 32
Cowry shell, 256
Crocodile, 260, 264
Cross-cultural comparisons: burning bush, 180-181; Easter Vigil, 186, 201; empty tomb, 187-189; *Moby Dick*, 189-199, 201-202; Transfiguration, 189
Cult association, 38
Cults of affliction, 37-38

Dance, 75, 76
Dante, 17-18
Dawn, 76-77, 259
Dead, the malevolent, *see Ayikodjikodji*
Death, ritual, 177
Denotation, 162
Disappearance after killing: of *Kavula*, 110; of Jesus, 188; of Moby Dick, 194-195
Disease, 118
Disembowelling, 82-83, 128, 183
Disputes in *Chihamba*, 44-45, 51, 62, 79, 90, 149
Dissociation, state of, 256

Distant diviner, 313
Divination: defined, 15-16; likened to judicial process, 26, 233; incorporates theory of evil, 27; symbols as signs in, 207-209; consultation, 214-215, 217-218, 234, 236-237, 239-241, 276-285; classifications used for questioning, 218, 279-281; points in course of, *chidimbu*, 219, 240, 264, 322-323; as phase of social process, 234-242; interpretation of symbol constellations, 239-240; of hidden objects, 260-263; testing of powers of, 260-264, 333-334; questioning, 276-278
Divination, types of: basket, 213-242, 244-321; poison ordeal, 319-321; pounding pole, *mwishi*, 322-324; rattle, *dawulang'ang'a*, 324-326; calabash, *katuwa*, 326-328; bushbuck horn, 328-332; termite hill, *chiswa*, 333-334; clay pot, 334-335; duiker horn, 335-336; rattle, *yanzenzi*, 337; stick bundle, 337; tortoise-shell, 337-338
Divinatory symbolism: cognitive, 231-232; brittle segmentation of, 232-233
Diviners: personality of, 23-25; task of, 209; initiation of, 215, 245-267; moral condition of, 229; upholders of tribal morality, 241-242; tally kept by, 268; training of, 289-290; payment of, 291, 319; distant, 313; etiquette among, 313; assistant, 313-314
Divining objects, *tuponya* (sing. *kaponya*), 216-229; shaking up of, 214; category of *ankishi*, human figurines, 216-217
Divining objects
  Ax Handle, *Muhinyi*, 307, 315
  Carrying Cloth, *Ng'oji*, 307, 308-309
  Country, *Itang'wa*, 307, 310
  Chamutang'a, the Prevaricator, 221-224, 293-295
  Chief's Bracelet, *Lukanu*, 294, 299
  Dead, *Mufu*, 304, 305
  Drum, *Ng'oma*, 228, 307, 315-316

Duiker's Hoof, *Chikwa chankayi*, 307, 310
Elders, *ankishi*, 219-221, 300, 301-303
Fame, *Mpuhu*, 307, 314-315
Fowl, *Kaneng'a*, 307-308
Funeral Fires, *Majiku*, 299-301
Hyena, *Chimbu*, 300, 303-304
Katwambimbi, the Tale Bearer, 224-225, 294, 295-297
Little Calabash of Beer, *Kaswaha kawalwa*, 317-318
Mwaka, Longevity, 227-228, 304, 306-307
Path, *Njila*, 307, 309
Penis, *Ilomu*, 307, 310-312
Portuguese Money, 307, 314
red clay in mongoose pouch, 292, 300
Situtunga's Hoof, *Chipaji*, 307, 308
Smelted Iron, *Wutali*, 307, 309-310
Snake Familiar, *Chanzang'ombi*, 317
Tears, *Madilu*, 307, 312
Twister, *Matang'isha*, 307, 312-313
Waterfall Stone, *Nkumbilu*, 318-319
white clay, 292, 300
Witches' Familiars, *Nyikana yawandumba*, 317
Word, *Izu*, 304, 305-306
Yipwepu, Possessions, 225-227, 294, 297-299
Doctors, 38, 246
Dominant symbol, 160-161
Douglas, Mary, 19, 20
Dragging, 80, 81-82, 83-84
Dreams, 248, 249
Dualism, 16, 20
Durkheim, Emile, 23, 27, 33
Dying, place of, *ifwilu*, 142

Easter liturgy, 186, 201, 202
Eating without hands, 61
Eckhart, Meister, 23
Ecstasy, after killing *Kavula*, 185, 186
Empirical testing of medicines, 155-156
Empty tomb, 187-189
Encircling, 51, 53, 80-81, 84, 118, 124
Epilepsy, 256
Ernest Knight Collection, 117n
Esoteric knowledge, 208
Esoteric phase of cult, 38

Excretion, 52n, 108, 134n
Exegetic level of meaning, 172

Familiars, 115, 117, 282; *ilomba*, 116, 117; *andumba*, 117, 252
Fan of referents, 164
Fatalism, 198, 199
Feast, 149
Fence, in ritual, 84, 87, 107
Fiddling prohibition, 100
Foods, sacred, 62, 64, 78
Forks, *mpanza*, 82, 84, 263
Frame, diviner's, 210, 270
Freedom, 200
Free will in social process, 31
Freud, Sigmund, 30
Friendship, ritual, 105, 133, 158
Funeral, 56

Genet cat, 123, 293
Gennep, Arnold van, 33
Ghosts, 45-46
Gilson, Etienne, 18, 179-180
Girl's puberty ritual, *see Nkang'a*
Gluckman, Max, 238n
Goat, 259
Godhead, 23
God, Nzambi, 74, 171
Good and evil, 27, 238-239
Good man, the, 238
Goodness, 168-169
Grandfather, epithet of *Kavula*, 63, 74-75
Grave: in *Chihamba*, 87, 90, 112; baby's, 141; of Jesus, 188
Greeting, ritual, 102-105, 112-113, 122, 148
Grudges, 26, 58, 234, 235, 238, 283

Head, meaning "life," 105, 128, 135, 136
Headpads, *mbung'a*, 210
Hidden sense of symbol, 176
Hinduism, 19, 22
Hippopotamus, 71, 72, 73, 89; *ku-lembeka* rites of Chihamba, 151-153
Historicity of Christianity, 197
Hoe, 84, 85, 146
Hoof marks, as category, 218, 180
Hopping, 77-78

Horton, Robin, 18, 19, 21
Hunters' rituals, 57, 61, 246, 251, 266
Huxley, T. H., 195

Ibanda salt, 60-61
Ifwilu, place of dying, 142
Ihamba: tooth-removing ritual, 143; meanings of, 247
Ihung'u, place of suffering, 142
Ikamba daChihamba, "cassava of *Chihamba*" tree, 119-121, 131, 132, 133, 138-139; analysis of symbolic meaning, 166-171
Ilomba, sorcery familiar, 116-117
Immanence of *Kavula*, 183-184
Impersonation, ritual, 65, 66, 102, 105, 107-109
Individual, enemy of society, 27
Innocence of initiated candidates, 85, 86, 112, 115, 137
Instruction of candidates, 103-104
Interrogation of candidates, 64-72, 90, 98-100, 101, 109-111, 122, 123
Interpretation, 211
Intuitive approach to problem of ritual, 187
Invocation, 51, 53-54, 62, 63, 124-125, 153, 155
Isaku medicine, "in pouch," 51-59, 120, 122, 123, 257
Ishikenu, principal or dominant medicine, 160-161
  ikamba daChihamba, 125
  kapwipu, for Kayong'u ritual
  katochi, mukeketi, 83, 84, 151
  mucheki, 51, 55
  mukula, 64, 83, 84, 153
  musoli, 80, 143
  muyombu, 253
Isoli, site of revelation, 45, 78, 80, 103, 105, 107, 110-114; derivation of word, 57-58; construction of, 84, 86-87, 109
Itota, 102-103
Izawu pot, 127, 131, 135, 136, 137

Joke: cosmic, 20; in ritual, 19, 20, 91, 92, 95-96, 133

Jung, C., 175, 178, 207-208
Junod, H., 216n

Kantong'a: personal shrine, 28; rite, 124-132; universality of, 135, 137-138, 175; complex symbol, 163-165
Kapwipu fruit tree, 260, 322, 333
Kashinakaji, Windson, 41, 244
Kaswamang'wadyi grass, 210
Katawubwang'u, twin medicine, 50, 156
Katochi, white root, 151
Kavula, 73-75, 87; demi-god of thunder and lightning, 19, 21, 39, 67; ambiguity of, 21, 74, 179; sacrificed, 22, 28, 103, 114, 182-183; reconciles contrarities, 25, 174; as effigy, 28, 86-88, 103, 105, 110; afflicting spirit, 39, 74; male or female, 39, 74, 87, 173; named, 51, 63, 67, 74-75, 99, 100, 103; impersonation of, 65, 66, 102, 105, 107-109; throaty voice, 65, 108; interrogates patients, 65-72, 99, 107-111; sexual swearing, 68, 75; brought out of earth, like belly organs, 83; and the grave, 87, 90, 112; posture of, 87, 114, 139; greatness of, 112; power of, 113-114; *yibi* effigy of, 122; complex symbol, 163; not to be explained sociologically, 181-182, 186-187; transcendent, 181; variously distributed after *isoli,* 183; immanent, 183-184
Kayong'u, diviners' initiation, 46, 215, 245-267; spirit, 257
Kayong'u episodes: medicine collection, 251-253; patient is possessed by spirit, 255-258; patient bites off head of red cock, 258-260; test divination with earth crocodile, 260-264; washing with medicine, 264-265
Keith, J. L., 171
Kierkegaard, Søren, 20
Killing: of *Kavula,* 105, 108-114; of patients, symbolically, 123; of white hen for *kantong'a* shrine, 127, 135, 136; of *ikamba daChihamba* root, 133-134; of Jesus, 188; of red cock, with the teeth, in *Kayong'u,* 259

kishi (root), mystical-human, 216
Ku-bola, to encircle and stamp flat, 84
Ku-busa, to start, to open up and disembowel, 82-83, 128, 136
Ku-jilola, rite of lifting taboos, 147, 148-150
Ku-lembeka, first phase in ritual of affliction, 38, 150-157, 249
Ku-pandula, leaf-smacking rite, 153, 264
Ku-solola, to reveal, make visible, 15, 83, 180
Ku-tumbuka, last phase in ritual of affliction, 38

Lambakasa, Chihamba doctor, 62, 106, 115, 119-121, 131
Langer, Suzanne, 162, 163
Latent sense of symbol, 164-165, 176
Lawrence, D. H., 196
Leaf-smacking rite, 153, 264
Leech, 322, 323
Life, *wumi,* 135-136
Lightning, 49, 153, 188
Liminality, 33, 189
Literary critics, 30
Lourie, 73, 153
Luweji Ankonde, 274-275
Lwalu, see Winnowing basket

Manifestation of spirit, 39, 246, 247
Manifest senses of symbol, 164, 176
Manyosa, 51
Marginals, 23-25
Meal, cassava, 86, 105, 107, 112
Meaning of symbols, 162-171
Medicine, *mutumbu,* 54; poultice, 116; meaning of names of, 118-119; principal, *see Ishikenu*
Medicine as complex symbol
    isaku, "in pouch," 51-59, 120, 122, 123, 257
    izawu, pot, 127, 131, 132, 135, 136, 137
    kantong'a bundle, 124-132, 175
    mpelu, personal magic, 272-274, 322
    nfunda bundle, 161
    nsompu, washing, 62, 75, 153, 252
    sweeping, 144, 145

Medicines
  chinang'amu, parasitic plant, 265, 266
  kabwititeng'i, "throw away" leaves,
    151, 152
  kapwipu fruit tree (*Swartzia madagas-
    cariensis*), 260, 322
  katawubwang'u, twin tree, 50, 156
  katochi, white root, 151
  lweng'i, strong-smelling plant (*Draecens
    reflexa var. nitens*), 322, 323
  mucha fruit tree (*Parinari mobola*), 52,
    58
  mucheki, white root, 51, 55, 60
  mudyi, milk tree (*Diplorrhyncus mossam-
    bicensis*), 51, 97, 121, 139-142
  muhotuhotu, "with falling leaves," 121,
    144, 145
  muhuma, "butting" tree, 264-265
  mukeketi, white root, 151, 152
  mukombukombu, sweeping, 116, 118,
    121, 144, 154
  mukula, blood tree (*Pterocarpus angolen-
    sis*), 64, 116, 118, 142-143, 153,
    154
  muleng'u fruit tree, 151, 152
  muneng'a, tear tree, 252, 254, 255, 262
  munkalampoli, thorn tree, 52, 57, 153
  muntung'ulu, with rootlets, 116, 118
  museng'u, flowering tree, 52, 59
  musojisoji, with red gum, 151
  musoli, tree of revelation, 52, 57-58,
    121, 143-144, 153
  mutantamu, parasitic plant, 266
  mutete, "cutting up" tree, 266-267
  mutuhu, "leaping" tree, 52, 59
  mututambulolu, "with bees hovering,"
    121, 144-145
  muyombu, tear tree, 47, 253-254
  mwang'ala, "scattering" tree, 116,
    117-118, 153
  ntotu, flotsam, 151
  wutotu, with white gum, 168
Melland, Frank, 166, 171, 283
Melville, Herman, 182
Men and women in *Chihamba*, 74, 173
Milk, 104, 140
Moby Dick, 182, 189-199, 201-202
Mode of affliction, 38
Mode of spirit manifestation, 246
Mongoose, 257, 292

Moonlight, 105, 119
Mortar, 82, 84, 85, 103
Mothers, 140
Mpanda, slave yoke, 89, 97-98, 101-
  102
Mpang'u, mysteries, 91, 97
Mpelu, personal magical medicine,
  272-274, 322
Mpemba, white clay, 46, 47, 50-51, 56,
  153, 168
Mucha, fruit tree, 52, 58
Mucheki, tree with white root, 51, 55, 60
Muchona, informant: for *Chihamba* ritual,
  40-41, 155-156; enacts greeting of
  Kavula, 103; on divination, 244
Mudyi, milk tree, 51, 97, 121, 139-142
Mufu, ghost, 45-46, 74, 188
Mukala, hunter spirit, 46
Mukanda, see Boys' circumcision
Mukanza Village, 40, 41
Mukishi, ancestor spirit, 212; in *Chihamba*,
  45-46, 47, 74, 87, 114, 120, 123, 137;
  of *Kayong'u*, 247, 249, 257
Mukoleku barrier, 78-80, 90, 270
Mukula, blood tree, 50, 61, 64, 121,
  142-143, 153, 154
Mukundu, see Red clay
Muloji, witch or sorcerer, 210; *see also*
  Witches *and* Sorcery
Multiplicity of referents, 174
Mulusa, J. K., 339-342
Muneng'a, tear tree, 252, 254, 255, 262
Musambanjita tree, or *ikamba daChihamba*,
  analysis of, 165-167
Musoli, tree of revelation, 52, 57-58, 121,
  122, 143-144, 153
Musolu, chief's rain ritual, 58
Muyeji, patient, candidate, *see* Candidate
Muyombu, tear tree, 47, 54, 253-254
Mwaji, poison ordeal, 319-321
Mwishi, pounding pole divination,
  322-324
Mwiyanawu, vengeance medicine, 278n
Mysteries, *mpang'u*, 91, 97
Myth of Ndembu, foundation, 275-276

Nakedness, 89, 94-95
Names changed in ritual, 254, 258,
  266-267
Naming, 45, 67, 69, 71, 112, 132

Ndembu, conditions of hardship among, 25

Needle, 84, 85, 160, 215, 263

Ng'ombu yakusekula, basket divination, 213-242, 244-321

Ng'unda, praise cry, 75-76, 90, 157

Nkaka, see Grandfather

Nkang'a, girl's puberty ritual, 46, 47, 56, 139

Nkula, ritual for women' reproductive troubles, 58, 63, 135, 143, 276

Nominal source of meaning, 166

Nshimba, genet cat, 123, 293

Nsompu, washing medicine, 62, 75, 152, 255

Nsomu, nerve of tusk, 210-211

Nyaluwema, Chihamba organizer, 44, 50, 56, 74

Nyamakang'a, afflicting ancestress, 51, 54, 74

Nyamukola, principal Chihamba patient, 44, 54, 60

Operational level of meaning, 172

Orectic quality of symbols, 231, 233

Pad marks, as category, 218, 280

Paradox, ritual, 182-185

Paranoid style of diviners, 24-25, 27

Parrot feathers, 146, 273

Patient, 38; see also Candidates in Chihamba

Placenta, 141-142

Planting a shrine, 28, 126, 136-137

Points in course of divination, chidimbu, 219, 240, 264, 322-323

Poison ordeal, 319-321, 333-334

Pounding-pole divination, 322-324

Praising, 75-76, 90, 157

Prayer at tree, 120, 149; at village shrine before ritual, 47; at Kayong'u shrine, 252; see also Invocation

Principal medicine, see Ishikenu

Process, 33

Psychology, 30

Pure act, 19, 28, 200

Questioning by diviners, 216-217

Rain medicine, 58

Rattles, yileng'a, used in Chihamba: by adepts, 48, 63, 83, 86, 148; making of, 49-50; butt used to give medicine, 60, 148, 149; used by Kavula, 66, 68, 72, 107; butt used to "kill" Kavula, 103, 105, 109, 112; used by candidates, 112; stored under rafters, 116; butt used in the cutting of ikamba daChihamba root, 120, 134; butt used for kantong'a planting, 132

Razor, 84, 85, 86, 149, 260, 263

Reasonable man, the, 238

Red beads, 46, 80, 81

Red clay, mukundu, nkung'u, 218, 253, 261

Red cock, 76-77, 80, 109, 146

Religion, 32; centrality of, 31; not to be explained sociologically, 195

Resurrection, 193, 201

Reveal, make visible, ku-solola, Ndembu religious theme, 15, 83, 143-144, 180, 211-213

Revelation: rite of, 110-111, 113; see also Isoli and Musoli

Rimbaud, Arthur, 185

Rite of passage form, 249

Ritual: phases of, 39, 150, 249; drama, 177; not to be explained sociologically, 186, 195; and intuition, 187; special terms used in, 254, 258

Ritual man, the, 182

Rituals: of affliction, 27, 37-38, 245-246; girl's puberty, Nkang'a, 46, 47, 56; boys' circumcision, Mukanda, 47, 56; funeral, 56; hunters', 57, 251; Musoli, for rain, 58; Nkula, for women's troubles, 58, 276; Wubwang'u, twin, 141, diviner's initiation, Kayong'u, 215, 245-267; women's reproductive, 245-246

River ritual of Chihamba, 151-153

Running, in ritual, 89, 97, 98

Sacrifice, 22, 28, 103, 105, 109, 113, 177

Sakutoha, Chihamba doctor, 45, 51, 59

Salt, in ritual, 60-61, 146, 322, 323

Samadhi, 19

Sandombu, Chihamba organizer, 44, 51, 62, 106, 131

Sanyiwang'u, *Kayong'u* doctor, 250-251
Sapir, E., 232
Satori, 19
Semantics of symbolism, 162-168
Sexual swearing, 68, 75, 101
Shadow, *mwevulu*, 136
Shaking of divination basket, 214
Sharpness, 85, 215, 264
Shaving, 149
Short, R. J., 339
Shrines: village, 47; *isoli*, 83-88, 102, 105; *kantong'a*, 124-136; *muneng'a*, diviner's, 252, 254, 255, 262
Signifiant and signifié, 28; complexity ratio between symbol and meaning, 163
Signification, 162
Signs and symbols, 207-209, 231, 233, 234
Simmel, Georg, 33
Simultaneity, 131, 132, 153
Slaves, 89, 91, 93, 167
Social process, 234-242
Social structure, 19, 29, 173, 186, 237
Sociological aspect of symbolic action, 172
Sociological explanations, insufficient for religion and ritual, 186, 195
Sorcery, 221-222, 234, 235, 247-248
Spirit, *see Mukishi*
Spirit affliction, 38-39, 249
Srinivas, M. N., 32
Step by step questioning by diviner, 216-217, 279-282
String, for corpse's litter, 218, 276
Subject, user of symbols, 171-172
Substantial source of meaning, 166
Suffering, place of, *ihung'u*, 142
Symbol-function, 162, 163
Symbolic actions, 31, 159, 171-174, 176, 177
    anointing with white clay or medicine, 50-51, 120, 150
    beating, 90, 91, 97
    biting, 259
    blowing, 47, 48-49, 50
    breast-squeezing, 104, 105
    catching of candidates, 90-93
    chasing, 89-97, 101-102

clapping feet, 104
conflict, 90, 133
cutting open, starting, 82-83
disappearance, 110, 188, 194-195
disemboweling, 82-83, 128, 136
dragging, 80, 81-82, 83-84
earth-smearing, 104
eating without hands, 61
encircling, 51, 53, 80-81, 84, 118, 254
fitting arrowhead to shaft, 88-89
greeting, 102-105, 112-113, 148
hopping, 77-78
impersonation, 65, 66, 102, 105, 107-109
inserting arrow, 47, 77-78, 81
interrogation, 64-72, 90
invocation of spirits, 51, 53-54, 62, 63
killing, 105, 109-113, 127, 133-135, 188, 259
leaf-smacking, *ku-pandula*, 153, 262
naming, 45, 67, 69, 71
payment, 145
planting, 28, 126, 136-137
praising, 75-76, 90, 157
prayer, 47, 120, 149, 265
rattles, use of, *see* Rattles
resurrection, 193
revealing, 15, 83, 110, 113
rolling, 103
running, 89, 97, 98
sacrifice, 22, 28
sexual swearing, 68, 75, 101
shaving, 149
shooting arrow, 88-89
taboo, 71-72, 147, 283, 288-289
throwing, tossing, 63, 131-132, 150
touching, in human chain, 131
trembling, 256, 258
washing, 75, 132, 147-148, 264-265
whistling, 98
Symbolic articles, 159-162
    albino's hair, 273
    ants, 338
    arrow, 44, 47, 77, 84, 88-89, 269
    ax, 84, 85, 146
    beans, 70
    black mud, 134-135, 141, 151, 152, 255
    blood, 64; *see also* Blood *and Mukula*
    bow, 46, 84

Symbolic articles (*cont.*)
  cassava, 70, 138-139
  castor-oil leaf, 78
  charcoal, 211, 273
  crocodile, 260, 264
  cross, 51, 122, 189
  fire, 47, 106
  head, 83, 105, 135
  headpad, 210
  hoe, 84, 85, 146
  goat, 259
  goat's heart, 260, 262
  Goliath beetle, 273
  isaku, rat-skin pouch, 52
  leech, 322, 323
  liver of a witch, 273
  medicines, *see* Medicines
  milk, 104
  mudyi, milk tree, 51, 98, 139-142
  mukula, blood tree, 50, 64, 79, 118,
      142-143
  musoli, tree of revelation, 52, 57-58, 80
  needle, 84, 85, 260, 263
  nerve of tusk, 272-273
  payment objects, 145-147
  rattle, *chileng'a*, 48, 49-50
  razor, 84, 85, 86, 149
  red beads, 46, 80, 81
  red clay, 218, 253, 261
  red cock, 76-77, 80, 109
  red feather of parrot, 273
  root from under circumcision fire, 274
  salt, 60-61, 146
  skin from chief's forehead, 272
  white articles, list of, 168
  white beads, 44, 45-46, 84, 112, 121,
      149
  white beer, 54, 62, 63, 126, 148, 149
  white clay, *mpemba*, 46, 47, 50-51, 56,
      153, 168
  white hen, 127, 135
  winnowing basket, 50, 215
  yokes for slaves, 97-98
Symbolic qualities
  ambiguity, 21, 74, 179, 189
  darkness, 119
  innocence, 85, 86, 112, 115, 137
  light, 119
  limpness, 210-211

  nakedness, 89, 94-95
  sacredness, being set apart, *chakum-
      badyi*, 79
  sharpness, 85, 215, 264
  simultaneity, 131, 132
  universality, 135, 137-138
  uprightness, 52, 56, 84, 126, 134
  whiteness, 28, 46-47, 54-55, 86, 140,
      168-169; at empty tomb, 188; at
      Transfiguration, 189; in *Moby
      Dick*, 190-193
Symbolic relationships
  adepts and candidates, 91-93, 96-98,
      101
  chief, 103, 173, 188, 190
  friendship, *wubwambu*, 105, 133, 158
  grandfather, 63, 74-75
  joking, 91, 92, 95-96, 133
  mother, 139-140
  Mother of Huntsmanship, 250
  mother of *muneng'a*, 255
  slave, 89, 91, 93
Symbolic space, 28
  backwards position, 80, 81, 90
  barrier, *mukoleku*, 78-80
  bush, 153-154
  death, place of, *ifwilu*, 142
  divination site, 269
  fence, *chisolu*, 84, 87, 107
  forks, 82, 261, 263
  hut of patient in village, 51, 79, 89-
      90, 93, 99, 101
  isoli, place of revelation, 80, 86-87, 103,
      105, 107, 109-114
  open air for sleeping, 115-116
  path taken by divination party,
      268-269
  payment, place of, 145
  river, 151-153
Symbolic time, 189
  dawn, 76-77, 259, 324-326
  evening, 102, 105-106
Symbol/meaning complexity ratio, 163
Symbols: signifiants and signifiés, 28;
  chinjikijilu, Ndembu definition, 55,
  195; semantics of, 162-171; multiplicity of referents of, 164-165, 168-
  169, 174; and signs, 207-209, 231,
  233, 234; and the unconscious, 232-

354 Index

Symbols (cont.)
234; analysis of dominant, 266-267

Taboos: at *Chihamba*, 71-72, 100, 147-148; for diviners, 283, 288-289
Talenu, journal, 339
Testing: of medicines, 155-156; divination powers, 260-264, 333-334
Therapy, 185-186
Thomism, 18
Thunderstorms, metaphor of, 19, 39
Time, as indivisible, 19
Transcendence of *Kavula*, 181
Transfiguration, 189
Trembling, 256, 258
Turner, Victor: *Schism and Continuity in an African Society*, 19, 37, 40, 186; *The Forest of Symbols*, 30

Unconscious and preconscious, 175
Unitary flow of experience, 16
Universal benefit of *kantong'a* and its medicines, 135, 137-138
Unmasking, 16-17
Unpredictable, the, 200
Uprightness, 52, 56, 84, 126, 134

Vernacular texts, 8-9

War of all on all, 25
Washing, 75, 132, 147-148, 264-265
Water, as category, 218, 280
Weber, Max, 33
White articles, list of, 168
White beads, 44, 84, 85, 112, 121, 149
White beer, 54, 62, 63, 126, 148, 149
White clay, 47, 50-51, 153

White, C. M. N., 213, 243, 250n, 282, 320n
White hen, 127, 135
Whitehead, A. N., 174-175, 176
Whiteness: and killing, 178; negative aspects of, 191-193
White symbolism, 197-198; in Dante, 17; in *Chihamba*, 28, 46-47, 54-55, 86, 119, 180-181; in *Nkang'a*, 140; list of meanings, 168-169, 191-192; in other cultures, 178; at empty tomb, 188; in *Moby Dick*, 190-202; of Easter liturgy, 201, 202
Widest unity and narrow loyalties, expressed by *Chihamba*, 173
Wild animals, as category, 280
Winnowing basket, 47-48, 50, 215
Witchcraft, 227-228, 234, 235, 252
Witches, 211
Witchfinding, legislation against, 243
Wittgenstein, L., 32
Women: originators of *Chihamba*, 56, 113; first at tomb, 188; reproductive troubles of, 245-246
Wubwambu, ritual friendship, 105, 133, 158
Wubwang'u, twin ritual, 141
Wuta wawufuku, sorcerer's night-gun, 247-248
Wutooka, whiteness, 47; *see also* White symbolism
Wuyang'a, *see* Hunters' rituals

Yibi rite, 121-123, 134
Yileng'a (plu.), *see* Rattles
Yokes, slave, 89, 97-98, 101-102

Zen, 19, 20
Zuliyana, *Chihamba* patient, 44

REVELATION AND DIVINATION
IN NDEMBU RITUAL

Designed by R. E. Rosenbaum.
Composed by Vail-Ballou Press, Inc.,
in 11 point linofilm Janson, 3 points leaded,
with display lines in Helvetica.
Printed offset by Vail-Ballou Press
on Warren's No. 66 text, 50 pound basis,
with the Cornell University Press watermark.
Bound by Vail-Ballou Press
in Columbia book cloth
and stamped in All Purpose foil.